Frommer's®

Florence & Tuscany day BY day

1st Edition

by Darwin Porter &
Danforth Prince

Wiley Publishing, Inc.

Contents

Published by:

Wiley Publishing, Inc.

111 River St.
Hoboken, NJ 07030-5774

ISBN-13: 978-0-7645-7615-7
ISBN-10: 0-7645-7615-1

Editor: Maureen Clarke
Production Editor: Heather Wilcox
Photo Editor: Richard Fox
Cartographer: Andrew Murphy
Production by Wiley Indianapolis Composition Services
Savvy Traveler illustrations by Rashell Smith and Karl Brandt

For information on our other products and services or to obtain technical support, please contact our Customer Care Department within the U.S. at 800/762-2974, outside the U.S. at 317/572-3993 or fax 317/572-4002.

Wiley also publishes its books in a variety of electronic formats. Some content that appears in print may not be available in electronic formats.

Manufactured in China

5 4 3 2 1

A Note from the Publisher

Organizing your time. That's what this guide is all about.

Other guides give you long lists of things to see and do and then expect you to fit the pieces together. The Day by Day guides are different. These guides tell you the best of everything, and then they show you how to see it in the smartest, most time-efficient way. Our authors have designed detailed itineraries organized by time, region or special interest. And each tour comes with a bulleted map that takes you from stop to stop.

Hoping to relive the glory days of the Forentine Renaissance, or to tour the highlights of Siena? Planning a drive through Chianti Country, or a tour of Tuscany's most charming small towns? Whatever your interest or schedule, the Day by Days give you the smartest route to follow. Not only do we take you to the top sights and attractions, but we introduce you to those special "finds" that turn tourists into travelers.

The Day by Days are also your top choice if you're looking for one complete guide for all your travel needs. The best hotels and restaurants for every budget, the greatest shopping values, the wildest nightlife—it's all here.

Why should you trust our judgment? Because our authors personally visit each place they write about. They're an independent lot who say what they think and would never include places they wouldn't recommend to their best friends. They're also open to suggestions from readers. If you'd like to contact them, please send your comments my way at mspring@wiley.com, and I'll pass them on.

Enjoy your Day by Day guide—the most helpful travel companion you can buy. And have the trip of a lifetime.

Warm regards,

Michael Spring

Michael Spring,
Publisher
Frommer's Travel Guides

About the Authors

A team of veteran travel writers, **Darwin Porter** and **Danforth Prince** have produced numerous titles for Frommer's, including best-selling guides to Italy, Rome, Venice, Spain, France, the Caribbean, England, and Germany. Porter's international biographies, published in many languages, document 20th-century legends such as Humphrey Bogart, Katharine Hepburn, and Howard Hughes. His latest (Feb. 2006) focuses on the scandalous life of Marlon Brando. Prince is the president of Blood Moon Productions and other media-related entities.

Acknowledgments

A deep feeling of gratitude goes to our editor, Maureen Clarke, for her guidance in producing this pioneering little guide. Steadfast and unwavering, she showed razor-sharp skills as an editor, a keen insight into how to cut and shape material, and a dedication to the job rarely seen in an editor today. That she did all this with a certain style and grace was an added bonus.

An Additional Note

Please be advised that travel information is subject to change at any time—and this is especially true of prices. We therefore suggest that you write or call ahead for confirmation when making your travel plans. The authors, editors, and publisher cannot be held responsible for the experiences of readers while traveling. Your safety is important to us, however, so we encourage you to stay alert and be aware of your surroundings.

Star Ratings, Icons & Abbreviations

Every hotel, restaurant, and attraction listing in this guide has been ranked for quality, value, service, amenities, and special features using a **star-rating system.** Hotels, restaurants, attractions, shopping, and nightlife are rated on a scale of zero stars (recommended) to three stars (exceptional). In addition to the star-rating system, we also use a **kids icon** to point out the best bets for families. Within each tour, we recommend cafes, bars, or restaurants where you can take a break. Each of these stops appears in a shaded box marked with a coffee-cup-shaped bullet.

The following **abbreviations** are used for credit cards:

AE	American Express	DISC	Discover	V	Visa
DC	Diners Club	MC	MasterCard		

Frommers.com

Now that you have the guidebook to a great trip, visit our website at **www. frommers.com** for travel information on more than 3,000 destinations. With features updated regularly, we give you instant access to the most current trip-planning information available. At Frommers.com, you'll also find the best prices on airfares, accommodations, and car rentals—and you can even book travel online through our travel booking partners.

A Note on Prices

Frommer's provides exact prices in each destination's local currency. As this book went to press, the rate of exchange was 1€ = US$1.30. Rates of exchange are constantly in flux; for up-to-the-minute information, consult a currency-conversion website such as www.oanda.com/convert/classic.

In the Take a Break and Best Bets section of this book, we have used a system of dollar signs to show a range of costs for one night in a hotel (the price of a double-occupancy room) or the cost of an entrée at a restaurant. Use the following table to decipher the dollar signs:

Cost	Hotels	Restaurants
$	under $100	under $10
$$	$100–$200	$10–$20
$$$	$200–$300	$20–$30
$$$$	$300–$400	$30–$40
$$$$$	over $400	over $40

An Invitation to the Reader

In researching this book, we discovered many wonderful places—hotels, restaurants, shops, and more. We're sure you'll find others. Please tell us about them, so we can share the information with your fellow travelers in upcoming editions. If you were disappointed with a recommendation, we'd love to know that, too. Please write to:

Frommer's Florence & Tuscany Day by Day, 1st Edition
Wiley Publishing, Inc. • 111 River St. • Hoboken, NJ 07030-5774

16 Favorite **Moments**

16 Favorite **Moments**

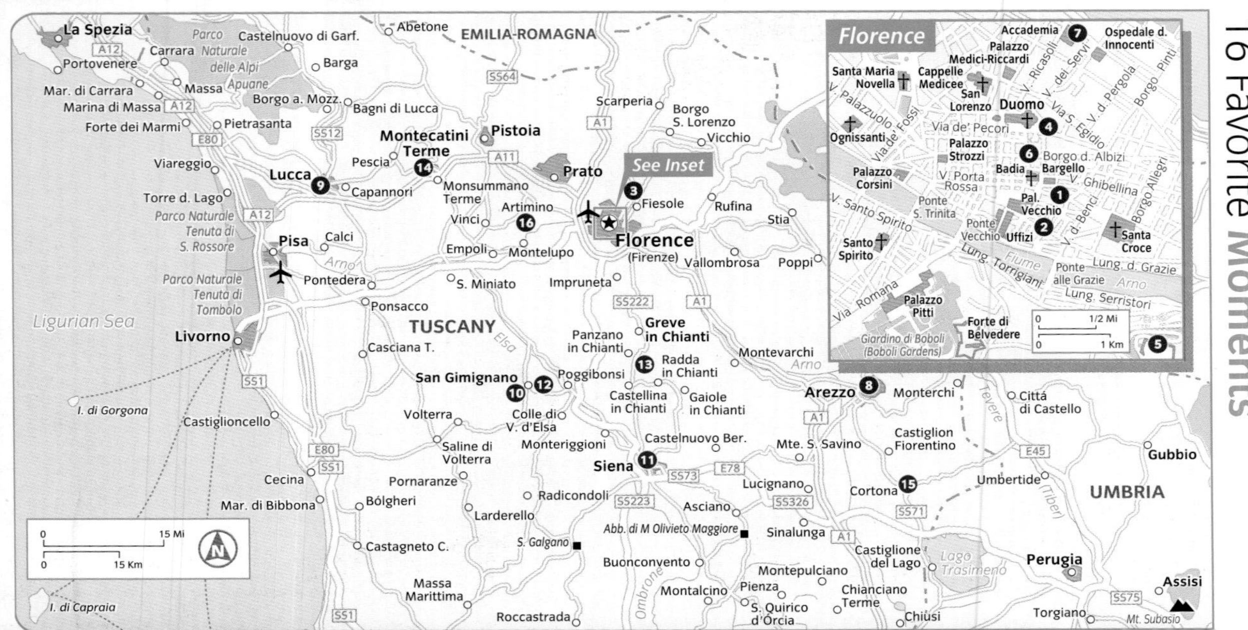

The treasures of the Uffizi and Michelangelo's *David* are the start of an awe-inspiring journey into Tuscany, but there is so much more to the region than Florence. Beyond the city that gave birth to the Renaissance, Tuscany is one of the world's most beautiful districts—with its snow-capped mountains, stately cypresses, Tyrrhenian Sea coastline, and silver-green olive groves. With Chianti's vineyards, Pisa's Tower, San Gimignano's medieval "skyscrapers," and the wealth of Florentine art and architecture, it's difficult to single out 16 highlights, but this list is our best attempt to do so.

1 Eating the world's best gelati. At Florence's **Gelateria Vivoli,** Via Isola della Stinche 7R (☎ 055-292344), in a back street near Santa Croce, you'll find the finest ice cream anywhere. From Marengo (meringue) to candied orange peels with chocolate: You name it, it's here. Vespa-riding punks and contessas alike come for their daily fix. *See p 28.*

2 Sitting in a cafe on Florence's Piazza della Signoria. Sip espresso on Tuscany's grandest, most beautiful square—the site of Girolamo Savonarola's infamous "bonfire of the vanities." From a comfortable perch, you'll behold Benvenuto Cellini's *Perseus* with the head of Medusa, a replica (to scale) of Michelangelo's *David,* the Uffizi, and Palazzo Vecchio. Coffee never tasted so good. *See p 13.*

Neptune, *one of the Piazza della Signoria's many marble deities.*

Cafe tables on the Piazza della Signoria in Florence.

3 Walking the ancient road from Fiesole to Florence. At twilight, start at Fiesole's Piazza Mino and follow the road of the ancients that linked this hill town with Florence, below. Untamed vegetation pours over the high walls that line the way past gnarled olive trees, private gardens, and 18th-century architecture. Prepare yourself for the stunning panoramic vista that will open suddenly.

The real thing: Michelangelo's David *at the Accademia.*

❹ **Taking a hackney ride** (horse and carriage) through historic Florence will make you feel like Henry James with a young woman in tow. Painted black, with fire engine red wheels, the carriage passes through the 13th-century heart of the city. *See p 24.*

❺ **Basking in the lights of the Renaissance,** at twilight, from the Piazzale Michelangelo. The bronze *David* here may be *faux,* and tourists abound, but the view of the city twinkling from this balustraded terrace may rank among the greatest you've seen. ***See p 15.***

❻ **Strolling the floodlit streets of Florence at night,** when everything from the Duomo to the Uffizi takes on even greater drama. Stand on the Ponte Vecchio and watch the Arno flow. ***See p 15.***

❼ **Standing in awe at the foot of Michelangelo's *David*.** Even if you've seen the *Venus de Milo,* the massive genius of Michelangelo's masterpiece, at the Accademia, may bowl you over—even from behind its Plexiglas barrier protecting it from fanatics. After all these centuries, it is still miraculously alive, embodying the ideals of the High Renaissance. ***See p 15.***

❽ **Following the Piero della Francesca trail.** His best work is the fresco cycle at the basilica of San Francesco in Arezzo (p 124), including *Legend of the True Cross.* Monterchi's museum (p 118) features the only pregnant Madonna in Italian art, and Sanselpolcro has two minor and two major works—including the 1463 *Resurrection of Christ* (often

Florence at night from the Piazzale Michelangelo.

A Tuscan vintner in the fertile Chianti region south of Florence.

hailed as "the best picture in the world"). *See p 81, 118, and 124.*

❾ **Biking along the city walls of Lucca.** Traverse 16th-century ramparts so thick they now function as a narrow, tree-lined promenade. Kids and octogenarians alike peddle Tuscany's greatest biking trail, 5km (2⅔ miles) in length. The chestnut and ilex trees are compliments of Marie Louise of Bourbon, from the 1800s. *See p 135.*

❿ **Dine al fresco in autumn.** What could be finer than a *bistecca alla fiorentina* dripping with olive oil and fresh herbs, grilling over a chestnut wood fire? One served outdoors, of course, in Tuscany in autumn. When the leaves are turning red and gold, regional staples—black truffles, grilled pheasant, hare with pappardelle—seem to taste their best. Try La Vecchie Mura, in San Gimignana. *See p 161.*

⓫ **Attending Palio, Siena's medieval costumed pageant** and Italy's grandest festival. This breakneck, bareback horse race around dirt-packed historic Piazza del Campo takes place in July and August. Beyond the race, it's bacchanalia—with 3 days of parades and heavy partying. *See p 164.*

⓬ **Scaling the Torre Grossa in the quintessential Tuscan town of San Gimignano.** Its skyline is still pierced by at least 14 medieval towers (locals call them "skyscrapers"). Climb the Torre Grossa ("Big Tower"), from 1311, for the single most memorable view of the Tuscan countryside. *See p 157.*

⓭ **Tasting the wine in Chianti country.** In the green vineyard-studded hills between Florence and Siena grows Italy's most famous

Pomp and circumstance overtake Siena during the Palio festival.

Da Delfina, outside Florence.

product. Against a backdrop of ancient villages and crenellated castles from the Middle Ages, you can sample the *vino*, from vineyards in Castellina, Greve, and Radda. *See p 157.*

⑭ **Taking the waters at Montecatini.** In the "Valley of Mists" lies Montecatini Terme, grande dame of all Italian spas. Giuseppe Verdi composed *Othello* while taking the waters here, but you can just relax, in mudpacks, drinking mineral-rich waters as radioactive vapors are steamed in your face. *See p 110.*

⑮ **Discover your favorite Tuscan hilltown.** Our vote goes to Cortona, one of the great cities of the Etruscans, surrounded by olive groves and vineyards on a rich plain of the Valdichiana. To huff and puff up and down its narrow, steep, cobbled streets is to wander back into the Middle Ages. *See p 128.*

⑯ **Dining Tuscan-style in the country at Artimino.** A 15-minute train ride outside Florence, **Da Delfina,** Via della Chiesa, Artimino (☎ 055-8718119), is wonderful and earthy, in a medieval walled village. Follow the smell of freshly caught fish, grilling over a wood-burning fireplace, served with produce from the nearby fields. *See p 43.* ●

The lush Tuscan countryside viewed from a San Gimignano "skyscraper."

1 Strategies for Seeing **Tuscany**

Strategies for Seeing **Tuscany**

Tuscany isn't Tokyo or New York; racing around the region trying to "see" everything runs against the grain and the pace of the place, and may prevent you from *experiencing* it. It's tempting to want to make tracks, given that there is so much to see within a relatively small region easily traversed by car. But structuring a relaxed itinerary makes for a memorable trip. In this chapter we provide some suggestions for maximizing your time in Tuscany.

Rule #1: Keep your expectations reasonable.

Consider the experience of two couples we know who recently visited the region. One couple fashioned an aggressive itinerary that encompassed most of the major towns covered in chapter 6. And while they were able to say they saw town after town, church after church, and artwork after artwork, they spent 3 to 4 hours a day stuck in the car, fighting traffic, the heat, and crazy truck drivers. The other couple decided to take on less turf and, naturally, didn't see as much; they even missed Cortona and some of our other favorite towns. Instead, they spent an entire afternoon in a Montepulciano cafe, splitting a chilled bottle of Orvieto Classico, staring over a wrought-iron balcony at a church in the distance. In hindsight, they considered that stop the

The countryside near Panzano, in Chianti Country.

pinnacle of their trip, writing, "We wouldn't have traded that lazy Tuscan afternoon for the world."

Rule #2: Remember, distances between towns are short. Visiting Tuscany is as easy as traveling around a small state in the U.S. You can drive from Florence to San Gimignano or Siena in less than an hour. The entire Chianti wine country is only 48km (30 miles) from north to south, and 32km (20 miles) at its widest point. What's more, it begins only 4km (½ mile) south of Florence. You can even drive from Florence west to Pisa in an hour. Once you veer off the autostrada, the roads become secondary, but unless you're going to the most remote hamlet in Tuscany, they're generally well maintained and signposted. The only problem in summer will be the heavy traffic caused by thousands of other visitors who also want to navigate the region by car.

Rule #3: Decide whether to hotel hop or stay in one place. Checking in and out of hotels is often a boring hassle—involving luggage transfers, packing and unpacking, registering and checking out, and other technicalities that can drain pleasure from a vacation. Because most Tuscan towns are within easy reach of one another, you can set up camp in the same hotel for 3 nights—in Siena, for example—and venture to smaller towns nearby on day trips. From Siena, you can easily visit San Gimignano, Volterra, or even the Chianti wine country

Tuscany is an ideal place to while away the hours in an outdoor cafe.

without wasting too much time in the car. You'll save a lot of wear and tear on your soul with this tack, reserving your energy for hotel changes required by longer hauls.

Rule #4: Plan your excursions around lunch.
If you're driving from town to town, plan to reach your destination by noon. Restaurants usually serve until 2 or 2:30pm, but you'll need time to park (which is often tricky in these overcrowded towns) and to locate the address of your restaurant. If you don't want to follow a schedule, pack a lunch before setting out and follow your bliss to the ideal picnic spot somewhere under the Tuscan sun.

Rule #5: Don't follow these ideas to the letter; use them as building blocks for your trip.
This guide was designed to help you piece together your own dream getaway. You can plan your time in Florence using one section and then hop about Tuscany, in the next few days, using another. It's like an a la carte menu—select one item from column A and another from column B, according to your own tastes and interests, to make the most of our advice. ●

Pick Your Point of Entry

No direct flights run to Tuscany's two airports, in Florence or Pisa, from the United States or Canada. But Tuscany is easy to access from either Rome or Milan by plane, car, or train. Rome is the most hassle-free gateway and the best point of entry if you're starting your trip in Florence—about an hour away by plane and 3 hours by train. You can also rent a car in Rome and drive north to Florence 277km (172 miles) on the fast-moving A1 autostrada. (Milan is slightly farther—298km/183 miles northwest of Florence—but worth the extra distance if you find a cheaper flight there.) If you're beginning your trip in northwest Tuscany—in Pisa or Lucca—we suggest you fly into the airport at Pisa, which is larger than the airport at Florence. If your goal is to visit destinations in southern Tuscany, such as Montepulciano and Pienza, we'd abandon the plane option and plan to drive north from Rome. For complete details about reaching Tuscany by plane, or the different options for getting between airports and your final destination, see the "By Plane" section in "Getting There/Getting Around" in Savvy Traveler (p 184).

2 The Best of Florence

Best of Florence in One Day

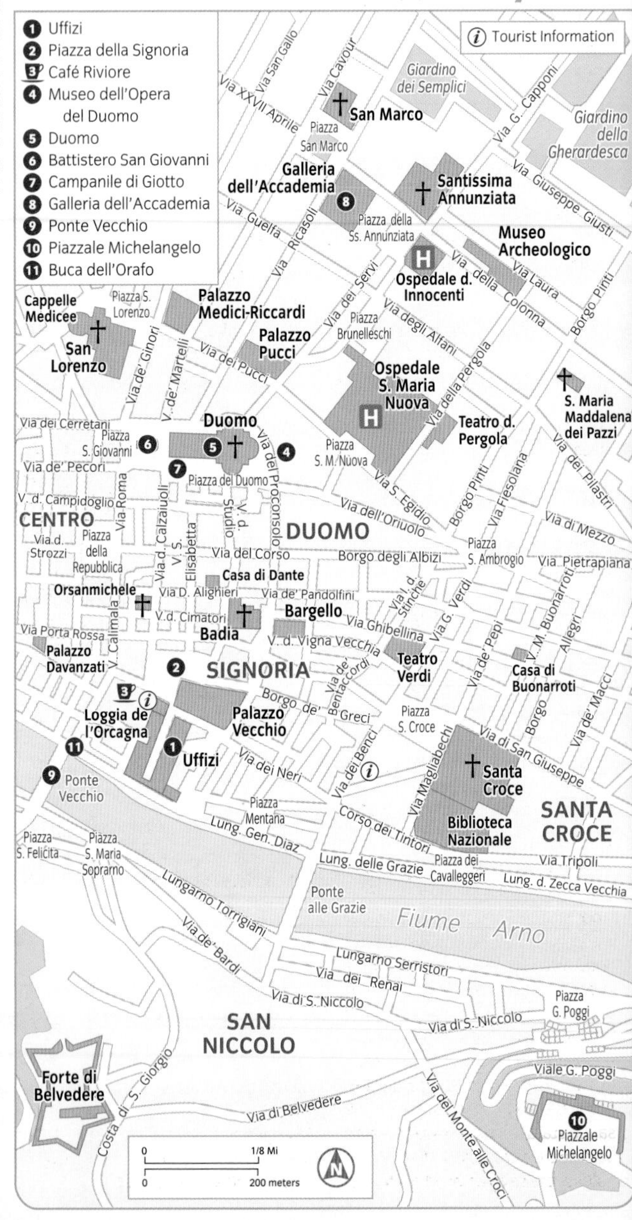

Florence in 1 day? *"Impossibile,"* a Florentine might tell you before throwing up his hands in despair and walking away, convinced you are mad. But 1 day in Florence is better than none—provided you rise with the roosters and move with steely discipline and stamina, to make the most of it. This "greatest hits" itinerary begins with the highlights of the Uffizi, the most rewarding and time-consuming stopover. After lunch at the Piazza della Signoria, you'll take in the city's majestic ecclesiastical complex: the Duomo, the Baptistery, and Giotto's Bell Tower. Then you'll round out the day with a trek to see Michelangelo's *David* at the Accademia—a mandatory call—followed by a shopping stroll across the Ponte Vecchio and a Tuscan meal in an authentic *buca* (cellar). **START: Take buses A, B, 14, or 23 to the Uffizi.**

1 ★★★ Uffizi. This is one of the world's greatest museums and the single best repository of Renaissance art. In room after room, you'll confront masterpiece after masterpiece—including Leonardo da Vinci's *Annunciation* (with an angel that could be Mona Lisa's brother), Michelangelo's *Holy Family,* Sandro Botticelli's *Birth of Venus,* Peter Paul Ruben's voluptuous nudes, and more. In Italian, *uffizi* means offices, and that's what Vasari deigned this building to be in 1550. But it's come a long way, bambino. The Uffizi will dazzle you with the greatest Florentine paintings of the 14th and 15th centuries—with works by Giotto to Caravaggio and beyond. (Serious art devotees may want to spend the entire day here.) *3 hr. See p 33 for details.*

2 ★★ Piazza della Signoria. The monumental heart of Florence (and Tuscany's most famous square) is an open-air museum of sculpture, dominated by Michelangelo's *David* (a copy of the original, which used to stand here). The powerful mass of the Palazzo Vecchio dominates one end of the square; another is defined by the 14th-century Loggia della Signoria, filled with ancient and Renaissance statues (the most celebrated being Bevenuto Cellini's *Perseus* holding the severed head of Medusa).

Hercules, David, and other superheroes loom over the Piazza della Signoria.

Also check out Giambologna's *Rape of the Sabines,* one of the great Mannerist sculptures. *45 min. See p 27, bullet 5 for full details.*

3 ★ Café Riviore. Regrettably filled with tourists and overpriced, it occupies one of the greatest pieces of real estate in the world. Smartly clad waiters hustle to deliver lunch platters and elegant sandwiches—as though anyone's paying attention to anything but the view. *Piazza della Signoria (at Via Vacchereccia 5R). ☎ 055-212412. $–$$$.*

Titian's Venus of Urbino *is a hallmark of the Uffizi collection.*

❹ ★★ **Museo dell'Opera del Duomo.** For connoisseurs of Renaissance sculpture, this museum across from the Duomo is a shrine, hosting everything from an unfinished, heart-wrenching Michelangelo *Pietà* to its premier attraction—the restored panels of Lorenzo Ghiberti's *Gates of Paradise.* The works here were deemed too precious to be left to the elements, and were moved inside. 🕒 *1 hr. See p 30, bullet ⓮.*

❺ ★★ **Duomo.** Consecrated in 1436, one of Europe's most majestic cathedrals rests under Filippo Brunelleschi's revolutionary dome, a triumph of engineering over gravity. The symbol of Florence itself, it's a tourist stamping ground of horrendous proportion—but justifiably so. It's part-church, part-candy cane, part-zebra—in stripes of marble-white, bottle-green, and pink. The interior, by contrast, is spartan but with one of Europe's most classic views from the top of the cupola. 🕒 *45 min. See p 29, bullet ⓫ for details.*

Michelangelo's David *draws throngs of admirers to the Accademia.*

❻ ★★★ **Battistero San Giovanni.** On a hurried first-day tour of Florence, you need invade the inner precincts of the Baptistery only to take in the magnificent 13th-century mosaics lining the inner dome. The excitement is outside, in the world-famous bronze doors. Sure, they're replicas (the original work is in the Museo dell'Opera del Duomo); but even the copies are masterpieces. Ghiberti's East Doors, facing the Duomo—a commission he won in 1401 through a competition against the city's greatest artists—are widely credited with having launched the Renaissance. 🕒 *30 min. See p 29, bullet ⓭ for full details.*

❼ ★★ **Campanile di Giotto.** An ideal companion to Brunelleschi's dome, this Gothic bell tower was completed at the end of the 14th century long after Giotto, its creator, had died (in 1337). Walk 414 steps to the top of the campanile for a panoramic view of the Duomo and

Florence. It's roughly the same vista as from the Duomo, but with a view onto the cathedral itself. 30 min. *See p 29, bullet* ⓬ *for full details.*

❽ ★★ **Galleria dell'Accademia.** You've seen the mock of Michelangelo's *David* all over the world. This gallery has the real thing (1501–04)—a monumental icon of youthful male beauty and a stellar example of Michelangelo's humanism. It can require an hour-long wait, unless you reserve space. *15 min., without a wait. Via Ricasoll 60. ☎ 050-2388609. 8€. Tues–Sun 8:15am–7pm. Bus: B, D, or 12.*

❾ ★★ **Ponte Vecchio.** The Ponte Vecchio, as its name suggests, is the city's oldest bridge; its latest incarnation dates to 1345, but the shops along it have been taking advantage of all the foot traffic since at least the 12th century. Originally occupied by blacksmiths, butchers, and tanners, the shops that flank the bridge have mostly sold gold and silver since the reign of the Medicis. (Sunset is the ideal time to cross.) *30 min. See p 24, bullet* ❷ *for full details.*

❿ ★ **Piazzale Michelangelo.** For a final *arrivederci* to Florence, head for its most panoramic

The Duomo (rear view).

piazza, laid out in 1885. From this balustraded, 1885 terrace, the city of the Renaissance unfurls before you. View it at twilight as the lights of the city twinkle on. In the center of the square is a monument to Michelangelo. *30 min.*

11 ★ **Buca dell'Orafo.** For your final meal in Florence, head for this famous cellar restaurant, in the former workshop of a Renaissance goldsmith, for Tuscan cuisine served at communal tables. It's on an arched alleyway near the Ponte Vecchio. (If you want to dine with locals, book a late table.) *2 hr. See p 43 for full details.*

An evening stroll on the Ponte Vecchio.

Best of Florence in Two Days

On your second day in Florence, spend the morning wandering Oltrarno, the district on the left bank of the Arno. The great attraction here is the *Palazzo Pitti* and the adjacent *Giardino di Boboli.* Even if you take all morning, you will see only a part of the Pitti Palace's great collection of art, which encompasses not only Renaissance works, but painting and sculpture by later European masters. Stroll through the Boboli Gardens before a typical Oltrarno lunch in a Mamma Mia–type trattoria, before heading back to the Right Bank for a grand array of treasures. These include the Medici Chapels (with Michelangelo's grand sculptures), Filippo Brunelleschi's Basilica di San Lorenzo, and the art-filled town hall, Palazzo Vecchio. START: **Take bus D, 11, 36, 37, or 68 to the Palazzo Pitti.**

1 ★★ Palazzo Pitti. This 15th-century Medici palace on the south side of the Arno is second only to the Uffizi in its wealth of artwork. The Galleria Palatina on the second floor, with its marvelous collection of paintings, is reason enough to go to Florence; we'd visit for the Raphaels alone. And the Palatina just primes you for what's to come: the city's most extensive coterie of museums—including exhibitions of costume, modern art, even the Medici's private digs. 🕘 *2 hr.* *See p 26, bullet 3 for full details.*

2 ★ Giardini di Boboli. Laid out between 1549 and 1656, this is the grand Renaissance garden of Europe. After a stroll through the garden, climb to the top of Fortezza di Belvedere for a panoramic view of the city, with its Renaissance spires. Before departing, stroll down the stunning Viottolone, an avenue of pines and cypresses. 🕘 *30 min.* *See p 27, bullet 4 for full details.*

Medici Skywalk

After Cosimo I de' Medici moved to the Pitti Palace, he commissioned Vasari to build a private aboveground tunnel to the Uffizi. The **Corridorio Vasariano,** built in 1565, runs along the Arno from the Pitti Palace to the Ponte Vecchio,

The Palazzo Pitti was Europe's grandest residence when it housed the Medicis.

Florence's town hall, the Palazzo Vecchio, on the Piazza della Signoria.

crosses the river above the bridge shops, then continues on to the museum that once served as the Medici offices. Lined with paintings and windows, it is open to visitors. ⌚ *1 hr. Reservations (required) 055-2654321; www.firenzemusei.it; 8.50€*. Tues–Sun 8:15am–7pm. Tours Tues, Wed, Fri–Sun. Bus: A, B, 23, or 71.

3 Mama Gina. This is the most famous—and one of the best—trattoria on the Left Bank of the Arno, ideal for a luncheon stopover after the Pitti and the Boboli Gardens. One of the succulent pasta dishes along with a garden salad makes for an ideal repast before you venture into the sun again. After lunch, you can head across the Ponte Santa Trinita bridge back to the Centro Storico of Florence. *See p 45 for full details.*

4 ★★ Cappelle Medicee. The big deal here is the celebrated Medici tombs by Michelangelo. Regrettably, two of his grandest creations honored unworthy members of the Medici clan. Nevertheless, the great artist portrayed them as idealized princes of the Renaissance: Michelangelo's *The Thinker* (Il Pensieroso), for example, adorned the tomb of Giuliano di Medici—a deranged young man who died an early death. Michelangelo's *Night* and *Day,* two allegorical figures, are two of the grandest pieces of sculpture in the world. ⌚ *15 min.* *See p 31, bullet 16 for full details.*

The Basilica di San Lorenzo's architects included Brunelleschi and Michelangelo.

Perseus *brandishes Medusa's head, outside the Palazzo Vecchio.*

5 ★★★ Basilica di San Lorenzo. Some of the greatest artists and architects, including Brunelleschi, worked to create this splendid church between the 15th and 17th centuries. Walk up the nave to explore Vecchia Sacrestia (Old Sacristy), Brunelleschi's grand creation, one of the first and finest works of the early Renaissance—made all the more enthralling by the 1460 pulpits of Donatello. As if this weren't bait enough, the Biblioteca Medicea Laurenziana, the library of the Medicis, was designed by Michelangelo himself. *1 hr.* *See also p 30, bullet 15 for full details.*

6 ★★ Palazzo Vecchio. In the heart of Florence, this massive 13th-century palace is still the town hall, putting to shame other city halls around the world. A highlight is the Salone dei Cinquecento, or hall of the 500, where the great council met. It's filled with Giorgio Vasari frescoes. The star attraction is Michelangelo's *Victory,* originally intended for the tomb of Pope Julius. *1 hr.* *See also p 28, bullet 6 for full details.*

7 Caffé Italiano. Ease into the Florentine night by heading directly north of Piazza della Signoria, site of Palazzo Vecchio, to this secret hideaway in the historic core. If you're rushed, stay downstairs and drink at the stand-up bar. Head upstairs for a more leisurely evening spent at dark wooden tables. Service is a disaster, but when your order comes, expect some of the best coffee and desserts in town. Our favorite? **Caffé-choc**—that's espresso laced with pure bitter chocolate powder. *Via della Condotta (between Via dei Calzaiuoli and Via del Proconsolo) 56R.* ☎ *055-291082.*

Docents in Renaissance garb run guided tours through the Palazzo Vecchio.

Best of Florence in Three Days

A 3rd day in Florence will yield just a glimpse of the city's treasures. The Museo Nazionale del Bargello is a worthy first stop, as the world's greatest repository of Renaissance sculpture. The Museo di San Marco, the former convent and cloisters where Fra Angelico lived and painted, is also rewarding. Few dare to sneak out of Florence without paying a visit to the Basilica di Santa Maria Novella and the Basilica di Santa Croce, two of Europe's grandest churches (Michelangelo and Galileo, among others, are buried in the latter). To escape tourists for a spell, retreat to Le Cascine, the city's premier park, which dates to the 15th century. Even better, head for the hills, for a romantic dinner in the hilltown of Fiesole.

1 ★★ Museo Nazionale del Bargello. This is a vast repository of some of the most famous Renaissance sculpture ever created, including Donatello's *John the Baptist* and his own bronze *David.* The Bargello also contains, along with countless other works, another Michelangelo *David*—created some 3 decades after the celebrated version in the Accademia. *1½ hr.* *See p 29, bullet 10 for full details.*

2 ★★ Museo di San Marco. This convent and cloisters are a museum honoring Fra Angelico. Cosimo il Vecchio chose Angelico to build and decorate this new convent, where he also lived, and where Girolamo Savonarola later resided as well. The Chiostro di Sant'Antonio was designed by Michelozzo di Bartolomeo. Angelico's famous *Last Judgment* and his sober masterpiece, *Annunciation,* are filled with a pacifying power, as are the walls of the monks' cells, which are also decorated with scenes that foster meditation. *1hr. Piazza San Marco 1. ☎ 055-294883. 4€. Tues–Fri 8:30am–1:50pm; Sat 8:15am–6:50pm. Bus: 1, 6, 7, 10, 11, 17, or 20.*

Donatello's David, *the first nude to appear after Roman times.*

3 ★ La Mescita. Florentines call this a *fiaschetteria,* while Americans might call it a "dive." By any name, it makes the best sandwiches in this part of town, and also peddles home-cooked platters of a few Tuscan dishes. If you're in the area for lunch, it's worth fighting for a table at this crowded, bustling joint where locals and university students flock. You'll eat smack up alongside Florentines and risk getting booted if you occupy a table for too long. *Via degli Alfani 70R (at Via dei Servi). ☎ 055-7591604. $. Bus: 31 or 32.*

The Bargello claims one of the world's finest troves of Renaissance sculpture.

Masaccio's Trinita, *at the Basilica di Santa Maria Novella.*

❹ ★★ **Basilica di Santa Maria Novella.** Built from 1246 by the Dominicans, this church is filled with some of Tuscany's grandest frescoes, notably the late-14th-century paintings by Andrea di Bonaiuto in the Cappellone degli Spagnoli. Other treasures include the famous *Crucifix* by Filippo Brunelleschi. ◷ *45 min.* *See p 31, bullet ⓱ for full details.*

❺ ★★ **Basilica di Santa Croce.** Locals call it "the Westminster Abbey of Tuscany," because this 14th-century church contains the tombs of the Renaissance's brightest lights—most notably Michelangelo and Galileo. Author John Ruskin made a classic comment about Santa Croce: "Wait then for an entirely light morning: rise with the sun and go to Santa Croce, with a good opera glass in your pocket." Some of the finest Renaissance sculptures in the world are waiting for you here. ◷ *1 hr.* *See p 28, bullet ❽ for full details.*

❻ ★ **Parco della Cascine.** The Giardini di Boboli is a common stop

The 11th-century Santa Maria Novella houses some of the city's finest frescoes.

Michelangelo's tomb, one of many in Santa Croce.

for travelers, but Le Cascine is relatively undiscovered by nonresidents, even though it's hard to miss—stretching 3km (1¾ miles) west of Piazza Vittorio Veneto, on the Arno. Le Cascine was once a dairy farm belonging to the Medici. In the 19th century, when Percy Bysshe Shelley composed *Ode to the West Wind* here, it was the haunt of fashionable carriages. Today, it's free from traffic and Renaissance masterpieces—it's just fresh air and greenery, with a swimming pool open to nonmembers. *Open all the time.* ⌚ *1 hr. Bus: 1, 9, 12, 26, 27, or 80.*

7 ★ Trattoria le Cave di Maiano. For your final good-bye to Florence, take a 15-minute ride to this converted farmhouse where Florentines escape the city heat on summer nights. The hearty regional cuisine—such as chicken roasted under a brick with peppers, and succulent pastas, such as green tortellini—is the finest in the area. Many adventurous diners walk the entire 8km (5 miles) back to Florence, with the city lights, twinkling in the distance, to lead the way. See p 3, 16 Favorite Moments, for details. ***Note:*** You can stop at any point along the way and board bus #7 back to town. ⌚ *4 hr., including dinner and the walk. For full details on the restaurant, see p 45.*

Centro Storico

In Florence's historic core—a flat, compact area known as Centro Storico—you can wander stone streets that remain essentially the same as they were when Michelangelo, Leonardo da Vinci, and Galileo trod the same paths. And even on the street, the art doesn't stop; it's seemingly everywhere one looks. Remember, though, to wear comfortable shoes and bring water. And, if you're traveling in July or August, be aware that walking the hot, crowded city streets is an intense, demanding experience. To fully visit all the attractions below would take 2 days—even 3 if you tend to linger over great art. START: **Take bus D, 11, 36, 37, or 68, which will deliver you across the Arno to the Pitti Palace.**

1 ★★★ Uffizi. On par with the Prado and the Louvre, this is one of the world's greatest art museums. No place has a more extensive collection of Renaissance masterpieces—including Michelangelo's *The Holy Family,* Leonardo da Vinci's *The Annunciation,* and Sandro Botticelli's *The Birth of Venus.* Gallery after gallery dazzles the viewer with works from the Medici private collections. You'll be tempted to spend 2 days here. 🕒 ***3 hr.*** *See p 33 (introduction) for full details.*

Botticelli's Venus, *at the Uffizi.*

❷ ★★ **Ponte Vecchio.** Built in 1354 across the Arno's narrowest stretch, the Ponte Vecchio's medieval character endures, despite the bustling modern commerce it supports. Italy's greatest goldsmith, Benvenuto Cellini, runs his business in the middle of the bridge—one of many jewelers who have replaced the medieval butchers and tanners who originally traded here. 🕘 ***30 min. Open anytime. Bus: B.***

The Ponte Vecchio has been a bustling commercial hub since the 14th century.

3 ★★ **Pitti Palace.** Luca Pitti, a rich importer of French fabrics, wanted a palace to outclass the Medicis—and in that he got his wish. Niccolò Macchiavelli hailed the *palazzo* as "grander than any other erected in Florence by a private citizen." When the Pittis went broke, the Medici moved in, making it the most splendid palace in Europe until Louis XIV built Versailles. In the 19th-century, the Pitti Palace sheltered the Italian royal family, when Florence was the capital. Victor Emmanuel III gave it to the state, which turned it into a series of world-class museums.

4 ★ **Giardini di Boboli.** The great landscape artist, Triboli, laid out these Renaissance gardens, through which the Medici romped, in the 16th century. Since opening to the public in 1776, Boboli has become the most famous and

Pitti Palace

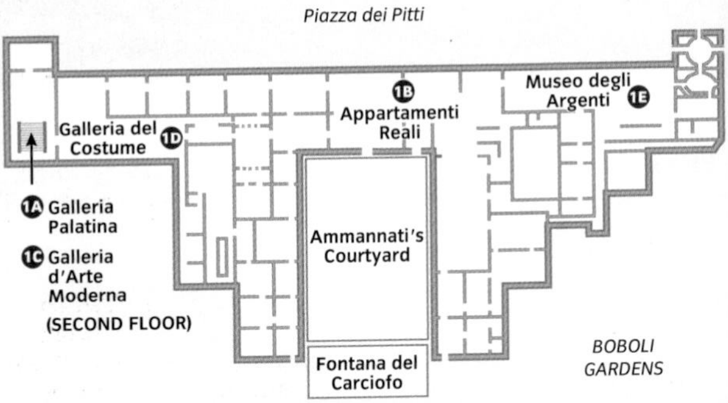

After climbing 140 steps, you enter the **3A** ★★★ ***Galleria Palatina.*** Head here if you have to skip everything else. It's filled with masterpieces from the High Renaissance and later eras, collected by the Medici. The most famous painting is Raphael's *Madonna of the Chair,* one of the six most renowned paintings in Europe. Baroque sumptuousness defines the **3B** ★ ***Appartmenti Reali,*** homes to the Kings of Savoy. Note Michelangelo da Caravaggio's *Portrait of a Knight of Malta.* In the shadow of the Renaissance rooms, **3C** ★ **the *Galleria d'Arte Moderna*** showcases the Macchiaioli, the 19th-century School of Impressionist painters in revolt against academicism. The **3D** ***Galleria del Costume*** is filled with 18th- to 20th-century clothing, including historic wardrobes such as Eleonora of Toledo's burial dress. On the ground floor, **3E** ***Museo degli Argenti*** is a camp glorification of the Medici household wares, with treasures in ivory and silver, among other metals. It's ostentatious but fun. ⌚ *2 hr. Piazza Pitti (across the Arno off Via Guicciardini).* ☎ *055-2388611. www.firenzemusei.it. Galleria Palatina 6.50€ adults, 3.25€ children. Other museums 5€ adults, 2.50€ children. Tues–Sun 8:15am–6:45pm. Bus D, 11, 36, 37, or 68.*

One of the many lavish, art-filled rooms in the Pitti Palace.

dazzling garden of Tuscany, filled with splashing fountains and elegant statuary such as *Venus* by Giambologna in the grotto of Buontalenti. The fountain—an obese Bacchus astride a turtle—is a copy of a statue depicting Pietro Barbino, Cosimo I's court jester. ⌚ *30 min. Piazza Pitti (at Via Romana).* ☎ *055-2651838. Admission 6€ including entrance to Museo degli Argenti (see above). June–Aug daily 8:30am–7:45pm; Apr–May and Sept–Oct daily 8:30am–6:30pm; Nov–Feb daily 8:15am–4:45pm; Mar daily 8:15am–5:30pm. Closed the 1st and last Mon of each month. Ticket office closes 1 hr. before gardens. Bus: D, 11, 36, 37, or 68.*

Bacchus in the Giardini di Boboli.

5 ★★ Piazza della Signoria. The center of civic life in Florence for centuries, this landmark square appropriately stands in the historic core dominated by the Palazzo Vecchio (p 28), the town hall. Michelangelo's *David* in front of the palace is a copy, but the late-14th-century Loggia della Signoria is an open-air museum that boasts plenty of original master works, including Benvenuto Cellini's *Perseus* holding the severed head of Medusa.

Ammannato's controversial fountain of Neptune inspired this chant in the 16th century: *Ammannato, Ammannato, che bel marmot rovinato!* (What beautiful marble you've ruined!) ⌚ *1 hr. Open anytime. Bus: A, B, 23, or 71.*

6 ★★ Palazzo Vecchio. This "Old Palace" became home to Cosimo I and the Medici in 1540, but it dates to the 13th century, when it was built by Gothic master builder Arnolfo di Cambio. (Di Cambio's 92m/308-ft. landmark tower, which still graces the Florentine skyline, was an engineering feat in its day.) The highlight of the interior is the Hall of the 500 *(Salone dei Cinquecento)*, frescoed by Giorgio Vasari and his assistants in the 16th century. (Alas, wax-pigment frescoes by Leonardo melted when braziers were brought in to speed up the drying process.) Michelangelo's sculpture *Victory* survives, thankfully, along with Donatello's famous bronze group, *Judith Slaying Holofernes*, created in 1455. You can also visit the private apartments of Eleanor of Toledo, the Spanish wife of Cosimo I, and the chamber where religious zealot Girolamo Savonarola endured a dozen torture sessions, including "twists" on the rack. ⌚ *1 hr. Piazza della Signoria (at Via Vacche Reccia). ☎ 055-2768465. Admission 6€. Mon–Wed and Fri–Sun 9am–7pm; Thurs 9am–2pm. Ticket office closes 1 hr. before palace. Bus: A, B, 23, or 71.*

7 ★ Café Riviore. Have a coffee at this landmark cafe—the best positioned in Florence for taking in the glories of the Piazza della Signoria. *See p 13, bullet* **3** *for full details.*

8 ★★ Basilica di Santa Croce. The statue of Dante in the square is lifeless, but Santa Croce is the pantheon of Florence, with monuments to Galileo, Michelangelo, Dante, Petrarch, and other creators of western civilization. Ignore the hideous facade and head inside for the galaxy of great Renaissance sculpture, such as Donatello's famous *Crucifixion*. Check out Filippo Brunelleschi's Cappella del Pazzi, a masterpiece of Renaissance design, and take in Giotto's masterful 1320 frescoes depicting the life of St. Francis. ⌚ *1 hr. Piazza Santa Croce 16 (at Via de Benci). Free admission to church, 4€ to cloisters and museum. Church Mon–Sat 9:30am–5pm; Sun 1–5:30pm. Museum and cloisters Mon–Sat 9:30am–5:30pm; Sun 1–5:30pm. Bus: B, 13, 23, or 71.*

Rape of the Sabines *in the Piazza della Signoria.*

9 Vivoli. A block west of Piazza Santa Croce, this little hole-in-the-wall *gelateria* serves the world's best ice cream. Just choose your flavor: fig, melon, chocolate mousse, even rice. Or try candied lemon peels with creamy vanilla or *Semifreddi,* with a base of cream instead of milk. Our all-time favorite, *Zabaglione,* tastes like eggnog. ***Via Isola delle Stinche 7R (at Via della Vigna Vecchia). ☎ 055-292334. Closed Jan and 3 weeks in Aug; dates and opening hours vary.***

⑩ ★★ Museo Nazionale del Bargello. This grim fortress—once a place for public hangings—centers around a courtyard with a loggia and portico. The second-floor sculpture collection is the Renaissance's finest, including Donatello's *David* (the first free-standing nude since the Roman era), two Donatello versions of *John the Baptist,* and a less famous *David* by Michelangelo. ***1½ hr. Via del Proconsolo 4 (at Via Ghibellina). ☎ 055-294883. www.sbas.firenze.it. Admission 5€, daily 8:30am–1:50pm. Closed 2nd and 4th Mon and 1st, 3rd, and 5th Sun of each month. Bus: A, 14, or 23.***

⑪ ★★ Il Duomo (Cattedrale di Santa Maria del Fiore). The world's largest cathedral in its day, the "Duomo" still ranks fourth in size. From 1294 to 1436, builders labored and taxpayers paid for the work, but the flamboyant neo-Gothic structure wasn't complete until the 19th century. The facade is a polychrome jumble of marble stripes in sugarcane colors, but few fault the dome Brunelleschi imposed over it, 105m (351 ft.) off the ground; climbing it is one of the great joys of visiting Florence. You must mount 463 spiraling steps to the ribbed dome for a sublime panoramic view. Afterward, you needn't waste too much time here; much of the art, frescoes, votive offerings, pews, and memorials were swept away or moved elsewhere for safekeeping. Once on the street again, walk around to the eastern side of the Duomo to be awed by its sheer mass and its stunning marble mosaic decorations. ***45 min. Piazza del Duomo (at the northern end of Via Calzaiuoli). www.operaduomo.firenze.it. Free admission to cathedral; 6€ dome. Mon–Wed 10am–7pm; Thurs 10am–3:30pm; Sat 10am–4:45pm; Sun 1:30–4:45pm. Bus: 1 or 3.***

⑫ ★★ Campanile di Giotto. Giotto, Andrea Pisano, and Francesco Talenti collaborated to create this bell tower next to the Duomo. They created visual harmony with three colors of marble. The tower's bells are called *Grossa, Beona, Completa, Cheirica,* and *Squilla* (or Big, Tipsy, Finished, Priestling, and Shrieker). Climb the tower's 414 steps for a panoramic view of Florence and a dazzling perspective on Brunelleschi's dome. Visible for miles, the tower rises 81m (269 ft.) from the ground. ***30 min. Piazza del Duomo (at the northern end of Via Calzaiuoli). ☎ 055-2302885. Admission 6€. Daily 8:30am–7:30pm. Last admission 40 min. before closing. Bus: 1 or 3.***

⑬ ★★★ Battistero San Giovanni. This 11th- and 12th-century octagonal baptistery, named after Saint Giovanni (John the Baptist), is

The Campanile di Giotto, or bell tower, with the best view of Brunelleschi's dome.

visited mainly for the gilded bronze doors on three of its eight sides. The doors are copies; the originals are in the Duomo Museum (see below). The most magnificent are Lorenzo Ghiberti's east doors, which the typically critical Michelangelo hailed as "The Gates of Paradise." The panels illustrate scenes from the Old Testament. Beating out Brunelleschi in a famous competition, Ghiberti also designed the north doors, and Andrea Pisano made the impressive south doors in 1336. Dominated by a figure of Christ, the 13th-century mosaics inside are also worth a peek. *Piazza San Giovanni (off Piazza del Duomo). ☎ 055-2302885. Admission 3€. Mon–Sat noon–7pm, Sun 8:30am–2pm. Last admission 30 min. before closing. Bus: 1 or 3.*

14 ★★ **Museo dell'Opera del Duomo.** The "loot" ripped from the Duomo, the Baptistery, and Giotto's Campanile (including Ghiberti's *Gates of Paradise*) ended up here, near Florence's ecclesiastical complex. For openers, Michelangelo carved another *David,* on display in the courtyard. Rarer and more beautiful, Michelangelo's *Pietà,* originally intended for the artist's tomb, is now on the mezzanine. Upstairs are joyous *cantorie*—one by Donatello, the other by Luca della Robbia. With clashing symbols and sounding brass, these *cantorie* say "praise the Lord" in marble. Sharing the room with the *cantorie* is Donatello's *Magdalene,* one of his most celebrated penitent works, from 1454. ⏲ *1 hr. Piazza del Duomo 9 (at the northern end of Via dei Calzaiuoli). ☎ 055-2302885. Admission 6€. Mon–Sat 9am–7:30pm; Sun 9am–1:30pm. Last admission 40 min. before closing. Bus: 1 or 3.*

Lorenzo Ghiberti's Gates of Paradise.

15 ★★★ **Basilica di San Lorenzo.** The overall effect of this basilica, which houses the tombs of many a Medici (see also Cappelle Medicee, below), is almost Byzantine; one Bulgarian critic called it "a Florentine Hagia Sophia looming over a souk" (a reference to the nearby Mercato di San Lorenzo; p 56). The Medicis shelled out big bags of gold for it, however. The taller of the two domes at the chancel shelters the Cappella dei Principi, the shallower cupola covering Michelangelo's New Sacristy. Commissioned in 1516, Michelangelo's model for the facade was deemed unacceptable to the Medici and so went to Brunelleschi, whose greatest achievement is the Old Sacristy at the end of the north transept. There Donatello created two pulpits with dramatic bronze panels in the nave. ⏲ *1hr. Piazza San Lorenzo (at Via Del Canto dei Nelli). ☎ 055-216634. Free Admission. Daily 10am–5pm. Bus: 1, 6, 7, 11, 17, 33, 67, or 68.*

16 ★★ **Cappelle Medicee.** Make a fast trek to the Sagrestia Nuova, Michelangelo's first realized architectural work—begun in 1520, but left unfinished until 1534. On the left, the tomb of Lorenzo, Duke of Urbino, bears the artist's reclining figures representing *Dawn* and *Dusk.* On the right, the tomb of Giuliano, Duke of

The ceiling of the 11th- and 12th-century Battistero San Giovanni.

Nemours (and youngest son of Lorenzo the Magnificent), features Michelangelo's allegorical figures of *Day* and *Night*. Michelangelo's New Sacristy was intended as an addition to Brunelleschi's Old Sacristy in San Lorenzo proper (see above). Michelangelo never completed the other two tombs commissioned to him, but in 1521 he did finish the deeply moving *Madonna and Child*, for the tomb of Lorenzo de Medici the Magnificent. *15 min. Piazza Madonna degli Aldobrandini 6 (behind San Lorenzo where Via del Gigli and Via Faenza converge). 055-2388602. Admission 6€. Daily 8:15am–4:30pm. Closed 2nd and 4th Sun and 1st, 3rd, and 5th Mon of each month. Bus: 1, 6, 7, 11, 17, 33, 67, or 68.*

17 ★★ Basilica di Santa Maria Novella. The green and white marble facade was created in the 15th century. The interior dates to the 13th century. By the 1800s, this Romanesque and Gothic structure in the city of the Renaissance had become "the church for foreigners," attracting expatriate literati, including Percy Bysshe Shelley, Henry James, Ralph Waldo Emerson, even Henry Wadsworth Longfellow. Giovanni Boccaccio used the church for scenes in his *Decameron*. Of the many frescoes adorning the church, Domenico Ghirlandaio's are the finest. Ostensibly, they depict scenes in the lives of the Virgin Mary and St. John the Baptist, but they're also a dazzling portrait of everyday life in Renaissance Florence. If time remains, visit the cloisters and the splendid Spanish Chapel, frescoed by Andrea di Bonaiuto in the 14th century. *45 min. Piazza Santa Maria Novella (at Via della Scala). 055-215918. Admission free to church, 2.70€ to cloisters and Spanish Chapel. Church Mon–Thurs 9:30am–5pm, Fri 1–5pm; Sat 9:30am–5pm, Sun 1–5pm. Cloisters and Spanish Chapel Sat and Mon–Thurs 9am–5pm, Sun 9am–2pm. Bus: A, 6, 9, 11, 36, 37, or 68.*

The Best of the Uffizi

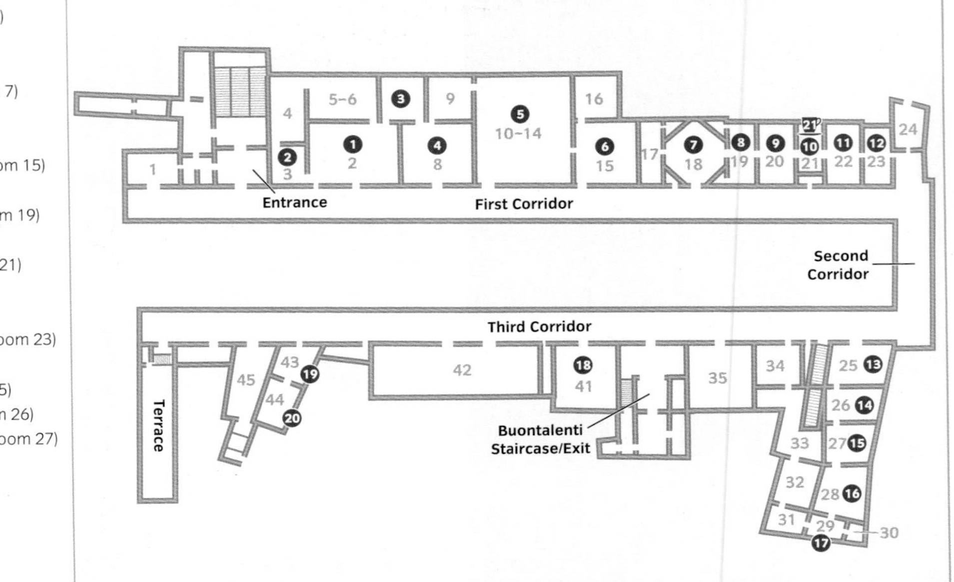

1. Giotto and Cimabue (Room 2)
2. 14th Century Siense paintings (Room 3)
3. Masaccio and Uccello (Room 7)
4. Fra Filippo Lippi (Room 8)
5. Botticelli (Room 10-14)
6. Da Vinci and Verrocchio (Room 15)
7. La Tribuna (Room 18)
8. Perugino and Signorelli (Room 19)
9. Dürer (Room 20)
10. Bellini and Giorgione (Room 21)
11. Dutch and Flemish Renaissance (Room 22)
12. Mantegna and Correggio (Room 23)
13. Michaelangelo & Florentine artists (Room 25)
14. Raphael and del Sarto (Room 26)
15. Fiorentino and Pontormo (Room 27)
16. Titian (Room 28)
17. Il Parmigianino (Room 29)
18. Rubens (Room 41)
19. Caravaggio (Room 43)
20. Rembrandt (Room 44)
21. Uffizi Cafe

Once the Medici business offices, the Galerie degli Uffizi ★★★ is now the world's best introduction to Renaissance painting. If you don't reserve tickets, you can wait for 6 hours in summer, when security guards have to close certain galleries at times for crowd control. Visitors from North America can book tickets before they go from **Select Italy** (☎ 847/853-1661, 800/877-1755; www.selectitaly.com). **Firenze Musei** also takes reservations (☎ 055-294883; www.firenzemusei.it). START: **Take the A, B, 23, or 71 bus to Piazzale degli Uffizi 6 (at Via Lambertesca). Trip length: 3 hr. minimum.**

❶ **Room 2:** This salon showcases the works of Giovanni Cimabue (1240–1302), often called the father of modern painting, and his pupil, Giotto (1276–1337)—both rebels from Byzantium. Still linked to Byzantine art, Cimabue's *Santa Trinita Maestà* (1280) approaches realistic painting. Three decades later, Giotto painted the greatest Maestà of them all, the *Orgissanti Maestà*.

The Medici's former offices, the Uffizi has the world's best Renaissance art collection.

❷ **Room 3:** This is a showcase of 14th-century Sienese master paintings—none finer than Simone Martini's *Annunciation* (1313), showing a horrified Mary learning of her imminent immaculate conception. The Lorenzo brothers, Pietro and Ambrogio, also created masterpieces displayed in this room, before the Black Death of 1348 claimed their lives; the chief work is Ambrogio's *Presentation at the Temple* (1342).

❸ **Room 7:** Renaissance innovations in painting were possible in part because of Masaccio (1401–28) and Paolo Uccello (1397–1475) and their revolutionary use of perspective. Look at Uccello's *Battle of San Romano* (1456), depicting a Florentine victory over the Sienese army. A rare piece by Masaccio (he was dead at 27) is *Madonna and Child with St. Anne* (1424).

Caravaggio's Medusa.

❹ **Room 8:** Numerous paintings by Fra Filippo Lippi (1406–1469) are showcased in this early Renaissance salon. One of our favorites is *Madonna and Child with Two Young Angels*—a portrait of the randy monk's mistress.

5 Rooms 10–14: These rooms feature the most famous paintings in Florence, Sandro Botticelli's *Birth of Venus* and *Primavera* (allegory of Spring).

6 Room 15: Art lovers flock here to see the stunningly beautiful *Annunciation* by Leonardo da Vinci. (1452–1519). Leonardo is believed to have painted the angel on the far left and the landscape, from 1472 to 1475. The *Baptism of Christ* is by his master, Andrea del Verrocchio (1435–88).

The Holy Family, a rare painting by Michelangelo Buonarroti.

7 Room 18: Called *La Tribuna,* this octagonal room is the most lavish salon, made of lapis lazuli for air, red walls for fire, green *pietra dure* for earth, and mother-of-pearl for water. Its showcase is the *Medici Venus,* a copy of a Greek original. The baroque artist Angelo Bronzino painted the celebrated portrait of Eleonora of Toledo, wife of Cosimo I. When the Medici tombs were opened in 1857, her body was discovered buried in the same satin dress she wore in the painting. You can also view Raphael's *St. John the Baptist in the Desert* (1518).

Leonardo da Vinci's Annunciation *(detail).*

8 Room 19: Pietro Perugino's (1446–1523) *Madonna* and his stern *Portrait of Francesco delle Opere* shine brightest here.

9 Room 20: This gallery exhibits paintings of Germans who worked in Florence. Albrecht Dürer (1471–1528) was the master of the German Renaissance. Contrast his *Adam and Eve* with the one by Lucas Cranach (1472–1553). Dürer's work is a study of the body; Cranach's shows a more erotic bent. Dürer's *Adoration of the Magi* is also not to be missed. Hans Bruegel (1568–1625) is represented by his *Il Grande Calvario,* a Calvary scene.

10 Room 21: Venetian masters of the 15th century shine in this *sala*—especially Giovanni Bellini (1430–1516). His *Sacra Allegoria* is his most memorable work here, showing an advanced understanding of perspective.

11 Room 22: Dutch and Flemish paintings of the Renaissance, including more German works, grace this gallery. Our favorite is *Portrait of Sir Richard Southwell* by Hans Holbein the Younger (1497–1543).

12 Room 23: This gallery is a showcase for Andrea Mantegna's triptych of the *Adoration of the Magi, Circumcision,* and *Ascension* painted from 1463 to 1470. There are also three noted works by Antonio da Correggio (1489–1534).

⓭ **Room 25:** This gallery houses Michelangelo's only painting in Florence—a tondo (round painting) of the *Holy Family,* commissioned by the Doni Family and often called the *Doni Tondo* (1506–08). The muscular forms show Michelangelo's preference for sculpture. Michelangelo even designed the elaborate frame.

⓮ **Room 26:** This salon of High Renaissance painting is dominated by the serene *Madonna del Cardellino* by Raphael Sanzio (1483–1520), one of the world's most celebrated works. Another remarkable version of the Virgin is *Madonna of Harpies* by Andrea del Sarto (1486–1530), one of the first Mannerists.

⓯ **Room 27:** Early Florentine Mannerism reaches a fever pitch in this room dedicated to Rosso Fiorentino (1485–1541), Del Sarto's star pupil. Fiorentino is best appreciated in his *Moses Defends the Daughters of Jehro* (1523), which owes a heavy debt to Michelangelo. Del Sarto's other Mannerist pupil, Jacopo Pontormo (1494–1557), is represented by his *Supper at Emmaus.*

⓰ **Room 28:** This *sala* is dedicated to Titian Vercellio (1488–1566). Of all the postcards sold at the Uffizi, none—not even Botticelli's *Primavera*—tops the sale of Titian's *Venus of Urbino,* lounging nude on her bed.

⓱ **Room 29:** The late Mannerist master Il Parmigianino (1505–40) dominates this gallery. His *Madonna and Child* is one of the most celebrated paintings in the Uffizi.

⓲ **Room 41:** This room is dedicated to Peter Paul Rubens (1577–1640) and his voluptuous nudes. You can also see his fat *Baccanale.*

⓳ **Room 43:** Michelangelo Caravaggio is the star painter here, especially his marvelous *Medusa* painted with oil on cloth. His *Adolescent Bacchus* is also arresting.

⓴ **Room 44:** Compare the two self-portraits by Rembrandt—one in his youth, the other as a senior citizen.

21 The **Uffizi café,** a bar atop the loggia, serves cold drinks and espresso. *3hr. Piazzale degli Uffizi 6 (at Via Lambertesca).* *055-23885. www.polomuseale.firenze.it/English/Uffizi. Admission 6.50€. Tues–Sun 8:30am–6:50pm (last entrance 4:45pm). Bus: A, B, 23, or 71.*

Sandro Botticelli's Primavera.

Florence's Best **Small Museums**

In the shadow of the Uffizi and the Pitti Palace, the small museums of Florence are often overlooked by visitors. But Florence has even more to offer than those vast repositories of Renaissance art. Away from the tourist-trodden paths are one of Tuscany's greatest archaeological museums, an offbeat museum of science, and several church museums housing relatively unknown Renaissance masterpieces. **START: Take bus 6, 31, or 32 to the Piazza della S.S. Annunziata to see the best of these museums, beginning immediately below.**

1 ★★ Museo Archeologico. A marvelous *palazzo* is home to one of the world's greatest collections of Egyptian and Etruscan artifacts, much of it collected by the Medici. "The great looter," Leopold II, acquired much of this treasure trove in the 1830s.The *Arezzo Chimera* (a lion with a goat protruding from its back) is a 5th-century masterpiece. Room XIII contains the celebrated *Idolino*, a nude bronze lad (perhaps a Roman statue created during the time of Christ). *1 hr., 15 min. Via della Colonna (off Piazza della S.S. Annunziata). ☎ 055-23575. Admission 4.15€. Nov–Aug Mon 2–7pm; Tues, Thurs 8:30am–7pm; Wed, Fri–Sun 8:30am–2pm; Sept (as above) and also Sat 9pm–midnight. Oct (as above) except for Sun (9am–8pm). Bus: 6, 31, or 32.*

A detail from Andrea Orcagna's Tabernacle at Orsanmichele.

2 ★ Museo di Storia della Scienza. This museum houses such treasures as the lens Galileo used to discover the four moons of Jupiter; an alchemist's laboratory; Galileo's right hand and middle finger, stolen when he was being buried at Santa Croce; and amazingly realistic anatomical wax models. The 18th-century surgical implements will make you cringe. *1 hr. Piazza dei Guidici (at the Uffizi). 055-2653130. Admission 6.50€ June–Sept Mon, Wed–Fri 9:30am–5pm; Tues and Sat 9:30am–1pm. Off season Mon, Wed–Sat 9:30am–5pm, Tues 9:30am–1pm. Bus: 13, 23, 62.*

3 ★★ Orsanmichele. This Gothic grain warehouse from 1337 was turned into a church that today contains an upstairs museum. Check if it's open (its hours are erratic). The landmark building contains fine frescoes by Sandro Botticelli depicting scenes from the life of St. Augustine. Of exceptional beauty is the bronze copy of Donatello's marble of *St. George*, the first relief carving to create the illusion of perspective. Andrea Orcagna's elaborate Gothic *Tabernacle* (1349–59) is one of the finest in Italy, housing the *Image of the Virgin* (1347) by Giotto's student, Bernardo Daddi. In the nearby Church of Orsanmichele you can feast your eyes on such works as Lorenzo Ghiberti's bronze of *St. John the Baptist* (1413–16), the first life-size bronze of the Renaissance, and Donatello's remarkable *St. Mark* in marble (1411–13). *45 min. Via Arte della Lana 1 (at Via dei Calzaiuoli). 055-284944. Free admission. Church hours erratic; call for information. Museum daily 9–11:45am, Sat–Sun 1–1:45pm (but don't count on these hours). Bus: A.*

4 ★ Museo di Santa Maria Novella. Attached to the Basilica of Santa Maria Novella (p 31) are the green cloisters *(Chiostro Verde)*, open to the public as a museum. These cloisters are the most richly decorated in Florence. The 15th-century frescoes are among the most mysterious and disturbing paintings of the Florentine Renaissance—one for example, depicts the *Drunkenness of Noah*. The walls and vault of the adjacent Cappella degli Spagnoli (Spanish Chapel) are covered with gorgeous frescoes by Andrea di Bonaiuto (ca. 1365), depicting such scenes as the *Crucifixion* and the *Resurrection*. *45 min. Piazza Santa Maria*

St. Mark, *one of several Donatello figures that grace the facade of Orsanmichele.*

Novella (at Via Benci). ☎ 055-282187. Admission 2.60€ Wed–Mon 9am–2pm. Bus: A, 6, 11, 12, 36, 37, or 68.

❺ **Museo Opificio delle Pietre Dure.** This unique museum grew out of the Medici's passion for *pietre dure*, a type of mosaic work made from semi-precious stones and marble, starting in the 16th century. The craft is sometimes erroneously called "Florentine Mosaic." Since 1796 this workshop has been dedicated to restoring *pietre dure* works. Attached is a small museum with some of the better examples of this art form—not the tawdry souvenirs hawked all over town. ⌚ *30 min. Via degli Alfani 78 (at Via Ricasoli). ☎ 055-294883. Admission 2€ Mon–Sat 8:15am–2pm (Thurs until 7pm). Bus: 6, 11, 17, 31, or 32.*

❻ **Museo dell'Opera di Santa Croce.** Sometimes this museum is called the Museo Cimabue because it is host to what's left of the artist's once magnificent *Crucifixion*, the most tragic victim of the devastating flood of 1966. This is a critical work that bridged the gap between Byzantine art and the coming Renaissance. The museum, a former convent, also harbors the Cappella Pazzi, entered through the cloisters. The early Renaissance chapel, by Filippo Brunelleschi, is one of the most beautiful and serene in Tuscany. ⌚ *40 min. Piazza Santa Croce 16 (at Via de Benci). ☎ 055-244619. Admission 4€ to cloisters and museum. Museum and cloisters Mon–Sat 9:30am–5:30pm; Sun 1–5:30pm. Bus: B, 13, 23, or 71.*

❼ **Museo Horne.** English-born Herbert Horne, an art historian—and not a rich one at that—immortalized himself by collecting the nucleus of this collection, including minor masterpieces by major artists such as Fra Filippo Lippi and Simone Martini. His greatest acquisition was the Giotto portrait of St. Stephen, dating from the early 14th century. The building housing the museum is a 15th-century *palazzo* built for the powerful Corsi family. ⌚ *45 min. Via dei Benci 6 (at Lungarno delle Grazie). ☎ 055-244661. Admission 5€. Mon–Sat 9am–1pm (in summer also Tues 8:30am–11pm). Bus: B, 13, 23, or 71.*

❽ **Museo Stibbert.** Frederick Stibbert (1838–1906), half-Italian, half-Scotsman, was an eclectic collector, as the 50,000 objects d'art

The breezeways of Santa Croce, wherein lie the tombs of Michelangelo and Galileo.

Santa Maria Novella's green cloisters are among Europe's most richly embellished.

(tapestries, antiques, porcelain, paintings) in these 57 rooms testify. As you'll see, Stibbert also had a fetish about arms and armor. *45 min. Via Stibbert 26 (at Via Vittorio Emanuele II). 055-475520. Admission 5€. Mon–Wed 10am–4pm; Fri–Sun 10am–6pm. Bus: 4.*

9 Sinagoga & Jewish Museum. This Moorish-Byzantine synagogue was built in the 1870s but badly damaged by the Nazis in 1944. It is used today by Florence's 1,000-strong Jewish community. A small museum upstairs contains an exhibit of the Jewish ghetto that existed in Florence until it was disbanded in 1859. *45 min. guided tour. Via Farini 4 (off Piazza d'Azeglio). 055-2346654. Admission 4€. June–Aug Sun–Thurs 10am–6pm; Apr–May and Sept–Oct Sun–Thurs 10am–5pm; Nov–Mar Sun–Thurs 10am–3pm. Bus: C, 6, 31, or 32.*

10 Cenacolo di Santo Spirito Museo. This is the refectory of the church of Santo Spirito, standing on Piazza Santo Spirito, across the Arno. The square is beloved by Florentines because it's evocative and not overrun by visitors. The church was based on designs by Brunelleschi, but remained uncompleted until 1487, after his death. The interior is calm and rational with its soaring forest of columns. Don't miss the baroque altar with a coborium inlay of *pietre dure* dating from 1607. Works by Jacopo della Guercia and two reliefs attributed to Donatello are among several works in the old refectory. *30 min. Piazza Santo Spirito 29 (at Via Sant'Agostino). 055-287043. 2.20€. Tues–Sat 10:30am–1:30pm. Bus: D, 6, 11, 36, 37, or 68.*

11 Il Borgo Antico. Stop in for a memorable pasta dish or a heaping salad at this popular dive frequented by students and the young at heart who wander off the beaten trail. Our favorite salad is made with shrimp, avocado, and fresh mozzarella. The pizzas are great, too. After a day of museum hopping, this is a welcome break and it's never touristy. *Piazza Santo Spirito 6R. 055-210437. Bus: D, 6, 11, 36, 37, or 68.*

The piazza outside Santa Maria Novella is a popular resting place.

The Best Dining in Florence

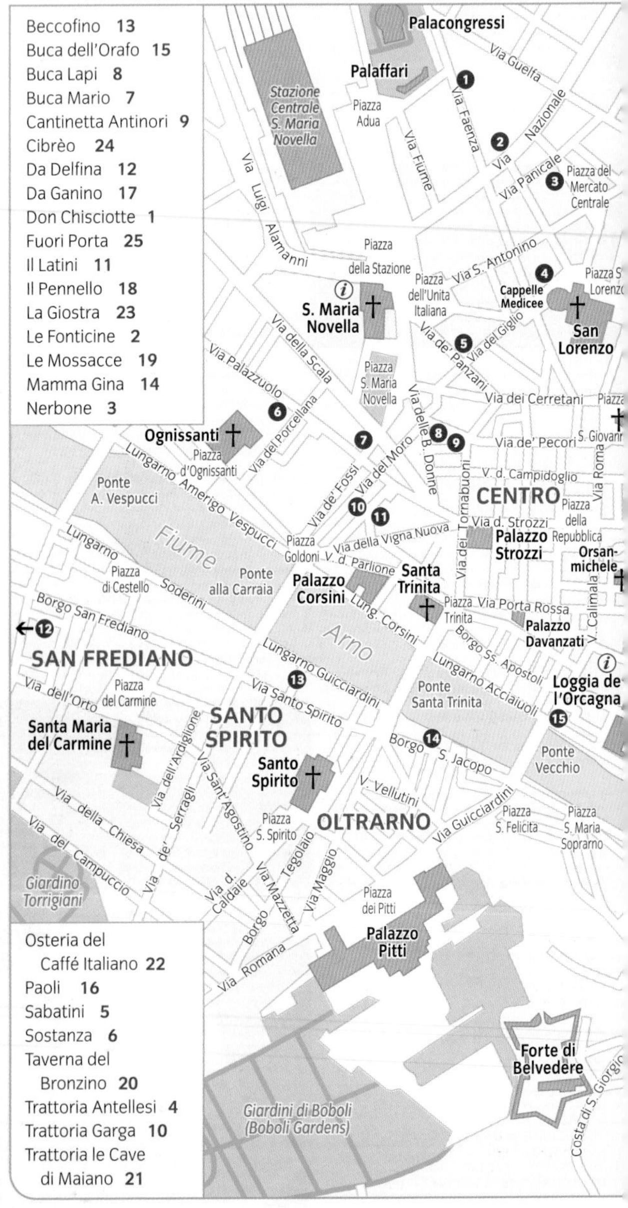

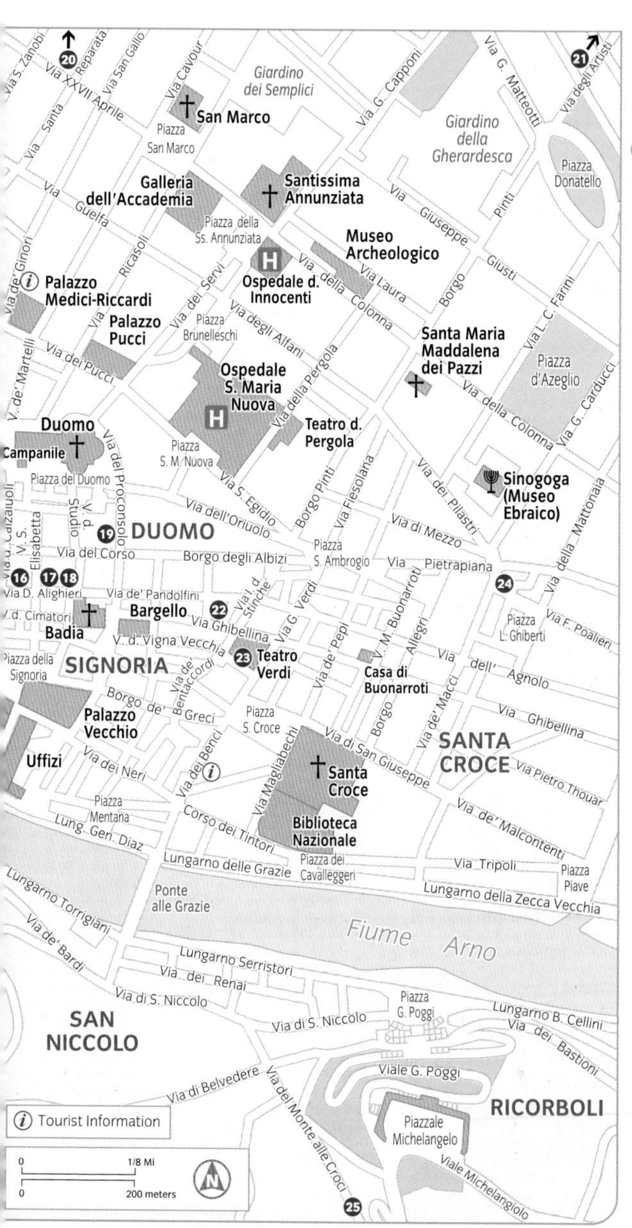
Giardino dei Semplici
San Marco
Piazza San Marco
Galleria dell'Accademia
Santissima Annunziata
Piazza della Ss. Annunziata
Museo Archeologico
Ospedale d. Innocenti
Giardino della Gherardesca
Piazza Donatello
Palazzo Medici-Riccardi
Palazzo Pucci
Piazza Brunelleschi
Ospedale S. Maria Nuova
Santa Maria Maddalena dei Pazzi
Piazza d'Azeglio
Duomo
Campanile
Piazza S. M. Nuova
Teatro d. Pergola
Sinogoga (Museo Ebraico)
Piazza del Duomo
DUOMO
Piazza S. Ambrogio
Bargello
Badia
Piazza L. Ghiberti
SIGNORIA
Piazza della Signoria
Teatro Verdi
Casa di Buonarroti
Palazzo Vecchio
Piazza S. Croce
SANTA CROCE
Uffizi
Santa Croce
Piazza Mentana
Biblioteca Nazionale
Piazza dei Cavalleggeri
Piazza Piave
Ponte alle Grazie
Fiume Arno
Piazza G. Poggi
SAN NICCOLO
RICORBOLI
Piazzale Michelangelo
Via S. Zanobi
Via XXVII Aprile
Via Santa Reparata
Via San Gallo
Via Cavour
Via G. Capponi
Via G. Matteotti
Via degli Artisti
Via Guelfa
Via Giuseppe Giusti
Pinti
Via de' Ginori
Via Ricasoli
Via dei Servi
Via della Colonna
Via Laura
Borgo Pinti
Via L. C. Farini
Via degli Alfani
Via dei Pucci
V. de' Martelli
Via della Pergola
Via della Colonna
Via G. Carducci
Via del Proconsolo
Via S. Egidio
Via dei Pilastri
Via dell'Oriuolo
Via Fiesolana
Via di Mezzo
Via della Mattonaia
V. d. Studio
V. S. Elisabetta
Via del Corso
Borgo degli Albizi
Via Pietrapiana
Via D. Alighieri
Via de' Pandolfini
Via I. d. Stinche
Via G. Verdi
V. M. Buonarroti
Allegri
Via F. Poalieri
V. d. Cimatori
Via Ghibellina
Via de' Pepi
V. d. Vigna Vecchia
Via de' Bentaccordi
Via dell' Agnolo
Borgo de' Greci
Via de' Macci
Via Ghibellina
Borgo
Via di San Giuseppe
Via Magliabechi
Via dei Benci
Via dei Neri
Via Pietro Thouar
Via de' Malcontenti
Corso dei Tintori
Lung. Gen. Diaz
Lungarno delle Grazie
Via Tripoli
Lungarno della Zecca Vecchia
Lungarno Torrigiani
Via de' Bardi
Lungarno Serristori
Via dei Renai
Via di S. Niccolo
Via di S. Niccolo
Lungarno B. Cellini
Via dei Bastioni
Viale G. Poggi
Via di Belvedere
Via del Monte alle Croci
Viale Michelangiolo
16
17
18
19
20
21
22
23
24
25
Tourist Information
0
1/8 Mi
0
200 meters
N

Dining Best Bets

Best Wine Tavern
★ Cantinetta Antinori $$ *Piazza Antinori 3 (p 43)*

Best Seafood
★★ Don Chisciotte $$$ *Via Ridolfi 4R (p 44)*

Most Quintessential Florentine Trattoria
★ Sabatini $$ *Via de'Panzani 9A (p 45)*

Best Family Favorite
★ Sostanza $ *Via del Porcellana 25R (p 45)*

Best Tuscan Cuisine
★ Taverna del Bronzino $$ *Via della Ruote 27R (p 45)*

Most Innovative Cuisine
★★★ Cibrèo $$$ *Via Verrocchio 8R (p 43)*

Best Mediterranean Cuisine
★★★ Beccofino $$$ *Piazza degli Scarlatti (p 43)*

Best Bagnato
★ Nerbone $ *Mercato Centrale (p 45)*

Best Roast Meats
★ Il Latini $$ *Via del Palchetti 6R (p 44)*

Best Countryside Dining
★★ Da Delfina $$ *Via della Chiusa, Artimino (p 43)*

Best Farmhouse Dining
★ Trattoria le Cave di Maiano $$ *Via della Cave 16, Fiesole (p 45)*

Most Authentic Florentine Cuisine
★ Dan Ganino $ *Piazza dei Cimatori 4R (p 44)*

Best Italian Cuisine
★ Paoli $$ *Via dei Tavolini 12R (p 45)*

Best Antipasti
★ Il Pennello $ *Via Dante Alighieri 4R (p 44)*

Best Ice Cream
★★★ Vivoli $ *Via Isole delle Stinche 7R (p 28)*

Il Latini is a Florence institution.

Florence Restaurants A to Z

★★★ Beccofino OLTRARNO *MEDITERRANEAN/TUSCAN* Le Cirque's Francesco Bernardinelli returned home to open this restaurant. His Mediterranean dishes with a twist win raves. *Piazza degli Scarlatti (at Lungarno Guicciardini).* ☎ *055-290076. Entrees 19€–24€. AE, MC, V. Dinner Mon–Sat. Bus: C, 6, 11, 36, 37, or 68.*

★ Buca dell'Orafo CENTRO STORICO *FLORENTINE* This cellar trattoria once housed a Renaissance goldsmith. Now, locals and visitors here share communal tables and Tuscan peasant food. *Volta dei Girolami 28R (at Ponte Vecchio).* ☎ *055-213619. Entrees 10€–18€. AE, MC, V. Lunch, dinner Tues–Sat. Closed Aug and 2 weeks in Dec. Bus: 23 or 71.*

Buca Lapi CENTRO STORICO *TUSCAN* Huddled under the Palazzo Antinori since 1880, this is Florence's most glam *buca* (cellar), under vaulted ceilings. Expect regional classics such as *bistecca alla fiorentina* prepared with decades-old recipes. *Via del Trebbio 1R.* ☎ *055-213768. Main courses 12€–25€. AE, DC, MC, V. Dinner Mon–Sat. Closed 2 weeks in Aug. Bus: 6, 11, 14, 17, 22, 36, 37, or 68.*

★ Buca Mario CENTRO STORICO *FLORENTINE* This century-old workman's tavern in the cellar of the 1886 Palazzo Niccolini turns out classic regional fare. *Via Rosina 2R (at Piazza Mercato Centrale).* ☎ *055-218550. Entrees 15€–23€. AE, MC, V. Lunch Fri–Tues, dinner daily. Closed Aug. Bus: 10, 12, 25, 31, 32, or 91.*

★ Cantinetta Antinori CENTRO STORICO *FLORENTINE/TUSCAN* For 600 years, the Antinori family has dazzled with ingredients and wines from their own farms and vineyards, served in a 15th-century *palazzo. Palazzo Antinori, Piazza Antinori 3.* ☎ *055-292234. Entrees 13€–22€. AE, DC, MC, V. Lunch, dinner Mon–Fri. Closed: Aug. Bus: 6, 11, 36, 37, or 68.*

Da Delfina draws Florentines to the countryside.

★★★ Cibrèo CENTRO STORICO *MEDITERRANEAN* Fabio Picchi's innovative restaurant is one of Florence's finest. Simple soups share the menu with ventures like fricasseed cocks' combs and innards in an egg. Nearby Cibreino is less costly. *Via Verrocchio 8R.* ☎ *055-2341100. Entrees 20€–36€. AE, DC, MC, V. Lunch, dinner Tues–Sat. Closed late July to early Sept. Bus: B or 14.*

★★ Da Delfina ARTIMINO *TUSCAN* In a medieval walled village 15 minutes from Florence (8.9m), Artimino draws city folk to feast on dishes made with produce from nearby fields. *Via della Chiesa, Artimino (near Carmignano).* ☎ *055-8718119. Entrees 12€–15€. No credit cards. Lunch Tues–Sun, dinner Tues–Sat. From Santa Maria Novella, take the Signa train then a cab for 5 min.*

A traditional antipasti.

★ **Dan Ganino** CENTRO STORICO *FLORENTINE* Savvy foodies patronize this intimate tavern halfway between the Duomo and the American Express office. The chefs deliver reliably praiseworthy victuals, from succulent pastas to Tuscan white beans and juicy T-bones. *Piazza dei Cimatori 4R. ☎ 055-214125. Entrees 6€–20€. AE, DC. Lunch and dinner Mon–Sat. Bus: 14, 23, or 71.*

★★ **Don Chisciotte** CENTRO STORICO *ITALIAN/SEAFOOD* The fish served in this old Florentine *palazzo* is the city's freshest, brimming with zesty, unusual flavors. The chef's efforts have been called "quixotic." *Via Ridolfi 4R. ☎ 055-475430. Entrees 22€–25€. AE, DC, MC, V. Lunch Tues–Sat, dinner Mon–Sat. Bus: 20.*

★ **Fuori Porta** OLTRARNO *TUSCAN* Over the Arno, one of the city's best *enotecas* (wine taverns) offers 650 labels. Some 50 are sold by the glass, with a limited food menu. *Via del Monte alle Croce 10R. ☎ 055-2342483. Entrees 5€–9€. AE, MC, V. Lunch, dinner daily. Closed Aug 10–20. Bus: 13.*

★ **Il Latini** CENTRO STORICO *FLORENTINE* At this local dive, diners feast at communal tables on dishes such as *arrosto misto*—slabs of assorted meats fresh off the grill. *Via del Palchetti 6R. ☎ 055-210916. Fixed price 35€. AE, DC, MC, V. Lunch, dinner Tues–Sun. Closed 2 weeks in Aug. Bus: C, 6, 11, 36, 37, or 68.*

★ **Il Pennello** CENTRO STORICO *FLORENTINE/ITALIAN* Florence's oldest trattoria is going strong, with hot young Tuscan chefs and a vast antipasti table. *Via Dante Alighieri 4R. ☎ 055-294848. Entrees 7.50€–13€. Fixed-price 20€. AE, DC, MC, V. Lunch, dinner Tues–Sat. Closed 3 weeks in Aug. Bus: 14, 22, or 23.*

★ **La Giostra** CENTRO STORICO *TUSCAN* A Hapsburg prince with Medici blood welcomes guests to this adventurous restaurant, with some dishes based on Hapsburg family recipes. *Borgo Pinti 12R. ☎ 055-241341. Entrees 12€–24€. AE, DC, MC, V. Lunch, dinner daily. Bus: A, B, C, 14, 23, 71 or 80.*

Le Fonticine CENTRO STORICO *TUSCAN/BOLOGNESE* Silvano Bruci's trattoria is *the* place to go for Italian soul food (based on his wife's Bolognese family recipes). *Via Nazionale 79R. ☎ 055-282106. Entrees 8.50€–19€. AE, DC, MC, V. Lunch, dinner Tues–Sat. Closed 2 weeks in Aug. Bus: 7, 10, 11, 12, 25, 31, 33, or 70.*

Le Mossacce CENTRO STORICO *TUSCAN/FLORENTINE* Midway between the Duomo and the

Bargello, this *osteria* from 1942 hires trustworthy waiters eager to recommend Florence's best cannelloni or chestnut flour cake. *Via del Proconsolo 55R. ☎ 055-294361. Main courses 3.50€–9€. AE, DC, MC, V. Open Mon–Fri for lunch and dinner. Closed Aug. Bus: 14.*

Mamma Gina OLTRARNO *TUSCAN* The food isn't what it was when Mama Gina was in charge, but her recipes still make this place an excellent choice for lunch near the Pitti Palace. *Borgo San Jacopo 37R. ☎ 055-2396009. Entrees 10€–20€. AE, DC, MC, V. Lunch, dinner Mon–Sat. Closed 15 days in Aug. Bus: D.*

★ **Nerbone** CENTRO STORICO *FLORENTINE/TUSCAN* Hasten to this 1872 five-table dive for the *bagnato* (boiled beef sandwich) dipped in meat juices. *Mercato Centrale (Via dell'Ariento entrance, stand #292). ☎ 055-219949. Entrees 3€–7€. No credit cards. Lunch Mon–Sat. Closed 2 weeks in Aug. Bus: 12, 25, 31, or 32.*

★ **Osteria del Caffè Italiano** CENTRO STORICO *WINE BAR/TUSCAN* Umberto Montano's wine bar, in a 13th-century *palazzo*, has the city's best Tuscan *salumi* and fine wines by the glass. *Via Isola delle Stinche 11–13R. ☎ 055-289368. Entrees 11€–25€. MC, V. Lunch, dinner Tues–Sun. Bus: A or 14.*

★ **Paoli** CENTRO STORICO *TUSCAN/ITALIAN* Between the Duomo and Piazza della Signoria, this 1824 restaurant in 13th-century digs is touristy, but the Italian cuisine is superb. *Via dei Tavolini 12R. ☎ 055-216215. Entrees 11€–19€. AE, DC, MC, V. Lunch, dinner Wed–Mon. Closed 3 weeks in Aug. Bus: A.*

★ **Sabatini** CENTRO STORICO *FLORENTINE/INTERNATIONAL* Tripe and beefsteak fans flock to this quintessential Florentine trattoria. *Via de'Panzani 9A. ☎ 055-211559. Entrees 11€–30€. AE, DC, MC, V. Lunch, dinner Tues–Sun. Bus: 1, 6, 14, 17, or 22.*

★ **Sostanza** CENTRO STORICO *FLORENTINE* Known as *il troia* (the trough), this trattoria serves huge portions of peasant food at crowded communal tables. *Via del Porcellana 25R. ☎ 055-212691. Entrees 7.50€–18€. No credit cards. Lunch, dinner Mon–Fri. Closed Aug and 2 weeks at Christmas. Bus: 12.*

★ **Taverna del Bronzino** CENTRO STORICO *TUSCAN* In Bronzino's converted studio, chefs ply diners with some of Florence's most refined regional cuisine. *Via delle Ruote 27R. ☎ 055-495220. Entrees 14€–20€. AE, DC, MC, V. Lunch, dinner daily. Closed Aug. Bus: 12 or 91.*

Trattoria Antellesi CENTRO STORICO *FLORENTINE* Only the best, freshest Tuscan field and farm ingredients are served at this trattoria in a 15th-century building near the Medici Chapels. *Via Faenza 9R. ☎ 055-216990. Entrees 10€–16€. AE, DC, MC, V. Lunch, dinner daily. Bus: 1, 6, 7, 11, 17, 33, 67, or 68.*

Trattoria Garga CENTRO STORICO *FLORENTINE/TUSCAN* Between Ponte Vecchio and Santa Maria Novella, a young crowd gathers for dishes such as angel-hair with orange and lemon zest. *Via del Moro 48R. ☎ 055-2398898. Entrees 20€–27€. AE, DC, MC, V. Dinner Tues–Sun. Bus: 6, 9, 11, 36, 37, or 68.*

★ **Trattoria le Cave di Maiano** FIESOLE *TUSCAN* This former farmhouse is known for its herb-flavored roast lamb and homemade ice cream with raspberries. *Via delle Cave 16 (between Florence and Fiesole). ☎ 055-591133. Entrees 7€–19€. Fixed-price lunch 30€–65€. AE, DC, MC, V. Lunch, dinner daily. Closed 1 week in Feb. Bus: 7.*

The Best Lodging in Florence

San Marco
Galleria dell'Accademia
Santissima Annunziata
Museo Archeologico
Palazzo Medici-Riccardi
Palazzo Pucci
Ospedale d. Innocenti
Ospedale S. Maria Nuova
Santa Maria Maddalena dei Pazzi
Duomo
Campanile
Teatro d. Pergola
Sinogoga (Museo Ebraico)
DUOMO
Bargello
Badia
SIGNORIA
Teatro Verdi
Casa di Buonarroti
Palazzo Vecchio
Uffizi
SANTA CROCE
Santa Croce
Biblioteca Nazionale
Fiume Arno
SAN NICCOLO
RICORBOLI
Piazzale Michelangelo
Giardino dei Semplici
Giardino della Gherardesca
Piazza Donatello
Piazza d'Azeglio
Tourist Information
0 1/8 Mi
0 200 meters

Hotel Best Bets

Best for Families
Annabella $ *Via Fiume 17 (p 49)*

Best Boutique Hotel
★ Gallery Hotel Art $$$$ *Vicolo dell'Oro (p 49)*

Most Glamorous Hotel
★★★ Grand Hotel $$$$ *Piazza Ornissanti 1 (p 49)*

Best for Value
★ Pensione Maria Luisa de'Medici $ *Via del Corso 1 (p 50)*

Most Ancient Address
Porta Rossa $$ *Via Porta Rossa 19 (p 50)*

Best for Art Lovers
★ Relais Uffizi $$ *Chiasso del Buco 16 (p 51)*

Best Left Bank Retreat
★ Villa Carlotta $$ *Via Michele di Lando 3 (p 51)*

Most Luxurious Enclave
★★★ Villa San Michele $$$$$ *Via Doccia 4, Fiesole (p 51)*

Best View
★ Grand Hotel Cavour $$ *Via del Pronconsolo 3 (p 49)*

Best Location
★ Hermitage Hotel $$ *Vicolo Marzio 1 (p 49)*

Most Artistic Hotel
★★★ J.K. Place $$$ *Piazza Santa Maria Novella (p 49)*

Best for Tradition
La Scaletta $ *Via Guicciardini 13 (p 50)*

Best Locanda (Inn)
Locanda de' Ciompi $ *Via Pietrapiana 28 (p 50)*

Most Welcoming
★ Mario's $ *Via Faenza 89 (p 50)*

Best Palazzo Living
★ Monna Lisa $$ *Borgo Pinti 27 (p 50)*

The lobby bar of Tornabuoni Beacci.

Florence Hotels A to Z

Annabella CENTRO STORICO Many rooms in this small, well-run hotel are big enough for three or four guests. The 20th-century *palazzo* has been tastefully updated. *Via Fiume 17. ☎ 055-281877. www.hotelannabella.it. 15 units. Doubles 90€–300€ w/breakfast. AE, DC, MC, V. Bus: 22, 36, or 37.*

Casci CENTRO STORICO Antonio Rossini *(The Barber of Seville)* once stayed in this old hostelry near the Duomo. Renovations have upgraded it without destroying its old charm. Some family suites sleep four to five. *Via Cavour 13. ☎ 055-211686. www.hotelcasci.com. 24 units. Doubles 90€–150€ w/breakfast. AE, DC, MC, V. Bus: 1, 7, 25, or 33.*

★ **Gallery Hotel Art** CENTRO STORICO This boutique hotel run by the Ferragamo family (the shoemakers) is a bastion of grand comfort. *Vicoli dell'Oro 5. ☎ 055-27263. www.lungarnohotels.com. 74 units. Doubles 286€–375€ w/breakfast. AE, DC, MC, V. Bus: 1, 10, 11, or 17.*

★★★ **Grand Hotel** CENTRO STORICO The Grand is sumptuous—with large bathrooms and Renaissance or Empire bedrooms done in silks, brocades, frescoes, and antiques. *Piazza Ornissanti 1. ☎ 800-3253589 or 055-288781. www.luxurycollection.com/grandflorence. 107 units. Doubles 583€–685€. AE, DC, MC, V. Bus: 6 or 17.*

★ **Grand Hotel Cavour** CENTRO STORICO Opposite the Bargello, this 13th-century *palazzo*'s rooftop terrace has stunning panoramic views. Traditional bedrooms are comfy, but some are too small. *Via del Proconsolo 3. ☎ 055-266271. www.albergocavour.it. 105 units. Doubles 150€–280€ w/breakfast. AE, DC, MC, V. Bus: 14, 23, or 71.*

★★ **Helvetia & Bristol** CENTRO STORICO This restored Belle Epoque *palazzo*, in the city's most elegant section, has lavish bedrooms and a Winter Garden. *Via dei Pescioni 2. ☎ 888-7700447 or 055-211686. www.royaldemeure.com. 67 units. Doubles 200€. AE, DC, MC, V. Bus: 6, 11, 36, or 37.*

★ **Hermitage Hotel** CENTRO STORICO The Hermitage has a terrace over the Arno and small to midsize rooms with 17th- and 19th-century antiques; some bathrooms have Jacuzzis. *Vicolo Marzio 1. ☎ 055-287216. www.hermitagehotel.com. 28 units. Doubles 195€–245€ w/breakfast. MC, V. Bus: B.*

★★ **Hotel J and J** CENTRO STORICO This 16th-century former monastery, with vaulted ceilings and frescoes, has some of the city's largest rooms. *Via di Mezzo 20. ☎ 055-26312. www.jandjhotel.com. 20 units. Doubles 283€–315€ w/breakfast. AE, DC, MC, V. Bus: A.*

★★ **Hotel Torre Guelfa** CENTRO STORICO Florence's tallest privately owned tower graces this 14th-century *palazzo* near the Ponte Vecchio. Rooms have canopied iron beds. *Borgo SS. Apostoli 8. ☎ 055-2396338. www.hoteltorreguelfa.com. 21 units. Doubles 145€–185€ w/breakfast. AE, MC, V. Bus: D, 11, 36, 37, or 68.*

★★★ **J.K. Place** CENTRO STORICO This refined hotel has elegant rooms with four-poster beds and fireplaces, a glass-covered courtyard, a rooftop terrace, and a splendid library. *Piazza Santa Maria Novella 7. ☎ 055-2645181. www.jkplace.com. 20 units.*

Doubles 285€–470€ w/breakfast. AE, DC, MC, V. Bus: 14 or 23.

La Scaletta OLTRARNO If you like vintage charm, check into this aging *palazzo* across the Arno and hang out on its flower-bedecked terrace, with a 360-degree view over the Boboli Gardens. *Via Guicciardini 13. ☎ 055-283028. www.lacaletta.com. 13 units. Doubles 119€ w/breakfast. MC, V. Bus: D, 11, 36, or 37.*

Locanda de' Ciompi CENTRO STORICO This small inn in a restored, 1600s building has individually decorated bedrooms in the antique Florentine style, with great use of color. *Via Pietrapiana 28. ☎ 055-2638034. www.locandadeciompi.it. 5 units. Doubles 94€–130€ w/breakfast. AE, MC, V. Bus: B, 13, 23, or 71.*

★ **Loggiato dei Serviti** CENTRO STORICO A monastery in 1527, this comfortably elegant hotel has beamed or vaulted ceilings and terracotta floors on one of the world's most beautiful squares. *Piazza Santissima Annunziata 3. ☎ 055-289592. www.loggiatodeiservithotel.it. 29 units. Doubles 130€–205€ w/breakfast. AE, DC, MC, V. Bus: 1, 7, or 17.*

★ **Mario's** CENTRO STORICO This little, spotless, home-style city inn has small to midsize bedrooms stylishly decorated and furnished for your comfort; some have small private gardens. *Via Faenza 89. ☎ 055-216801. www.hotelmarios.com. 16 units. Doubles 80€–165€ w/breakfast. AE, DC, MC, V. Bus: 10, 13, or 17.*

The lobby of the Hotel Torre Guelfa, in a converted 14th-century palazzo.

★ **Monna Lisa** CENTRO STORICO Behind a severe facade, this art-laden 14th-century *palazzo* takes top prize for old-world elegance. One might half expect Da Vinci to drop in for a stay. *Borgo Pinti 27. ☎ 055-2479755. www.monnalisa.it. 45 units. Doubles 182€–350€ w/breakfast. AE, DC, MC, V. Bus: A, 6, 31, or 32.*

★ **Morandi alla Crocetta** CENTRO STORICO In a 16th-century convent, this *pensione* evokes the era when British travelers sought private homelike lodgings with family heirlooms. *Via Laura 50. ☎ 055-2344747. www.hotelmorandi.it. 10 units. Doubles 177€–220€. AE, DC, MC, V. Bus: 6, 7, 10, 17, 31, or 32.*

★ **Pensione Maria Luisa de'Medici** CENTRO STORICO In a 1645 *palazzo* with baroque art, this B&B is one of the city's most desirable, with large bedrooms (often with shared baths) up three flights of stairs. *Via del Corso 1. ☎ 055-280048. 9 units. Doubles 80€–95€ w/breakfast. No credit cards. Bus: A, 14, or 23.*

★ **Porta Rossa** CENTRO STORICO The second oldest hotel in Italy (from 1386), Porta Rossa has renovated, well-kept bedrooms, ample bathrooms, and a small terrace with a view. *Via Porta Rossa 19. ☎ 055-287551. www.hotelportarossa.it. 79 units. Doubles 148€–176€ w/breakfast. AE, DC, MC, V. Bus: A.*

★★ **Regency** CENTRO STORICO A citadel of taste and exclusivity, this intimate hideaway was converted from two posh 19th-century mansions on a wooded square at the eastern edge of town (though it

Guest quarters at the Hotel Torre Guelfa.

could well be in London). It's filled with antiques, carpets, wall fabrics, marble-clad bathrooms, and mirrored wall panels. *Piazza Massimo d'Azeglio 3. ☎ 055-245247. www.regency-hotel.com. 34 units. Doubles 305€–450€ w/breakfast. AE, DC, MC, V. Bus: 6, 31, or 32.*

★ **Relais Uffizi** CENTRO STORICO Beside the Uffizi, this hotel is a great value, in a 15th-century building with homey, midsize to large rooms and marble baths. *Chiasso del Buco 16. ☎ 055-2676239. www.relais.uffizi.it. 10 units. Doubles 220€ w/breakfast. AE, DC, MC, V. Bus: A, B, 23, or 71.*

★★ **Residenza dei Pucci** CENTRO STORICO Near the Duomo and Uffizi, this restored 19th-century town house has ample rooms with high ceilings, French tapestries, four-poster beds, and marble baths. *Via dei Pucci 9. ☎ 055-281886. www.residenzadeipuccii.com. 12 units. Doubles 80€–165€. AE, MC, V. Bus: 1, 6, 14, or 17.*

★ **Ritz** CENTRO STORICO This family-run budget hotel near the Uffizi has snug, comfy rooms overlooking the Arno and a view of Fiesole from the roof terrace. *Lungarno della Zecca Vecchia 24. ☎ 055-2340650. www.florenceitaly.net/ritz/index.html. 32 units. Doubles 110€–180€ w/breakfast. AE, DC, MC, V. Bus: 23.*

★ **Tornabuoni Beacci** CENTRO STORICO In a 16th-century palace, this timeworn favorite faces another century with genteel grace. The roof terrace bursts with flowers and panoramas. *Via Tornabuoni 3. ☎ 055-212645. www.bthotel.it. 28 units. Doubles 210€–250€ w/breakfast. AE, DC, MC, V. Bus: B, 6, 11, or 36.*

★ **Villa Carlotta** OLTRARNO This retreat in a residential neighborhood on the left bank of the Arno is lavishly renovated, with plenty of antiques and crystal. *Via Michele di Lando 3. ☎ 055-220530. www.hotelvillacarlotta.it. 32 units. Doubles 150€–299€ w/breakfast. AE, DC, MC, V. Bus: 11, 36, or 37.*

★★★ **Villa San Michele** FIESOLE Behind a facade designed by Michelangelo, this 15th-century Franciscan monastery is now a swank enclave in the hills, with a heated outdoor pool and Jacuzzis in the former "cell." *Via Doccia 4 (off Via Fra' Giovanni Angelico, Fiesole). ☎ 800-2371236 or 055-5678200. www.villasanmichele.com. 41 units. Doubles 811€ w/breakfast. AE, DC, MC, V. Closed mid-Nov to mid-Mar. Bus: 7.*

The Best Shopping in Florence

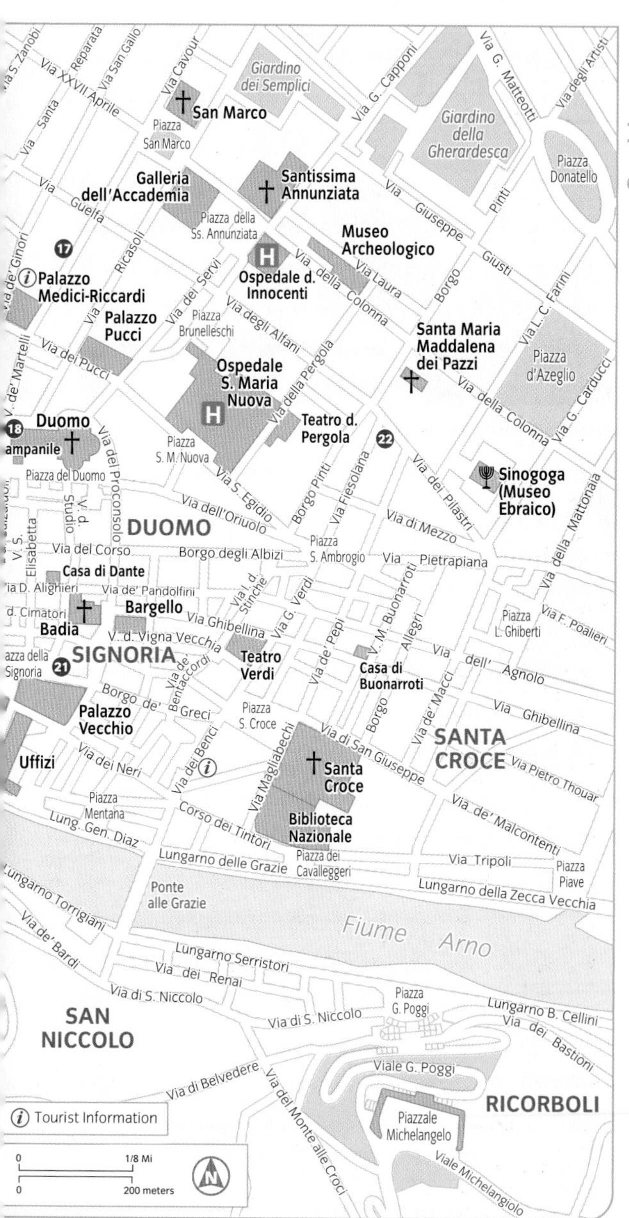
San Marco
Piazza San Marco
Giardino dei Semplici
Giardino della Gherardesca
Piazza Donatello
Galleria dell'Accademia
Santissima Annunziata
Piazza della Ss. Annunziata
Museo Archeologico
Ospedale d. Innocenti
Palazzo Medici-Riccardi
Palazzo Pucci
Piazza Brunelleschi
Santa Maria Maddalena dei Pazzi
Piazza d'Azeglio
Ospedale S. Maria Nuova
Teatro d. Pergola
Duomo
Campanile
Piazza del Duomo
Piazza S. M. Nuova
Sinogoga (Museo Ebraico)
DUOMO
Piazza S. Ambrogio
Casa di Dante
Bargello
Badia
SIGNORIA
Piazza della Signoria
Teatro Verdi
Casa di Buonarroti
Piazza L. Ghiberti
Palazzo Vecchio
Uffizi
Piazza S. Croce
SANTA CROCE
Santa Croce
Biblioteca Nazionale
Piazza Mentana
Piazza dei Cavalleggeri
Piazza Piave
Ponte alle Grazie
Fiume Arno
SAN NICCOLO
Piazza G. Poggi
Piazzale Michelangelo
RICORBOLI
Via XXVII Aprile
Via San Gallo
Via Cavour
Via G. Capponi
Via G. Matteotti
Via degli Artisti
Via Guelfa
Via Giuseppe Giusti
Via Ricasoli
Via dei Servi
Via della Colonna
Via Laura
Borgo Pinti
Via L. C. Farini
Via degli Alfani
Via dei Pucci
Via de' Martelli
Via della Pergola
Via G. Carducci
Via del Proconsolo
Via S. Egidio
Via dell'Oriuolo
Via Fiesolana
Via dei Pilastri
Via di Mezzo
Via della Mattonaia
Via del Corso
Borgo degli Albizi
Via Pietrapiana
Via de' Pandolfini
Via Ghibellina
Via G. Verdi
Via M. Buonarroti
Via dell' Agnolo
Via F. Poalieri
Borgo de' Greci
Via de' Macci
Via di San Giuseppe
Via Pietro Thouar
Via dei Neri
Via dei Benci
Via Magliabechi
Via de' Malcontenti
Corso dei Tintori
Lung. Gen. Diaz
Lungarno delle Grazie
Via Tripoli
Lungarno della Zecca Vecchia
Lungarno Torrigiani
Via de' Bardi
Lungarno Serristori
Via dei Renai
Via di S. Niccolo
Lungarno B. Cellini
Via dei Bastioni
Viale G. Poggi
Via di Belvedere
Via del Monte alle Croci
Viale Michelangiolo
Tourist Information
0 1/8 Mi
0 200 meters
N

Shopping Best Bets

Pucci's outpost in Florence.

Best Modern Art Gallery
★★★ Galleria Masini, *Piazza Goldoni 6R (p 55)*

Best Clothing for Men
★★ Giorgio Armani, *Via de Tornabuoni 48 (p 56)*

Best Clothing for Women
★★ MaxMara, *Via de Tornabuoni 66-70R (p 56)*

Best Leather Goods
★★★ Beltrami, *Via della Vigna Nuova 70R (p 56)*

Best Local Market
★★ Mercato di San Lorenzo, *Piazza San Lorenzo (p 57)*

Best Mosaics
★★ Le Pietre nell'Arte, *Piazza Duomo 36R (p 56)*

Best Florentine Paper Goods
★★★ Pineider, *Piazza della Signoria (p 57)*

Best Beauty Products
★★ Antica Farmacia Santa Maria Novella *(p 55)*

Best Shoes for Men and Women?
★★★ Salvatore Ferragamo, *Via de Tornabuoni 14R (p 57)*

Best Silver
★★★ Brandimartre, *Via Bartolini 18R (p 57)*

VAT Refund

Visitors from non-European Union countries who spend 155€ or more at any one shop are entitled to a value-added tax (VAT) refund that can save them 11% to 13%. To get a refund, pick up a tax-free form from the retailer. Present your unused purchases for inspection at the airport Customs office *(dogana)* or your point of departure. The inspector will stamp your form, enabling you to pick up a cash refund (minus commission) on the spot.

Florence Shopping A to Z

Florence is known for its showrooms of famous designers and also for its artisan workshops, turning out jewelry and leather merchandise of the highest quality. The most fashionable shops—and the most expensive—are clustered along **Via de Tornabuoni** in the center of town. **Via della Vigna Nuova** is the other fashionable shopping street.

Art

★★★ **Galleria Masini** CENTRO STORICO Florence's oldest gallery is the best, representing more than 500 of the country's most avant-garde painters. *Piazza Goldoni 6R. ☎ 055-294000. www.masiniart.com. AE, DC, MC, V. Bus: A, B, 14, or 23.*

Beauty Products

★ **Antica Farmacia del Cinghiale** CENTRO STORICO For 3 centuries, this apothecary has been dispensing herbal teas, fragrances, and potpourris. Its skin care products were used by the mistresses of the Medici. *Piazza del Mercato Nuovo 4-5R. ☎ 055-282128. AE, MC, V. Bus: A, B, 23, or 71.*

★★ **Antica Farmacia Santa Maria Novella** CENTRO STORICO Herbal secrets known to the Medicis are still sold here in a wonderfully antique atmosphere—potpourris, perfumes, scented soaps, and more. *Via della Scala 16N. www.smnovella.it/English.html. AE, MC, V. Bus: A, 6, 9, 36, 37, or 68.*

Books

★ **Franco Maria Ricci** CENTRO STORICO Florence's best art bookshop also sells homemade stationery and arts and crafts. *Via delle Belle Donne 41R. ☎ 055-283312. AE, DC, MC, V. Bus: A, 6, 9, 11, 36, 37, or 68.*

★ **Paperback Exchange** CENTRO STORICO New and used titles, all in English. *Via Fielsolana 31R. ☎ 055-2478856. www.papex.it/faq.html. AE, DC, MC, V. Bus: A or C.*

Ceramics & Pottery

★★ **Richard Ginori** SESTO FIORENTINO Exquisite porcelain and refined bone china are sold in a western suburb. Good buys in Murano glass. *Via Giulio Cesare 21, Sesto Fiorentino. ☎ 055-420491. www.richardoginori1735.com. AE, DC, MC, V.*

Department Stores

★ **Coin** CENTRO STORICO This department store in a 16th-century *palazzo* sells everything from affordable clothing for men and women, to Italian-designed kitchenware, to MAC cosmetics. *Via dei Calzaiuoli 56A. ☎ 055-280531. www.coin.it. AE, MC, V. Bus: A, B, 23, or 71.*

Fashionistas haunt the shops of Via Tornabuoni.

★ **La Rinascente** CENTRO STORICO This six-story emporium sells top Italian designers at affordable prices. *Piazza della Repubblica 1.* ☎ *055-219113. AE, DC, MC, V. Bus: 22, 36, or 37.*

Fashion for Men & Women

★★ **Emilio Pucci** CENTRO STORICO Even Marilyn left a request to be buried in her favorite Pucci dress. Today, the bright, busy patterns are in fashion again. *Via de Tornabuoni 20R.* ☎ *055-2658082. www.pucci.com. AE, DC, MC, V. Bus: B, 6, 11, or 36.*

★★★ **Giorgio Armani** CENTRO STORICO Expensive, tailored men's wear and accessories, always in fashion. *Via de Tornabuoni 48.* ☎ *055-2658121. www.giorgioarmani.com. AE, DC, MC, V. Bus: B, 6, 11, or 36.*

★★★ **Gucci** CENTRO STORICO Unforgettable luxury leather goods. *Via de Tornabuoni 73R.* ☎ *055-264011. www.gucci.com. AE, DC, MC, V. Bus: B, 6, 11, or 36.*

★★ **MaxMara** CENTRO STORICO The finest clothing for women, from hats to slacks. *Via de Tornabuoni 66-70R.* ☎ *055-214133. AE, DC, MC, V. Bus: B, 6, 11, or 36.*

Glass

★★ **Cose del '900** OLTRARNO Exquisite original Art Deco glass objects. *Borgo S. Jacopo 45R.* ☎ *055-283491. AE, MC, V. Bus: 11, 36, 37, or 68.*

Leather

★★★ **Beltrami** CENTRO STORICO This world-famous, Florence-based leathermaker offers stunning footwear, handbags, belts, briefcases, and luggage at good prices. *Via della Vigna Nuova 70R.* ☎ *055-2877779. AE, DC, MC, V. Bus: A.*

★★ **Bojola** CENTRO STORICO A leading retailer of Florentine leather goods. The store pioneered the '60s trend of combining leather and cotton fabric. *Via dei Rondinelli 25R.* ☎ *055-211155. www.bojola.it/english/info/html. AE, DC, MC, V. Bus: A, 6, 11, 12, 36, 37, or 68.*

Markets

★ **Le Pietre nell'Arte** CENTRO STORICO Artful mosaics by father

Patrons flock with religious devotion to the San Lorenzo market.

Leather goods are plentiful, well-crafted bargains in the San Lorenzo market.

and son Renzo and Leonardo Scarpelli. Visits to their workshop can be arranged. *Piazza Duomo 36R. ☎ 055-212587. AE, DC, MC, V. Bus: 1 or 3.*

★★ Mercato di San Lorenzo CENTRO STORICO At the most bustling market in Tuscany, vendors hawk quality leather goods, meat, fish, and cheese. You'll find some stylish, designer-label accessories at affordable prices. *Piazza San Lorenza. Bus: 1, 6, 7, 11, 33, 67, or 68.*

Paper & Stationery

★★ Il Papiro CENTRO STORICO Exquisite paper products, photo frames, and more. *Via Cavour 55R. ☎ 055-6499151. www.ilpapirofirenze.it. AE, DC, MC, V. Bus: 1, 7, 25, or 33.*

★★★ Pineider CENTRO STORICO Since 1774 customers from Napoléon to Elizabeth Taylor have ordered personal stationery, greeting cards, and handcrafted diaries here. *Piazza della Signoria. ☎ 055-284655. www.marcus.com. AE, DC, MC, V. Bus: B or D.*

Prints & Engravings

★ Giovanni Baccani CENTRO STORICO Collectors have been flocking to "The Blue Shop" since 1903 for exquisite prints, engravings of old Florentine scenes, triptychs, and handmade frames and boxes. *Via della Vigna Nuova 75F. ☎ 055-214467. AE, DC, MC, V. Bus: A.*

Shoes

★★★ Salvatore Ferragamo CENTRO STORICO Shoes are the big thing here, with some world-class fashionwear and accessories for men and women. *Via Tornabuoni 14R. ☎ 055-292123. www.salvatoreferragamo.it. AE, DC, MC, V. Bus: B, 6, 11, 32, or 36.*

Silver

★★★ Brandimartre CENTRO STORICO Heirloom quality goods include goblets and flower vases. *Via Bartolini 18R. ☎ 055-239381. AE, DC, MC, V. Bus: D or 6.*

The Best A&E in Florence

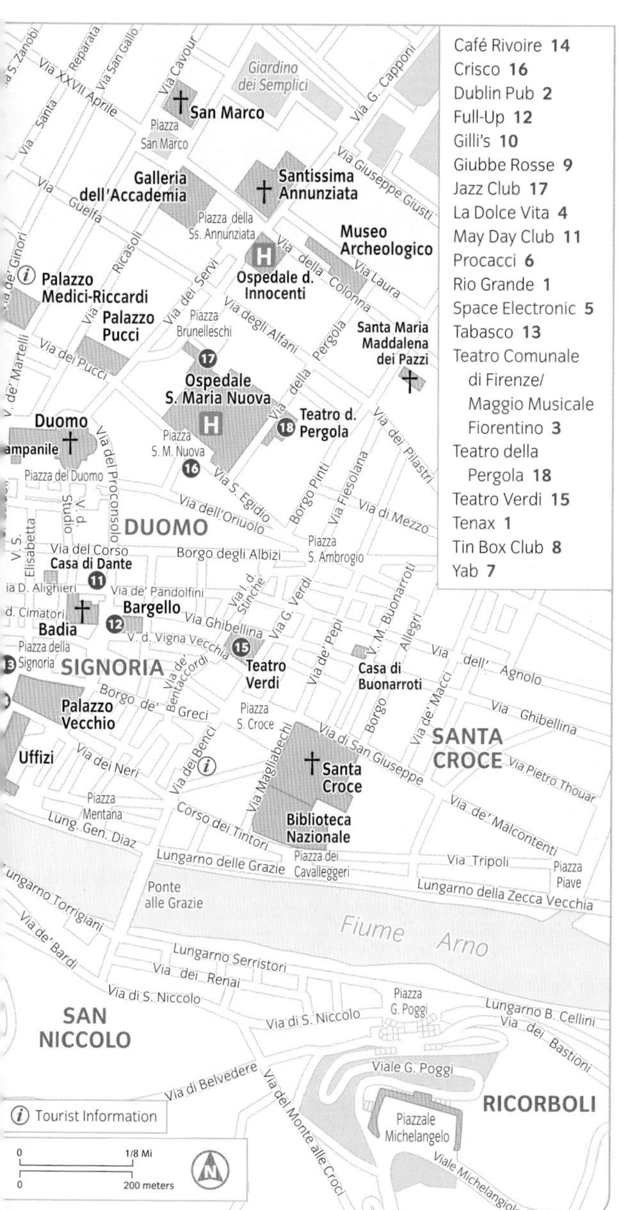
Café Rivoire 14
Crisco 16
Dublin Pub 2
Full-Up 12
Gilli's 10
Giubbe Rosse 9
Jazz Club 17
La Dolce Vita 4
May Day Club 11
Procacci 6
Rio Grande 1
Space Electronic 5
Tabasco 13
Teatro Comunale di Firenze/ Maggio Musicale Fiorentino 3
Teatro della Pergola 18
Teatro Verdi 15
Tenax 1
Tin Box Club 8
Yab 7
San Marco
Giardino dei Semplici
Galleria dell'Accademia
Santissima Annunziata
Museo Archeologico
Palazzo Medici-Riccardi
Palazzo Pucci
Ospedale d. Innocenti
Santa Maria Maddalena dei Pazzi
Ospedale S. Maria Nuova
Teatro d. Pergola
Duomo
DUOMO
Casa di Dante
Bargello
Badia
SIGNORIA
Palazzo Vecchio
Uffizi
Teatro Verdi
Casa di Buonarroti
SANTA CROCE
Santa Croce
Biblioteca Nazionale
Ponte alle Grazie
Fiume Arno
SAN NICCOLO
RICORBOLI
Piazzale Michelangelo
Tourist Information
0 1/8 Mi
0 200 meters

Nightlife/A&E Best Bets

Floodlit Centro Storico's cafes bustle at night.

Frat Party alla Florentine
★ May Day Club, *Via Dante Alighieri 16R (p 61)*

Best Cafe
★★ Gilli's, *Piazza della Repubblica 39R (p 61)*

Best Dance Club
★ Rio Grande, *Viale degli Olmi 1 (p 61)*

Best Gay Bar
★ Tabasco, *Piazza Santa Cecilia 3 (p 62)*

Best Irish Pub
★ Dublin Pub, *Via Faenza 27R (p 62)*

Best Jazz
★ Jazz Club, *Via Nuova de' Caccini 3 (p 62)*

Best Legitimate Theater
★★ Teatro della Pergola, *Via della Pergola 18 (p 62)*

Best Live Music
★★ Tenax, *Via Pratese 46A (p 62)*

Best Opera & Ballet
Teatro Comunale di Firenze, *Corso Italia 16 (p 62)*

Best Summer Festival
★★★ Maggio Musicale, *Corso Italia 16 (p 62)*

Club, Cafe & Concert Tips

Italian clubs are cliquey—people usually go in groups to hang out and dance exclusively with one another. Plenty of flesh is on display, but single travelers hoping to find random dance partners may often be disappointed.

Florence no longer has a glitterati or intellectuals' cafe scene. But if you want designer pastries and cappuccino served to you while you people-watch on a piazza, its high-toned cafes will do.

Florence is wanting for the musical cachet or grand opera houses of Milan, Venice, or Rome, but the city has two symphony orchestras and a fine music school in Fiesole. Florence's public theaters are respectable, and most major touring companies stop in town on their way through Italy. Tickets for all cultural and music events are available through **Box Office,** Via Alamanni 39 (☎ 055-210804; www.boxoffice.it).

Florence Nightlife/A&E A to Z

Bars & Lounges

★ **La Dolce Vita** OLTRARNO The owners covered the walls in mirrors so that beautiful people can dazzle themselves. *Piazza del Carmine.* ☎ *055-284595. Bus: D.*

★ **May Day Club** CENTRO STORICO The recorded music is cutting edge. Antique radios provide the decor for a young crowd. Occasional Japanese porn night with kinky-shaped sushi. *Via Dante Alighieri 16R.* ☎ *055-2381290. www.maydayclub.it. No cover. Bus: A.*

Cafes

★ **Café Rivoire** CENTRO STORICO The tables of this classy cafe open onto one of the world's most beautiful squares. Stick to the light snacks and drinks and ignore the main dishes. *Piazza della Signoria 4R.* ☎ *055-214412. Bus: A, B, 23, or 71.*

★★ **Gilli's** CENTRO STORICO Dating from 1789, this is the oldest, most beautiful cafe in Florence. *Risorgimento* leaders convened here in the 1850s to plot the unification of Italy. *Piazza della Repubblica 39R.* ☎ *055-213896. Bus: A or 22.*

★★ **Giubbe Rosse** CENTRO STORICO This fabled retreat of the Tuscan literati has been going strong since 1888. Full American breakfasts are the specialty. *Piazza della Repubblica 13–14R.* ☎ *055-212280. Bus: A or 22.*

★★ **Procacci** CENTRO STORICO This darling cafe/bar is beloved by *fashionistas.* Its specialty is a *panini tartufati,* an egg-shaped roll filled with white truffle paste. *Via de Tornabuoni 64R.* ☎ *055-211656. Bus: A or 22.*

Gilli's, the city's oldest cafe, popular by day and night.

Discos & Clubs

Full-Up CENTRO STORICO Sugar daddies meet hot models in this old cellar with a small dance floor blasting recorded music. It's a favorite expat dance club and piano bar. *Via della Vigna Vecchia 23-25R.* ☎ *055-293006. 5€–20€ cover. Bus: A, 14, or 23.*

★★ **Rio Grande** WEST OF CENTER The most popular dance club, with an older crowd. Music is mostly Latino. *Viale degli Olmi 1.* ☎ *055-331371. www.rio-grande.it. 16€ cover, including first drink. Bus: P.*

Space Electronic CENTRO STORICO Karaoke bar, pub, American-style bar, dance floor? One thing's sure: The second floor is definitely a disco with a space capsule hovering overhead. *Via Palazzuolo 37.* ☎ *055-293082. 15€ cover, including first drink. Bus: 26, 27, or 35.*

Yab CENTRO STORICO This 1980s-style disco is popular with 20-somethings. Expect surly bouncers and a rope line. *Via Sassetti 5R. ☎ 055-215160. 20€ cover, including first drink. Bus: A or 22.*

Gay Clubs

Crisco CENTRO STORICO The most famous cruising skin bar in Tuscany. Mr. Right is waiting. *Via Sant'Egidio 43R. ☎ 055-2480580. 9€–15€ cover. Bus: 1 or 3.*

★ **Tabasco** CENTRO STORICO The oldest gay dance club in Italy lives up to its fiery name, with smoke machines, strobe lights, and Tuscan studs. *Piazza Santa Cecilia 3. ☎ 055-213000. www.tabascogay.it. 10€–13€ cover. Bus: A, B, 23, or 71.*

Tin Box Club CENTRO STORICO The hottest dark room in Tuscany—for *young* gay men only. *Via dell'Oriuolo 19-21R. ☎ 055-2466387. 10€ cover. Bus: 1 or 3.*

Irish Pubs

★ **Dublin Pub** CENTRO STORICO Irish pubs are the rage in Florence, and this is the best of the lot. *Via Faenza 27R. ☎ 055-293049. Bus: A, 6, 11, 12, 36, 37, or 68.*

Jazz

★ **Jazz Club** CENTRO STORICO The best live jazz in town, in a smoke-filled basement. In summer the action moves to Parco di Villa Fabbricotti. *Via Nuova de'Caccini 3. ☎ 055-2479700. Membership 8€. Bus: A.*

Legitimate Theater

★★ **Teatro della Pergola** CENTRO STORICO This is the major classic theater of Tuscany, but you'd better speak Italian. *Via della Pergola 18. ☎ 055-22641. Tickets 7€–29€. Bus: 31 or 32.*

Live Music

★★ **Tenax** PERETOLA Tuscany's premier venue for rock and grunge bands. *Via Pratese 46A. ☎ 055-308160. www.tenax.org. 20€–25€ cover. Closed mid-May–Sept. Bus: 29 or 30.*

Opera & Ballet

★★★ **Teatro Comunale di Firenze/Maggio Musicale Fiorentino** CENTRO STORICO This is Florence's main cultural venue for opera, ballet, and classical concerts. *Corso Italia 16. ☎ 055-27791. Tickets 15€–150€. Bus: B.*

★★ **Teatro Verdi** CENTRO STORICO This is Tuscany's major hall for dance classical music, opera, and ballet, often with star performers. *Via Ghibellina 99. ☎ 055-2396242. 15€–83€. Bus: A.*

Summer Festivals

★★★ **Maggio Musicale** CENTRO STORICO This festival of opera, dance, and classical music is Italy's biggest and best. *Maggio Musicale Fiorentinio, Teatro Comunale di Firenze, Corso Italia 16. ☎ 055-27791. www.maggiofiorentino.com. May–June. Tickets 11€–85€. Bus: B.*

Jazz Club hosts musicians from around the world.

3 The Best Full-Day Tours of Tuscany

The Best of Tuscany in Three Days

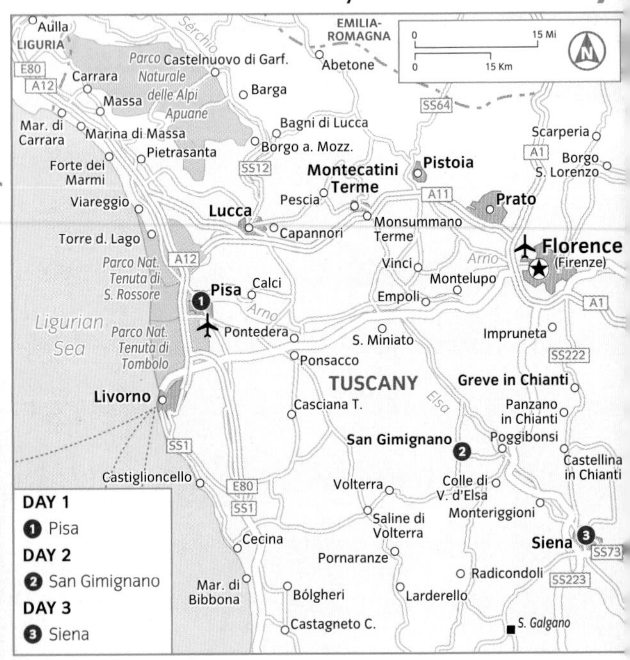

If you have only 3 days in Tuscany, you'll want to focus on Pisa, with its gravity-defying tower; San Gimignano, known for its 13 medieval "skyscrapers"; and Siena, Tuscany's best repository of art and architecture from the Middle Ages. From Florence, you'll shoot 81km (50 miles) west to Pisa, for day 1; 92km (57 miles) southeast to San Gimignano for day 2; and 40km (24 miles) southeast again to Siena. From Siena, it's 70km (43 miles) on the Firenze/Siena autostrada. START: **Florence. Trip length: 283km (174 mile) loop.**

Travel Tip

For detailed information on sights and recommended hotels and restaurants in this chapter, see the individual sections on Arezzo, Cortona, Lucca, Montepulciano, Pienza, Pisa, San Gimignano, Siena, and Volterra in chapter 6, "Charming Tuscan Towns & Villages."

Pisa is an hour west of Florence by car. Take the A11 and A12 west and follow signs.

❶ **Pisa.** Pisa is one of the easiest Tuscan cities to explore, because nearly all the major attractions center around Piazza del Duomo (also known as Campo dei Miracoli). Here you can visit the **Duomo** (the cathedral), the **Leaning Tower of Pisa,**

A carriage horse on Pisa's Campo dei Miracoli.

the **Battistero** (baptistery), the **Camposanto** (burial ground), and the **Museo dell'Opera del Duomo** (the cathedral museum).

Some visitors even manage to work in a quick look at the **Museo delle Sinopie** and **Museo Nazionale di San Matteo,** but you'd have to go at a breakneck speed that might make your trip less of a vacation. *The Pisa tourist board is on the Piazza del Duomo (☎ 050-560464; www.comune.pisa.it).*

After a night of Pisan fare at a local trattoria, bed down and head out the following morning to San Gimignano.

For detailed coverage of sights, hotels, restaurants, shops, and nightlife in Pisa, see p 150 of chapter 6.

La Bottega del Gelato After all those monuments, reward yourself with the best ice cream or *gelato* in Pisa in a wide range of flavors. We prefer the whisky cream, but grape and limoncello are also enticing. Two big scoops go for only 1.30€. *Open Mon–Tues and Thurs–Sun 11am–1am. Piazza Garibaldi 11. $.*

From Pisa, head east to San Gimignano along the Pisa/Livorno/Firenze autostrade until you near the town of Empoli and SS429. Take SS429 south until the turnoff heading southwest near the town of Poggibonsi; San Gimignano is signposted at this point. Cut west on S324 to San Gimignano.

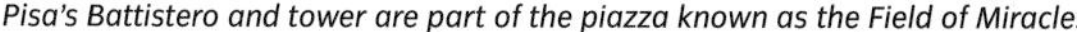

Pisa's Battistero and tower are part of the piazza known as the Field of Miracles.

San Gimignano's medieval towers overlooking the fields of Central Tuscany.

❷ San Gimignano. Arrive in San Gimignano as early as possible on the second day, so you'll be able to take in as much of the town as possible. Like Pisa, San Gimignano makes for a compact day trip because all its major attractions are in the Centro Storico, or historic core. Once you've parked and checked into a hotel, you can easily get around the town, with its 13 medieval towers, in 1 day. The Centro Storico centers around Piazza del Duomo and Piazza della Cisterna.

In just 1 day you can visit **Chiesa di Sant'Agostino,** the **Collegiata** (no longer a Duomo but the unofficial town cathedral), the **Museo Civico,** and **Torre Grossa,** with one of the most panoramic views in Tuscany. You might even have time left for a real-life horror show at the **Museo della Tortura.**

Travel Tip

For detailed coverage of sights, hotels, restaurants, shops, and nightlife in San Gimignano, see p 156 of chapter 6.

Siena is 40km (24 miles) southeast of San Gimignano. Head east on S324 to Poggibonsi and take

A cyclist on the Arno quays in Pisa.

Siena's serene medieval Piazza del Campo.

the Firenze/Siena autostrada south into Siena.

❸ **Siena.** After checking into a hotel in Siena, you face your busiest day. Begin at the **Piazza del Campo** (the main square) and take in such attractions as the **Museo Civico** (in the **Palazzo Pubblico**), even more of a highlight than the **Pinacoteca Nazionale** (Siena's picture gallery). You can also visit the Palazzo Pubblico itself and climb the **Torre del Mangia** for a panoramic view of the city and surrounding countryside. After lunch, head for the Duomo where you can easily spend 2½ to 3 hours at the cathedral, the **Museo dell'Opera Metropolitana,** and the **Battistero.**

If time remains, squeeze in some shopping and cafe time. *For detailed coverage of sights, hotels, restaurants, shops, and nightlife in Siena,* *see p 162 of chapter 6.*

Gelateria Brivido. This ice-cream shop serves Siena's best *gelato*—which can almost seem essential under the scorching Tuscan sun. It's standing room only as you place your order for flavors such as watermelon or kiwi. The *stracciatella* is irresistible. ***Via dei Pellegrini 1–3 (at Via di Città).*** *☎ 0577-280058. $.*

To return to Florence, where you began this whirlwind tour, take the Firenze-Siena autostrada the following morning. The return distance is 70km (43 miles).

Siena's landmark Torre del Mangia.

The Best of Tuscany **in One Week**

An extra 4 days in Tuscany means you can experience four more towns because driving distances in the region are so short and manageable. This weeklong itinerary expands on the 3-day tour to include Lucca, with its Roman roads ensconced in medieval ramparts; Pienza, the "ideal Renaissance city" built by Pope Pius II in the 15th century; Montepulciano, which yields one of the world's best wines, Vino Nobile; and Arezzo, Roberto Benigni's hometown and the setting for his film *Life Is Beautiful*. This itinerary should leave you time to relax a bit at each juncture. START: **Florence. Trip length: 407km (282 mile) loop.**

From Florence, Lucca is 72km (45 miles) west on the A11.

1 Lucca. At one time, Lucca was the unofficial capital of Tuscany, known to Caesar and Pompey. Today, it's celebrated for possessing the best-preserved Renaissance defense ramparts in Europe. Our recommendation is to ride along them on a bicycle.

In 1 busy day you can see the highlights of Lucca: the **Duomo,** the **Pinacoteca Nazionale,** and some of the grandest churches in Tuscany. Try to visit **San Frediano** and **San Michele in Foro,** if only to check out their facades.

A resident of San Gimignano.

Follow in Puccini's footsteps and dine on Lucchese fare in a trattoria that evening, before bedding down for the night. Head to Pisa the following morning.

For detailed coverage of sights, hotels, restaurants, shops, and nightlife in Lucca, see p 134 of chapter 6.

Leave Lucca early and drive 22km (14 miles) southwest on SS12 to Pisa.

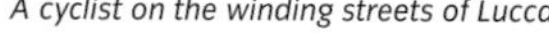

2 Pisa. Check into a hotel in Pisa and set about for one activity-filled day. For detailed suggestions on how to make the most of Pisa in just 1 day, see Day 1 in "The Best of Tuscany in Three Days," above.

For detailed coverage of sights, hotels, restaurants, shops, and nightlife in Pisa, see p 150 of chapter 6.

From Pisa, head east to San Gimignano along the Pisa/Livorno/Firenze autostrade until you near the town of Empoli and SS429. Take SS429 south until the turnoff heading southwest near the town of Poggibonsi; San Gimignano is signposted at this point. Cut west on S324 to San Gimignano.

3 San Gimignano. Arrive in San Gimignano in the morning and set about exploring the city, with its once-fortified medieval towers; this will be a highlight of your trip. For guidance, see San Gimignano, Day 2, in "The Best of Tuscany in Three Days," above.

For detailed coverage of sights, hotels, restaurants, shops, and nightlife in San Gimignano, see p 156 of chapter 6.

After an overnight stop, drive southeast to Siena for a 2-night visit.

A cyclist on the winding streets of Lucca.

Siena is 40km (24 miles) southeast of San Gimignano. Head east on S324 to Poggibonsi and take the Firenze/Siena autostrada south into Siena.

4 Siena. With a full week at your disposal, you'll probably want to spend at least 2 days in Siena. After Florence, it is the highlight of the Tuscan countryside, with its bounty of art and architecture left over from the Middle Ages.

For your first day, follow the outline for Day 3, Siena, in "The Best of Tuscany in Three Days," above.

For the second day, you should be able to visit the **Casa di Santa Caterina,** with mementos of Italy's patron saint; the **Pinacoteca Nazionale,** with its trove of some of the city's greatest art; **Chiesa di San Domenico** (also linked with St. Catherine); and the **Ospedale di Santa Maria della Scale,** also loaded with art treasures. Allow time in the afternoon for a short drive of 20km (12 miles) to **5 Monteriggioni,** the most perfectly preserved fortified village in Italy (full coverage, with driving directions, appears on p 170).

San Biagio, outside Montepulciano.

Casa di Santa Catarina in Siena.

For detailed coverage of sights, hotels, restaurants, shops, and nightlife in Siena, see p 162 of chapter 6.

Leave Siena early, the morning of your third day, and drive southeast 55km (33 miles) on SR2 to SS146 to Pienza.

6 Pienza. You can see all of Pienza's major attractions in about 3 hours, before heading out for your next stopover. The highlight of this model Renaissance town is **Piazza Pio II,** and the chief attractions are the **Duomo,** the **Museo Diocesano,** and **Palazzo Piccolomini.**

For detailed coverage of sights, hotels, restaurants, shops, and nightlife, see p 146 of chapter 6.

Montepulciano is 14km (8¾ miles) east of Pienza on SP146E.

7 Montepulciano. After spending the morning in Pienza, strike out for an afternoon in Montepulciano. Plan to arrive right after lunch, so you can visit Montepulciano's attractions before nightfall. The major sights here include the **Duomo, Tempio di San Biagio** (slightly out of the historic center), **Piazza Grande,** and **Palazzo Nobili-Targu**i. Visiting times are short for all these attractions, but you can do it all with some fast stepping. Plan to stay overnight in Montepulciano.

For detailed coverage of sights, hotels, restaurants, shops, and nightlife in Montepulciano, see p 142 of chapter 6.

Leave Montepulciano in the morning, driving 53km (33 miles) northeast to Arezzo. Head east on the SS327 toward the Firenze/ Roma autostrada. Head north on it until you reach the exit signposted to Arezzo.

8 Arezzo. For your final look at Tuscany, Arezzo won't disappoint; it's the chief reason to visit the northeastern part of the province. Its medieval streets were made for walking (in sensible shoes), but the chief attraction is the Piero della Francesca frescoes in the **Basilica di San Francesco.** If you're rushed, you can skip the **Duomo,** but don't miss the **Museo Statale d'Arte Medievale e Moderna** and **Santa Maria della Pieve.** For a memorable meal, and a fitting end to your Tuscan adventure, dine at **Buca di San Francesco** (p 127).

The Piazza Communale in Arezzo.

For detailed coverage of sights, hotels, restaurants, shops, and nightlife in Arezzo, see p 124 of chapter 6.

Arezzo is only 81km (50 miles) southeast of Florence, an easy drive on A1 the following morning.

A rear view of Pienza's cathedral, designed by Pope Pius II.

The Best of Tuscany **in Ten Days**

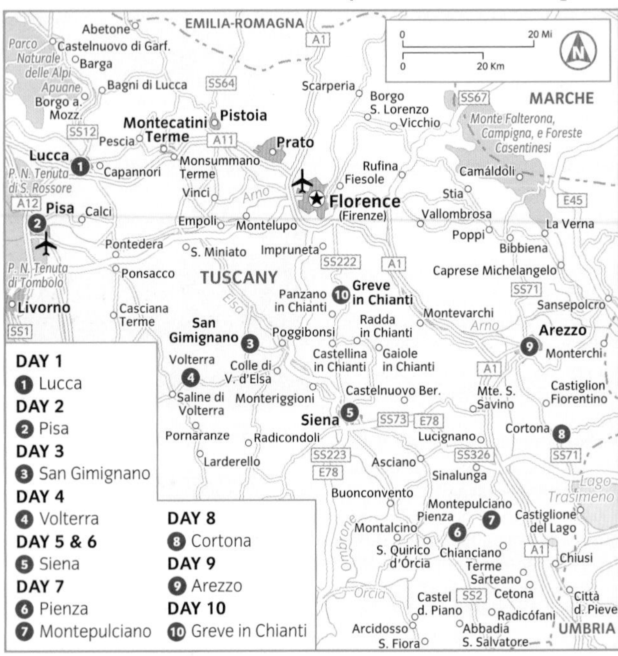

This tour is similar to Tuscany in 1 week, with a few additional stops: Etruscan Volterra, presiding over one of the highest points in the province; Cortona, another steeply pitched throwback to the Middle Ages; and the **Chianti country,** where you should have time to visit a vineyard or two before your return drive to Florence. START: **Florence. Trip length: 510km (305 miles) including return trip.**

From Florence, Lucca is 72km (45 miles) west on the A11.

1 Lucca. Head west from Florence for a 1-day visit to Lucca, celebrated for its Renaissance walls. A 1-day itinerary is detailed in Day 1, "The Best of Tuscany in One Week."

For detailed coverage of sights, hotels, restaurants, shops, and nightlife, see p 134 of chapter 6.

Leave Lucca early and drive 22km (14 miles) southwest on SS12 to:

2 Pisa. If you arrive early enough, you can see Pisa's sights before twilight, and then spend the night on the town. See Day 1, Pisa, in "The Best of Tuscany in Three Days."

For detailed coverage of sights, hotels, restaurants, shops, and nightlife, see p 150 of chapter 6.

From Pisa, take the Pisa/Livorno/Firenze autostrade east until you near Empoli and SS429. Take SS429 south until the turnoff,

Pedestrians on Volterra's city wall.

heading southwest near Poggibonsi. Cut west on S324 to:

3 San Gimignano. Leave Pisa early for a day in San Gimignano. For the 1-day tour, see San Gimignano under Day 2 in "The Best of Tuscany in Three Days."

For detailed coverage of sights, hotels, restaurants, shops, and nightlife, see p 156 of chapter 6.

From San Gimignano, drive 27km (17 miles) southwest to Volterra. Take the secondary road to Castel di San Gimignano on the SS68 to:

4 Volterra. If you arrive in the morning, you can cover Volterra's attractions in 1 day. By casually walking around, you can take in the **Duomo,** a major Etruscan treasure trove in the **Museo Guarnacci,** the **Palazzo dei Priori,** and **Teatro Romano.** Plan to spend the night.

For detailed coverage of sights, hotels, restaurants, shops, and nightlife, see p 174 of chapter 6.

From Volterra, drive east 50km (31 miles) to Siena. Take the SS68 east for 30km (19 miles) to the Firenze/Roma autostrada to:

5 Siena. As a travel destination, Siena is rivaled only by Florence. Because there is so much to see and do here, schedule at least a 2-night stopover.

See Day 3 and Day 4, Siena, in "The Best of Tuscany in One Week."

For detailed coverage of sights, hotels, restaurants, shops, and nightlife, see p 162 of chapter 6.

Leave Siena early, the morning of your third day, and drive southeast on SR2 to SS146 for 55km (33 miles) to:

6 Pienza. In the morning, take in Pienza's attractions. See Day 5, Pienza, in "The Best of Tuscany in One Week." After lunch in Pienza, continue to Montepulciano, for the afternoon and night.

For detailed coverage of sights, hotels, restaurants, shops, and nightlife in Pienza, see p 146 of chapter 6.

The Cortona countryside.

Volterra's city wall.

From Pienza, take the SS146 east for 13km (8 miles) to:

7 Montepulciano. For a half-day itinerary in Montepulciano, see Day 6, Montepulciano, in "The Best of Tuscany in One Week." Spend the night here and leave for Cortona in the morning.

For detailed coverage of sights, hotels, restaurants, shops, and nightlife, see p 142 of chapter 6.

From Montepulciano, ask for local directions to Cortona, a distance of 45km (28 miles).

8 Cortona. You can take in this medieval art town in 1 day. The chief attractions are **Museo dell'Accademia Etrusca, Museo Diocesano,** and **Santa Maria della Grazie al Calcinaio.** Stay the night and leave the next morning for Arezzo.

For complete coverage of Cortona, see p 128 in chapter 6.

From Cortona, drive north 34km (22 miles) on SS71 to:

9 Arezzo. Arezzo's chief attraction is the Piero della Francesca frescoes in the **Basilica di San Francesco.** Other attractions include the **Museo Statale d'Arte Medievale e Moderna** and the **Santa Maria della Pieve. The Casa di Vasari** and the **Duomo** are also intriguing.

For complete coverage of Arezzo, see p 124 in chapter 6.

From Arezzo, drive west, following the signs to the Firenze/Roma autostrada. Take it northeast toward Florence, to the western exit for Figline Valdarno. Follow this route (#236) west a distance of 71km (44 miles) to:

10 Greve in Chianti. On your way back to Florence from Arezzo, you can stop in **Chianti country.** Centered around Piazza del Mercatale, Greve is riddled with wine shops *(enoteche),* and you'll have time to visit a winery or two.

You can either bed down at a wine country inn or drive north into Florence and arrange transportation—home or elsewhere—the following day. Florence is 27km (17 miles) from Greve on the SS222.

For more detailed coverage of Chianti country, see p 102 in chapter 5, "The Best Regional Tours of Tuscany," and p 82, "Tuscany for Food & Wine Lovers," in chapter 4.

The fertile vineyards outside Greve, in Chianti country.

4 The Best Special-Interest Tours of Tuscany

Tuscany for Art & Architecture Lovers

During the Middle Ages and the Renaissance, artists who wanted to make a living went to Florence or Siena, where the rich, powerful churches and other wealthy patrons were. And for the most part, the art stayed where it was created. This doesn't mean you won't find great art elsewhere in Tuscany; Arezzo and Sansepolcro (see below), for example, have first-rate repositories of work by Piero della Francesco. But in general, art lovers will want to spend most of their time in Florence and Siena. Architecture buffs, on the other hand, have a much broader playing field in Tuscany, where even the old buildings and city plans in small towns such as Lucignano or Pienza attract admirers from all over the world. START: **Lucca is 72km (45 miles) west of Florence on the A11. Trip Length: 7 days.**

❶ **Lucca.** Inside its thick swath of Renaissance walls, bordered by gardens, Lucca still thrives within its medieval street plan. For architecture buffs, it's one of the most richly rewarding cities of Tuscany. Its Romanesque churches, best appreciated for their facades, exemplify the Pisan-Romanesque style, richly embroidered with polychrome

Garden statuary near the San Frediano tower in Lucca.

Travel Tip

For detailed information on sights and recommended hotels and restaurants, see the sections on Lucca, Pisa, San Gimignano, Siena, Pienza, Montepulciano, and Arezzo in chapter 6, "Charming Tuscan Towns & Villages."

marble insets and relief carvings by visiting Lombard and Pisan sculptors.

The main attractions, detailed under Lucca in chapter 6, include the **Duomo** or **Cattedrale di San Martino,** with its green and white marble facade designed by the Guidetto da Como; and the exceptionally tall **San Michele in Foro**—another stellar example of Luccan influence on the Pisan-Romanesque style and one of region's most beautiful church exteriors, with its delicately twisted columns and arcades.

Before the Pisan style of architecture swept through town here, the Lucca-Romanesque style prevailed. The church of **San Frediano** is a prime example, graced with white marble from the ancient Roman amphitheater.

In general, the streets of old town, **Città Vecchia,** are full of Gothic and Renaissance *palazzi*

Lucca's tall, delicately embellished San Michele in Foro.

and other delights. The town is well worth an entire day of your trip.

Take A12 south 21km (13 miles) and follow signs to Pisa.

2 Pisa. With its Leaning Tower, Pisa introduced the world to the Pisan-Romanesque style of architecture and sculpture—which flourished from the 11th to the 13th centuries, when the Pisan Republic was a powerful maritime city-state. Gothic sculpture flourished here as well, at the hands of sculptor Nicola Pisano (1220–80) and his son, Giovanni Pisano (1250–1315).

Touring Pisa is easy; its foremost monuments center around the Piazza del Duomo, the city's historic core (also known as the **Campo dei Miracoli,** or Field of Miracles). There's not a lot more to the town after you've spent a day taking in the sites on the main square.

Of course, the heavy, white marble **Leaning Tower** is the most compelling structure, with its six floors of circular galleries. It's famous for its tilt and its beauty, but also for the experiments Galileo conducted there (he dropped his mismatched balls from the top of the leaning side). Construction began in 1173 in the pure Romanesque style, and continued until 1350. Stainless steel cables keep the tower from toppling.

Pisa's Duomo, a model of the Pisan-Romanesque style.

The prototype for the Pisan-Romanesque style, the **Duomo** is an even greater treasure, particularly its west front with its four tiers of graceful marble columns. The fine Romanesque bronze panels on the south transept door date to the 12th century. The interior is also an impressive achievement for its nave, four aisles, and stunning pulpit, carved by Giovanni Pisano from 1302 to 1311.

The nearby **Battistero** is another stellar example of the Pisan Romanesque style. The roof is crowned by an unusual Gothic dome with four doorways, each decorated with fine carving. Papa

The nocturnal skyline of San Gimignano—Tuscany's "medieval Manhattan."

Pisano carved the impressive pulpit. If time remains, check out the **Museo dell'Opera del Duomo,** now the home of sculptures that were removed from the Piazza del Duomo for safekeeping. Some from the Romanesque period are masterpieces by unknown artists.

A fresco from the Collegiata.

From Pisa, head east to San Gimignano along the Pisa/Livorno/ Firenze autostrade until you near the town of Empoli and SS429. Take SS429 south until the turnoff heading southwest near the town of Poggibonsi; San Gimignano is signposted at this point. Cut west on S324 to San Gimignano.

❸ **San Gimignano.** Visitors can journey back to the Middle Ages in San Gimignano, Italy's best-preserved medieval town. Although San Gimignano is unique in appearance today, in the Middle Ages towns throughout Central Italy looked much like it.

Thirteen of 70 original towers are left standing since its heyday, from the 11th to the 13th centuries. More than defensive strongholds, the towers stood as symbols of a family's prestige and worth; the taller the tower, the more powerful the ruling dynasty.

Siena is 40km (24 miles) southeast of San Gimignano. Head east on S324 to Poggibonsi and take the Firenze/Siena autostrada south to the sign-posted exits.

❹ **Siena.** After Florence, Siena holds more pleasures for art and architecture lovers than any other Tuscan town. Our hurried tour calls for only 1 day here, but at least 2 days are preferable.

In the Middle Ages, Siena rivaled Florence as an art center until the Renaissance, when Sienese artists clung to Greek and Byzantine formulas and fell behind the times. Duccio di Buoninsegna and Simone Martini were pioneers in bringing greater realism to the more static Byzantine style with the flowing lines and expressive human features in their work. But the Black Death of 1348 also dealt a crippling blow to artistic aspirations in Siena.

Nicolo and Giovanni Pisano, who both worked on the **Duomo** (cathedral), were the first proponents of Gothic architecture in town. The Duomo is also a treasure trove of Tuscan and Sienese art, with Nicola Pisano's 13th-century pulpit, an undisputed masterpiece.

The **Pinacoteca Nazionale** is the greatest repository of Sienese art. It's not the Uffizi, but it houses an extensive collection of Sienese masterpieces created between the 13th and 16th centuries. Here you'll see works by all Siena's most famous artists, including Duccio and the great Simone Martini, the Lorenzetti brothers, Domenico Beccafumi, and Il Sodoma.

The **Palazzo Pubblico** houses the Sala della Pace with Amborgio Lorenzetti's fresco masterpieces *Effects of Good and Bad Government* (1335–50).

Some of the city's greatest sculpture is on display at the **Museo dell'Opera Metropolitana,** which is especially strong on sculpture by Duccio and Jacopo della Quercia, a towering figure in Gothic art.

Pienza is 55km (33 miles) southeast of Siena. From Siena, take the SS2 south to the SS146 and follow the signs.

5 Pienza. This village owes its overall look to Pope Pius II, who was born here in 1405. He set out to transform Pienza into a model Renaissance village and succeeded admirably. Bernardo Rossellino, a protégé of the great Renaissance theorist, Leon Battista Alberti, carried out the pope's mandate, creating a **Cattedrale** with a Renaissance facade, the **Palazzo Piccolomini** (Rossellino's masterpiece), and a main square that remains a Renaissance jewel.

Critics of the Vatican denounced all the money spent and called Pienza "the pope's folly." Pius died before the work was complete, but his achievement endures, helping to lure fans of great architecture to Tuscany.

Della Francesca's Resurrection in Sansepolcro.

From Pienza, drive 13km (8 miles) east to Montepulciano, following SS146.

6 Montepulciano. The trouble with visiting this idyllic town is that you may end up wanting to retire here. One of the region's highest hill towns, its architecturally harmonious medieval streets open onto panoramic views of the countryside. Spend a day wandering and discovering its treasures, beginning with the parade of Renaissance *palazzo* flanking its main street, "Corso."

The chief attractions are the **Duomo, Palazzo Neri-Orselli, Palazzo Nobili-Tarugi,** and **Tempio di San Biagio** (a masterpiece of High Renaissance architecture); everything centers around the monumental **Piazza Grande.** See p 142 for more details.

Montepulciano makes the best place in the area to stay for the

Backpackers take a break in Pienza's Piazza Pio II.

night. But after taking in its attractions and having lunch, you will still have time to explore Lucignano nearby in the afternoon.

From Montepulciano, drive east to the autostrada, taking it north toward Firenze but exiting at the signs for Lucignano, to the immediate west of the autostrada.

❼ **Lucignano.** This little town is unique in the annals of Italian hill towns for its street plan, which will have you going around in circles. Like a maze, it's laid out in four concentric ellipses, centering around four colorful squares. Visit its **Collegiata** and its **Palazzo Comunale.**

Return to Montepulciano and drive east to the autostrada. Take it north for 53km (33 miles) until the Arezzo turnoff.

❽ **Arezzo.** Arezzo marks the start of the **Piero della Francesca trail.** Della Francesca was a visionary early Renaissance master artist. A native of Sansepolcro, he created a dramatic style and explored the geometry of perspective. Born in the early 15th century, he spent his life painting and writing books on geometry and perspective until he went blind at the age of 60.

In the morning in Arezzo, you can visit his fresco masterpiece, the *Legend of the Holy Cross* (1452–66) on the walls of the apse at the church of **S. Francesco.** Treated with great realism, these frescoes evoke the Renaissance ideal of serenity and, in their subtle lighting techniques, a sense of timelessness.

In the afternoon, head east on Route 73 for 39km (64 miles), following the signs to Sansepolcro.

❾ **Sansepolcro.** We like to spend a lazy afternoon in Sansepolcro, wandering at leisure through the town's **Museo Civico** and returning time and time again to admire the paintings by native son della Francesca, including his *Resurrection* and his lovely polyptych of the *Virgin of Mercy.*

Art lovers will find much else to admire here, including works by Luca Signorelli and Jacopo Bassano. For more details, refer to Sansepolcro in chapter 5.

Spend the night in either Sansepolcro or Arezzo—both of which have adequate, if less than luxurious, accommodations.

Pope Pius II designed Pienza's historic core as the "ideal Renaissance city."

Tuscany for Food & Wine Lovers

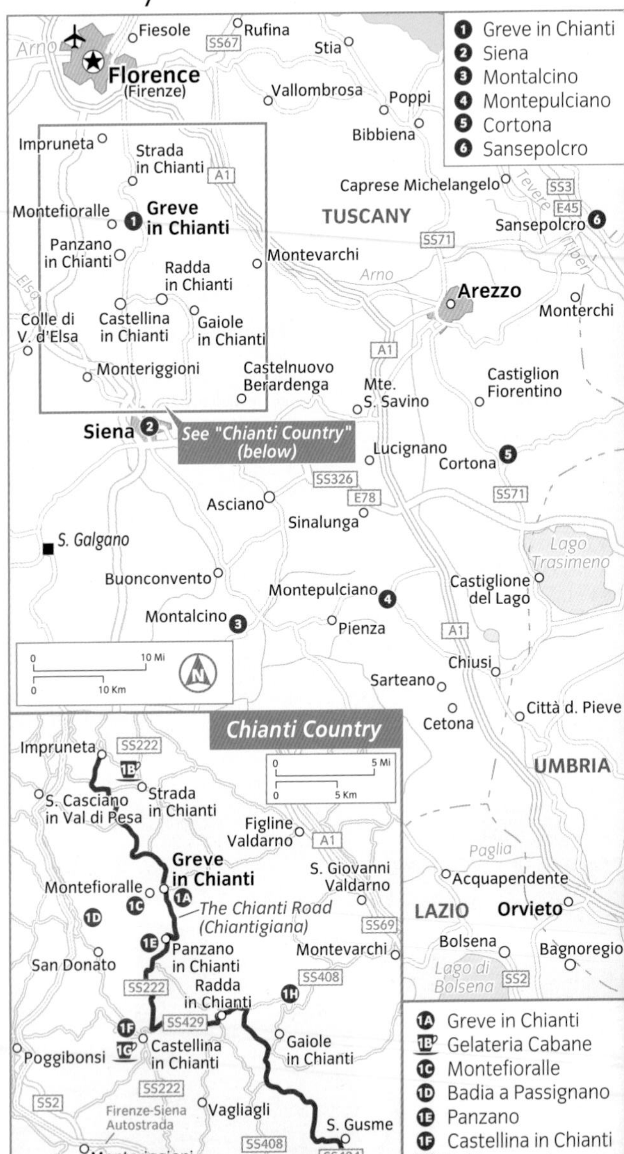

Gastronomes celebrate the fertile, sun-baked countryside of Tuscany for its olive groves and the extra-virgin oil they yield; for its Chianina cattle, acclaimed for producing the most succulent beefsteaks in Europe; and for its grapes, which give forth the world's best vintages of Chianti, in a region easily explored along the Via Chiantigiana (the Chianti Road). With such a bounty of fresh, locally available ingredients, it's only right that Tuscan food be a simply prepared, rural cuisine—known as *cucina povera.* Some recipes still served at regional trattorie were known to the Etruscans, or else were served at the tables of noble Renaissance families. This moveable feast was designed to help you experience the region at its most delicious. **START: Greve in Chianti (27km/17 miles south of Florence on the SS222). Trip length: 3–4 days.**

Travel Tip

For detailed information on sights and recommended hotels and restaurants, see Cortona, Montepulciano, and Siena in chapter 6, "Charming Tuscan Towns & Villages."

Greve in Chianti is 27km (17 miles) south of Florence along the SS222.

1 Chianti Country. Against a quintessential Tuscan landscape—with medieval wine castles and fields of gray-green olive groves—the Chianti Country south of Florence is home to some of Italy's best wineries and finest food producers, restaurants, and markets. You'll want to spend at least 2 days here. A good center for touring the area is its unofficial capital, **1A Greve in Chianti.** For more information, see Tour One, "Central Tuscany," on p 102 in chapter 5. *The Greve Tourist Information Center is at Viale Giovanni da Verrazano 33 (☎ 055-8546287).* In warm weather, head back north on SS222 from Greve for 8.2km (5 miles) to Strada. The ice cream from **1B Gelateria Cabane,** Via Mazzini 32 (☎ 055-8588659), is Tuscany's best. Ever have gray pistachio? It's gray here due to the absence of green coloring, and it's made from the finest quality Sicilian nuts. From Greve, follow signposts out of town .6km (1 mile) west to

Wine tasting is Chianti country's top sport.

A vineyard in Chianti country.

1C **Montefioralle.** This small hilltop village is the ancestral home of Amerigo Vespucci (1454–1512), the mapmaker and navigator for whom America was named. (It is said that Vespucci's niece, Simonette, was Sandro Botticelli's model for *Venus* in his celebrated painting *Primavera.*) This village is sleepy except in mid-September, when it hosts the Rassegna del Chianti Classico wine festival. But it's worth a quick stop. A signposted, potholed gravel road beyond Montefioralle continues for about 30 minutes to 1D **Badia a Passignano** (☎ 055-8071278), a 212-hectare (530-acre) property amid some of the best vineyards for producing Chianti Classico. In 1049, the Vallombrosian Order, a reformed branch of the Benedictines, took over this property. St. Giovanni Gualberto, who established the order here, died in 1073, and his relics are still preserved in the abbey. The original Romanesque church where the saint was buried received a baroque overlay in the 16th century. Ridolfo di Ghirlandio decorated the monks' refectory with one of his three representations of *The Last Supper* (1476). The on-site castle tower is from the 19th century. Antinori, winemakers since 1385, purchased the estate in 1987. You can visit the *bottega* (small store) on the grounds, purchase wines, and tour the historic cellars. La Bottega is in an 18th-century building near the abbey gate. Next to the shop is a good restaurant, l'Osteria di Passignano. From Montefioralle, follow the signposts south along a secondary road into 1E **Panzano,** a distance of 8.2km (5 miles). At the epicenter of Chianti Country, it's hailed as a *paese dei golosi* (village of gourmands). Foodies flock to the master butcher of Tuscany, **Dario Cecchini,** Via XX Lugglio 11 (☎ 055-852020)—the de facto community center, where news is dispensed about food parties, food festivals, food markets—whatever food events are happening. Cecchini's butcher shop is called "the Uffizi of Meat." Diehard Italian carnivores drive all the way from Rome and Florence to sample such delights as cured pig jowl or the quintessential Chianina steak, the single finest cut of this legendary beef we have ever eaten. Likewise, the best *salumi* in Tuscany is sold here. From Panzano, follow the signs 13km (8 miles) to 1F **Castellina in Chianti,** home to the region's finest wine restaurant: 1G **L'Albergaccio,** Via Fiorentina (☎ 0577-741042). At this restored stone barn, with a

The vineyards of Badia a Passignano.

One of the world's most prized wines, Brunello di Montalcino is produced in the vineyards outside this medieval hill town.

summer garden terrace, the wine list is unrivaled in Tuscany. Antipasti is prepared according to the season. Treats unique to the place include ravioli stuffed with salt cod and aromatic wood pigeon simmered in Chianti. For our final stopover, follow the signs east to Radda in Chianti. Continue east to **1H Badia a Coltibuono,** a distance of 21km (13 miles). Badia a Coltibuono, Coltibuono Nord Est (☎ 0577-749031), is one of the great Chianti estates. Made famous by its owner, Lorenza de' Medici (the maven of Italian cuisine), the estate is celebrated for its Chiantis (try the Sangiovetto label), virgin olive oils, and its cooking school. It was here that we learned to make gnocchi the right way. Fresh herbs and seasonal produce dominate the menu in the restaurant, the best place in Tuscany to order Chianina beef, one of the world's finest steak cuts. The wine list focuses on the estate's own production. *See inset map, p 82.*

From Greve in Chianti, the SS222 continues south to Siena, a distance of 42km (26 miles).

2 Siena. The Sienese are said to be "cursed" with the sweetest teeth in Tuscany. Since the 13th century, locals have been known for their candied fruit-and-almond cakes, among other baked goods.

Panforte and *pan pepato* are the two most famous such cakes, each baked from ancient recipes. *Pan pepato* is a flat, honey-sweetened cake filled with candied fruits and nuts and flavored with spices; the finishing touch is a dusting of ground pepper. *Panforte* is dusted with sugar instead. Torta Margherita, is named for Queen Margherita of pizza fame. *Ricciarelli* is a lozenge-shaped cake made from almond, sugar, and honey. Originally a jawbreaker to be dipped in wine, *cavallucci* is made with honey-coated, aniseed-flavored walnuts; for modern tastes, it has been softened. All of these cakes are available throughout the town but two co-owned bakeries do them the best: **Nannini-Coca d'Oro,** Via Banchi di Sopra 23 (☎ 0577-41591), and **Nannini,** Piazza Salimbeni (☎ 0577-281094).

From Siena drive south for 42km (25 miles), following the signs into Montalcino. Montalcino is 8km (5 miles) off the SS Via Cassia that runs between Siena and Rome.

3 Montalcino. This medieval hill town yields **Brunello di Montalcino,** one of the greatest wines in the world. Many wineries welcome visitors, and the town is filled with wine shops and *enoteche* (wine cellars).

The center of the town's foodstuffs, including its gourmet honey and its Pecorino cheese, is **Enoteca La Fortezza** (for more information, see p 117 under "Eastern Tuscany" in chapter 5).

One of Montalcino's many enoteche.

While in Montalcino you can also sample Brunello's "younger brother," the less noble **Rosso di Montalcino** made of the same grapes as its more famous counterpart. Taking far less time to age, this is a fruity red with Brunello's flavor but sold at a third of the price.

Our favorite vineyard and wine estate is **Col d'Orcia,** S. Angelo in Colle (☎ 0577-80891; www.coldorcia.com), which conducts wine-producing experiments with the University of Florence. Over the years, its owners have collected more than 50,000 bottles of old Brunello vintages and carefully preserved them. This is one of the largest local wine estates, with about 110 hectares (272 acres) of Sangiovese grapes, which produce both Brunello and Rosso. Itŝ star wine is *Poggio al Vento.* Limited tastings are available in the estate shop, but guided tastings and cellar visits are available by appointment.

For information on other wineries, check with the wine consortium at the center of town, inside the **Palazzo Comunale,** Costa del Municipio 1 (☎ 0577-848246).

For more information on Montalcino, see the Eastern Tuscany tour on p 114 in chapter 5.

From Montalcino, follow Route 146 east 32km (23 miles) to Montepulciano.

4 Montepulciano. This ancient town of Etruscan origin, dominating the Hills of the Valdichiana, is celebrated for its violet-scented, orange-speckled ruby wine, *Vino Nobile di Montepulciano,* famous since the 8th century. It has been called the "king of all wines," although Brunello is more beefy and is considered number one by most connoisseurs (see Montalcino, above).

As is the case with the Montalcino wine, a younger and less expensive *Vino Nobile di Montepulciano* exists. It is aged less and sold sooner. *For a complete rundown on Montepulciano, including hotels, restaurants, and how to taste its wines, see p 142 in chapter 6.*

From Montepulciano, head east to the autostrada, and take it north toward Florence. Continue until the turnoff for Perugia heading east. Take this autostrada to the junction with Route 71 going north into Cortona. The total driving distance between Montepulciano and Cortona is 32km (20 miles).

5 Cortona. Serious foodies, at least once in their tour of Tuscany, will want to stay at a grand regional inn specializing in the finest Tuscan cuisine and wines. Our candidate is **Il Falconiere** (recommended as both a country inn and a place to dine on p 131 and 133 of chapter 6). The summer dining terrace here opens onto views of the vineyard-covered hillsides. From a previous trip here, I vividly recall a pumpkin-coated homemade pasta with savory pheasant stuffing and an autumnal antipasti of a salt cod tartlet with herb-scented garbanzos.

Husband and wife Riccardo and Silvia Baracchi offer cooking classes at their restored 18th-century villa 4.5km (3 miles) north of Cortona. And Il Falconiere produces its own olive oil as well.

Sampling Vino Nobile di Montepulciano.

Follow the signs out of Cortona heading west to Route 71. Take this express highway north toward Arezzo until the junction with E78 east, toward Sansepolcro. The total distance between Cortona and Sansepolcro is 52km (32 miles).

6 Sansepolcro. This gastronomic center in Eastern Tuscany is relatively unknown to the average visitor. Beyond its excellent food and wine, it's home to masterpieces by Piero della Francesa. For a preview of the town's attractions and amenities, see p 119, in our tour of Eastern Tuscany, in chapter 5.

For gourmet dining, head for **Oroscopo di Paola e Marco,** Via Togliatti 68, Pieve Vecchia Nord-Ovest (☎ 0575-734875), a restored farmhouse with a creative *cucina* that uses only the finest regional ingredients. Two fixed-price menus—one five courses, another seven—will have you raving about Tuscan food and wine, and the owners' enthusiasm is contagious. Winemakers sometimes appear at special gourmet evenings to showcase their wines. You can also spend the night in one of the remodeled, affordable rooms upstairs—which is great if you've had too much *vino*.

When prepared properly, a *bistecca alla fiorentina* is the best in the world, especially when it comes from the indigenous purebred Chianina, a muscular beef cattle raised in this region. **Carni Shop,** Via dei Lorena 32 (☎ 0575-742924), sells it ready to cook. Rosangela Chieli operates the best pastry shop in town: **Pasticceria Chieli,** Via Fraternità 12 (☎ 0575-742026). Wait until you try the chocolate mousse, pine-nut-studded ricotta tarts, and the almond macaroons.

Classic breads, among the best in Eastern Tuscany, are baked fresh daily in a 15th-century building, at **Panificio La Spiga,** Via Santa Caterina 76 (☎ 0575-740522). The most acclaimed *gelateria* is **Gelateria Ghignoni,** Via Tiberina Sud 85 (☎ 0575-741900), 1km (½ mile) from the center on the road to Città di Castello. The shop's deep chocolate flavor is worthy of an award. But shrimp ice cream? How about porcini mushroom ice cream? Perhaps not, but if you're game, they've got it.

Casks of Chianti.

Tuscany for **Families**

An elderly Sienese noblewoman who lived in a decaying palazzo put the damper on our Tuscany for Families tour: "Tell people that Tuscany is an adult attraction," she said. "We have great art and architecture. We are not Disneyland." Fortunately, many of the palaces, castles, and fortified hilltowns of Tuscany look as though they had been created by Walt himself. So kids can be "lured" to cultural attractions—provided you don't call them that. With this tour, we tried to create a balance between cultural sites and activities that will please the entire family.

Travel Tip

For detailed information on sights and recommended hotels and restaurants in Lucca, Pisa, and San Gimignano, see each town in chapter 6, "Charming Tuscan Towns & Villages."

Drive west from Florence, toward Montecatini, to the turnoff heading north to Pescia, a distance of 64km (40 miles).

1 Pescia. In Pescia, **Giardino Zoologico Città,** Via Pieve a Celle 160 (☎ 0573-911219), has a total of 600 animals, including 30 species of reptiles. Visits require about 2 hours.

From Pescia, drive south for 5km (3 miles) to the little town of Collodi.

❷ **Collodi.** This is the hometown of Carlo Lorenzini who wrote *The Adventures of Pinocchio* in 1881. The world-famous children's story is celebrated in the **Parco di Pinocchio** (☎ 0572-429342) with diversions ranging from mosaic scenes about Geppetto and his fibbing puppet to a hedge maze and a children's museum. *Daily 8:30am–sunset; 8.50€ adults, 6.50€ children 3–14.*

From Collodi, take SP11 east to SS435 east for a total of 11km (7 miles) to Montecatini.

❸ **Montecatini.** This spa town near Collodi, with dozens of hotels, is the best place nearby to spend the night.

❹ **Lucca.** All family members will delight in walking or biking the 4km (2.4 miles) of Renaissance walls that ring the old town here. For other attractions, hotels, restaurants, and diversions, refer to "Lucca" in chapter 6.

The tilt of Pisa's tower has captivated children for centuries.

Despite all the old churches, Tuscany can appeal to kids.

❺ **The Garfagnana.** While still based in Lucca on Day 3, go to the **Lucca Tourist Office,** Piazza Santa Maria 35 (☎ 0583-919931), and get a map with detailed directions for exploring the **Garfagnana,** to the north of the city. Ideal for a day trip with kids, this section of northwestern Tuscany is riddled with rivers and valleys tucked between the Apennines and the Apuan Alps. Hiking and horseback riding trails run throughout the area. Once you're in the Garfagnana, more detailed information is available at the **Comunità Montana Garfagnana,** Piazza della Erbe (☎ 50983-644473), in Castelnuovo di Garfagnana, the stony capital of this region.

Orrido di Botri at Montefegatesi, a narrow natural gorge, is idyllic for a picnic on a hot day. Near Poggio, **Lago di Vagli,** an artificial lake, offers boats for rent. There are also many scenic walks in all directions starting from this lake.

At the **Grotta del Vento** (Cave of the Wind; ☎ 0583-722024), near Barga, you'll encounter the most dramatic caves in Tuscany. Wander into this subterranean landscape of tunnels, stalactites, stalagmites, emerald green pristine lakes, and underground rivers. A 1-hour tour guides you and your family safely through. Longer tours are more suited for adults and experienced "cavers." After a day in the Garfagnana, return to Lucca for the night.

From Lucca, continue west on the autostrada 28km (17 miles) to Viareggio.

6 Viareggio. Kids will be thrilled to break up their tour of Tuscan art cities by hanging out on the fine sandy beaches of this summer resort town. Several tourist boats run excursions through the beautiful bay, and the seaside boardwalk has plenty of places that peddle *gelato*.

From Viareggio, cut south on the autostrada to Pisa for 24km (15 miles).

7 Pisa. At the Campo dei Miracoli (Field of Miracles), all kids will want to climb to the top of the Leaning Tower, but the minimum age is 8 years old. Budding scientists of any age may stray into the Duomo and follow in the footsteps of Galileo. Another alternative for kids too young to climb the tower: Explore the old town walls and climb a medieval tower for a view of the city and the Arno river. The entire family can also walk to the river and board one of the many boats that offer hour-long rides.

Palio in Siena.

Pinocchio may well be Tuscany's most famous native son.

From Pisa, directions to San Gimignano are complicated. For details, refer to p 65 (Day 1 under "The Best of Tuscany in Three Days," in chapter 3).

8 San Gimignano. With its well-preserved medieval towers, San Gimignano is like a stage set for kids, who generally seem to love romping through its historic core. The adventure begins at the **Torre Grossa,** which families climb for a panoramic sweep of the Tuscan countryside. Parents have to make a decision about whether to subject their children to the **Museo della Tortura**—a Tuscan chamber of horrors, with horrendous instruments of torture—but most kids find these exhibits fascinating. For family outings, head to the **Rocca,** an old fort that's now a public park with trees and plenty of green space ideal for a picnic. Another stroll is a walk outside the old stone walls of this once-fortified town, or perhaps a visit to one of the **open-air markets** in the Piazza del Duomo on Thursday and Sunday. For a complete description of hotels, restaurants, and activities, refer to chapter 6.

From San Gimignano, travel 40km (24 miles) southeast on S324 to Poggibonsi, where you can hook up with the Firenze/ Siena autostrada. Head south and turn off at the exit marked Siena.

9 Siena. We saved the best for last. Siena is a year-round family attraction. If you're here in July and August for the famous 4-day **Palio** celebrations, the whole family can revel in the colorful parades with medieval costumes and banners and the anarchic horse races around Piazza del Campo.

In the center of town, climb the **Torre del Mangia,** the bell tower of the **Palazzo Pubblico,** for the most dramatic view of the city and the enveloping countryside. Even kids are fascinated by the Lorenzetti frescoes in the Palazzo Pubblico's **Sala della Pace**—often called "one big, long picture show."

The **Duomo** is jazzy enough to interest children who are normally bored with cathedrals. Its black and white floors are reminiscent of zebras, and even the art—such as a *Last Judgment* showing people squirming in hell—holds a morbid fascination for kids.

10 Monteriggioni. For an adventure after lunch, drive your kids to **Monteriggioni,** 20km (12 miles) northwest along SS2. It's the most perfectly preserved fortified village in Italy. Even Walt couldn't have done it better.

Return to Siena for the night.

Monterrigioni looks like the figment of a cartoonist's imagination.

Tuscany by **Rail**

Most of this guide has been structured for intrepid motorists who like to discover the countryside in their own set of wheels. But we recognize the increasing number of visitors who aren't so blessed, or who want to conserve fuel, or who simply prefer to see Tuscany by rail. Such visitors will miss discoveries in remote villages and towns that don't have train connections, but they will still be able to explore the most popular towns. To explore all of Tuscany, you'd have to double back to Florence many, many times and suffer unwieldy transfers, relying heavily on small country buses that don't always run on schedule. We've designed this 7-day tour to minimize hassle. By using Siena as a rail base, with a few additional connections made by bus, you can easily see many of the region's highlights.

Travel Tip

For detailed information on sights and recommended hotels and restaurants, see the Lucca, Pisa, Siena, San Gimignano, Volterra, Montepulciano, and Arezzo sections of chapter 6, "Charming Tuscan Towns & Villages."

An Italian train passing through the Tuscan countryside.

❶ **Lucca.** Within easy reach of Florence, Lucca receives trains from that city every hour, beginning daily at 5:10am and running up until 10:30pm. Trip time is 1½ hours, and fares are low—a one-way ticket is 4.75€. Trains from Florence pull into the station on **Piazza Ricasoli** (☎ 0583-47013), just outside the city walls.

❷ **Pisa.** Fortunately, to spend the following night in Pisa, you don't have to double back to Florence. Pisa and Lucca are among the few major cities in Tuscany that share convenient rail links with each other. The link between Pisa and Lucca is the most easy to use in all of Tuscany. Trains leave Lucca every 20 minutes daily, from 6:30am to 9:40pm daily, for the 30-minute trip. A one-way fare is 1.95€. Trains pull into Pisa at **Piazza della Stazione** (☎ 147-80888), at the southern end of town.

❸ **Siena.** To reach our next destination—which you can use as a base for a total of 4 nights—you have to double back from Pisa to Florence and change trains for Siena. During the day, trains depart Pisa to Florence once an hour, from 4:12am to 12:49am, for the 1-hour trip. It's 5.50€ one-way. In Florence, you can change trains at **Stazione Santa Maria Novella** (☎ 848-888088). Ten trains run from Florence to Siena daily, from 5:30am to 11:07pm, for the 1½-hour trip. It's 5.30€ for a one-way ticket. Trains arrive in Siena at **Piazza Rosselli** (☎ 147-80888), which is 15 minutes by frequent bus from the city center.

After seeing the sights of Siena, you can break up the trip and return to Florence. Or else you can spend another 3 nights in Siena, taking a series of day trips to some of the most enchanting towns of Tuscany, and return to Siena by nightfall. However, you'll have to rely on the bus instead of the train.

❹ **San Gimignano.** This hilltop fortress town with its famous towers is easily accessible from Siena's **Piazza Gramsci. TRA-IN/SITA** (☎ 0577-204246) runs more than 30 buses per day, linking Siena with San Gimignano. A one-way fare is 5€ and takes less than an hour. You can see the sights and take a bus back to Siena in time for dinner.

❺ **Volterra.** Try to get a direct bus between Siena and the ancient Etruscan town of Volterra. Otherwise, you'll have to change buses in Colle di Val d'Elsa. When you purchase the ticket, ask about the best connection between the two towns.

With views like this, who wants to have to keep an eye on the road?

TRA-IN (☎ 0577-204246) is your best bet for direct connections between Siena and Volterra. In Siena, you can purchase tickets for the 1½-hour trip at the underground terminal at Piazza Gramsci. A one-way ticket is 4.40€. Depending on the demand and the season, weekend service might be reduced. You can usually visit Volterra in the morning and afternoon, and return to Siena by nightfall.

❻ **Montepulciano.** Tuscany's highest hill town lies on the Siena-Chiusi rail line. But the train station (☎ 0578-20074) is 10km (6 miles) from the center of Montepulciano, to which it is connected by bus service. **LFI buses** (☎ 0578-31174) run between the terminus and Montepulciano, costing only 1€ for a one-way ticket. But summer schedules may be curtailed. If you're caught without a bus, it might cost from 13€ to 16€ to get to Montepulciano by taxi.

Involving less hassle, a **TRA-IN** bus (☎ 0577-204246) leaves from the underground terminal at Piazza Gramsci, in Volterra, and goes directly to Montepulciano in 1½ hours, costing 4.50€ for a one-way ticket.

Buses run between Montepulciano and Siena at the rate of 5 per

Tuscan cattle herders.

day. You have a choice of overnighting in Montepulciano or returning to Siena for the night.

At this point, you can break the trip and return to Florence. Or you can extend your journey 1 more day and travel to Arezzo.

❼ **Arezzo.** In northeastern Tuscany, the old city of Arezzo attracts fans of the artist Piero della Francesca. From the rail station in Florence, trains leave for Arezzo at the rate of 2 per hour daily from 4:30am to 9:50pm, taking 1½ hours and costing 5.10€ for a one-way ticket. For rail information, call ☎ 848-888088.

A Tuscan poppy field.

Rail Passes & Packages

For travel exclusively within Italy, Rail Europe's **Trenitalia** pass (www.raileurope.com) offers the best rates on Italy's national rail line: 3 days in 2 months are $168 for second-class travel; additional days, up to 7 days, are $23 each. **Trenitalia Saverpass** is an even better deal for two or more people traveling together: $143 for 3 days; $19 each additional day. Travelers under 26 save most: **Trenitalia Pass Youth** is $140 for 3 days; $19 for each additional day. Rates are good for consecutive or nonconsecutive travel.

Rail Europe's **Italy Fly 'n Drive** package is more expensive but optimal in Tuscany, where train service is limited. For $348, you get 4 days of unlimited second-class train travel in Italy and 2 days Hertz car rental with unlimited mileage; additional car days are $65. Two adults pay $564 ($282 per person) for the same 4-day period.

See the Rail Europe website for first-class fares and car upgrades.

Tuscany Outdoors

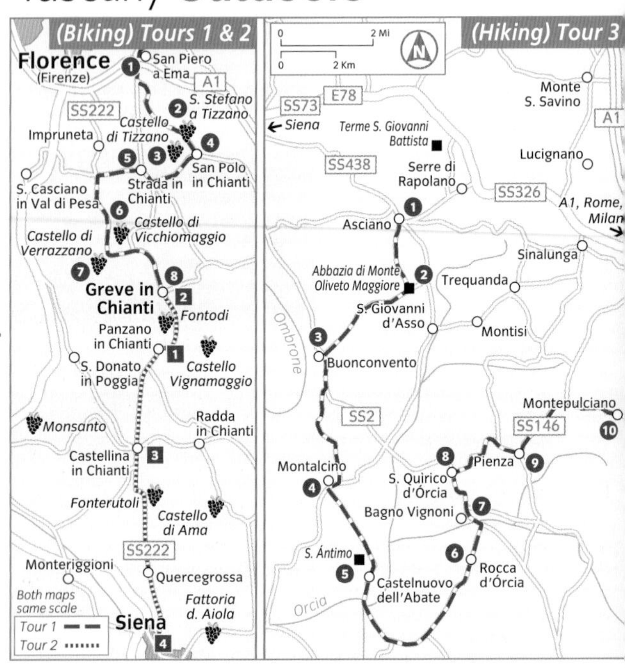

Most of the tours in this book were designed for motorists, but this one caters to bikers, hikers, and other outdoor enthusiasts who need to spike their tours of old churches with fresh country air. For fully guided cycling expeditions, contact **I Bike Italy** (☎ 561-3880783; www.ibikeitaly.com). Based in Florence, I Bike Italy offers 1- or 2-day tours from Florence to Siena. The same company leads extensive walking tours as well. **Club Alpino Italiano,** 7 Via E. Fonseca Pimental, Milan (☎ 02/2614-1378; www.cai.it), also arranges walking tours, of varying degrees of difficulty—from countryside rambles to serious mountain trekking expeditions.

Tour 1: Cycling Florence/ Chianti Country.

The most accessible and scenic route in Tuscany for cyclists is the Chianti Country, immediately south of Florence. You can extend this tour by 2 or 3 days by taking the suggested detours. If you're settling for a beautiful 1-day tour, head straight from Florence south to Greve in Chianti, the heart of the wine country, a full-day journey at a distance of 27km (17 miles). We recommend a 21-speed mountain bike for this trip. Stock up on supplies in Florence; you'll find dozens of idyllic places in

Tuscany is a challenging, rewarding destination for cyclists.

the countryside where you can stop for a picnic. START: **Florence. Trip length: 27km (17 miles)/1 day.**

Travel Tip

For more detailed information about stops along these tours, refer to our Chianti Road tours in the "Central Tuscany" section of chapter 5 (p 102) and in "Tuscany for Food & Wine Lovers," earlier in this chapter.

On your bicycle, cross the Ponte San Niccolò, spanning the Arno River at the eastern end of Florence, and follow the signs from Piazza Ferrucci to the town of Grassina and the SS222. This is the Chiantigiana or the celebrated Chianti Road. The route continues south on this road unless otherwise indicated. You'll make your first stop at Ponte a Ema, 4km (2.5 miles) south of Florence.

1 Oratorio di Santa Caterina dell'Antella at S. Piero a Ema. A wall fresco at this church traces the *Life of St. Catherine*. Spinello Aretino painted it in 1390. The apse displays more frescoes of St. Catherine—these painted by the "Master of Barberino" (ca. 1360).

2 Santo Stefano a Tizzano. Four kilometers (2½ miles) south of Florence, on a clearly marked road off the SS222, you'll come upon this vine-clad Romanesque church in Petigliolo. It was constructed by the Buodemontis, a local ruling family. Nearby, a sign points to:

3 Castello di Tizzano. This wine estate, amid vineyards, is a consortium of farms that produce the Gallo Nero label, a prestigious Chianti Classico. Visits are available by appointment only (☎ 055-482737 for reservations). If you've made a reservation, you can explore the 15th-century cellars on-site and purchase a bottle of *vin santo* for your picnic lunch—unless that would interfere with your peddling.

Poppy fields in Abbazia di Sant'Antimo.

4 San Polo in Chianti. Two kilometers (1¼ miles) south, you'll come upon this little town in the center of Tuscany's iris industry. An annual Iris Festival takes place here in May; dates vary. You can also visit the ancient church of San Miniato in Robbiana, consecrated in 1077.

From San Polo a by-road points the way west back to:

5 Strada in Chianti. Taking its name, Strada (street), from an old Roman road that ran through here, this town lies 14km (8½ miles) south of Florence. Immediately to its south, you pass by **Castello di Mugano,** one of the best preserved medieval castles in Tuscany. From this point, it's rolling countryside until you reach Vicchiomaggio.

Continue on the SS222 for 60km (37 miles) to:

6 Vicchiomaggio. The **Castello di Vicchiomaggio** (☎ 055-854078) once hosted Leonardo da Vinci. You can purchase their classic wines and a jar of honey, acclaimed as the best in Tuscany. Tours of the estate are limited to groups, but you can take part in free tastings at their roadside Cantinetta San Jacopo wine shop, on the SS222 at the signposted turnoff to the castle. The Vicchiomaggio control 120 hectares (300 acres) of land, of which 28 hectares (70 acres) are devoted exclusively to vineyards.

7 Verrazzano. With a name familiar to New Yorkers, from the bridge that links Brooklyn and Staten Island, this hamlet 49 km (30 miles) from Vicchiomaggio is named for Giovanni da Verrazzano, the first European colonial to sail into the harbor of New York in 1524. If time remains, you can follow the signposts to his birthplace, **Castello di Verrazzano** (☎ 055-854243). Take the route marked via San Martino in Valle to reach it. Its 10th-century tower is surrounded by

An invitation to cyclists.

15th- and 16th-century buildings. On-site visits to its ancient caves are possible Monday to Friday. You can also purchase bottles of red and white wines made on site.

Continue south on the SS222 for 110km (68 miles) to Greve.

8 Greve in Chianti. On the banks of the Greve River stands the wine country's unofficial capital. Head for the town square. You can overnight in Greve; few cyclists will have the stamina to bike back to Florence for the night. For more information about what to see and do in the area, refer to "The Chianti Road," in chapter 5.

Tour 2: Cycling Greve in Chianti/Florence.

The following morning, after an overnight in Greve, you can cycle back to Florence or continue on to Siena. The distance of 40km (25 miles) to Siena is longer than the distance between Greve and Florence, but with fewer distractions along the route. Leave Greve in the morning and set out along the SS222 again, following the signs to Siena. **START: Greve. Trip length: 40km (25 miles).**

1 Panzano. This village is 6km (3¾ miles) south of Greve and makes a worthwhile stopover for the sight of its medieval castle. For what to see and do in the area, refer to "Panzano" under "The Chianti Road," in chapter 5.

❷ **Fontodi.** In the heart of Chianti Country, 9.5km (6 miles) south of Greve, this long-neglected estate was recently restored. Now, it's turning out some of the region's finest vintages, including Chianti Classico, a blend of Sangiovese and other grapes aged in huge oak barrels. Visits are possible only by reservation. Via San Leolino 89 (☎ 055-852005; fax 055-852537). See "The Chianti Road," in chapter 5, for more details.

❸ **Castellina in Chianti.** Castellina is 21km (13 miles) north of Siena. Looking like a postcard left over from the *quattrocento,* Castellina is dominated by the imposing, crenellated **Rocca** (fortress) on its central square, and its medieval walls have survived more or less intact. Walk along **Via della Volte,** the most historic street, and stop in at one of the *bottegas* for lunch and a bottle of Chianti.

❹ **Siena.** The final destination of most cyclists in Tuscany, this is where you'll want to linger for a while, as time allows. For a complete preview of what to see and do here, refer to "Siena" on p 162 of chapter 6. From Siena, you can take your bike on the train back to Florence—unless, of course, you're game to repeat the entire 2-day trip north on your own steam!

Hoofing it through Tuscany.

Tour 3: Walking Siena/ Montepulciano.

This landscape southeast of Siena—one of Tuscany's most spectacular—can be covered on foot. The good thing about this tour is that you can break it up at almost any point along the route. At Asciano, Montalcino, Bagno Vignoni, Pienza, or Montepulciano, you can end the tour and head back to Siena. If you go all the way from Siena to Montepulciano, cutting south through Asciano and east toward Pienza, you will reach Montepulciano. This walk, depending on your pace, is more comfortably done in 3 to 5 full days, depending on how many of the suggested stopovers you make. START: **Siena. Trip length: 3–5 full days.**

Leave Siena via the SS326, signposted to Perugia. Turn right onto the SS438 leading to Asciano, a distance of 26km (16 miles) southeast of Siena.

❶ **Asciano.** Known as **Le Crete,** the landscape en route to Asciano is among the most dramatic in Tuscany. Asciano itself, girdled by ramparts from 1352, has as its chief attraction the **Museo d'Arte Sacre,** in the 14th-century Palazzo Corboli, Corso Matteotti 122.

Back on SS438, turn left onto SS451 and follow the signs for:

❷ **Abbazia di Monte Oliveto Maggiore.** The walk between Asciano and this monastery, founded in 1313, is 9km (5½ miles). Art lovers flock here to view the series of 36 frescoes by Luca Signorelli and Il Sodoma, which are among the masterpieces of the High Renaissance.

Back on the SS451, continue 9km (6 miles) along Via Cassia (SS2) to:

❸ **Buonconvento.** Ignore the industrial horror surrounding this little town and head for its historic medieval core. The **Museo d'Arte**

Sacre, Via Soccini 18, is filled with Renaissance masterpieces, including works by Duccio.

Continue south on SS2 for 11km (7 miles) and follow the signs into:

❹ **Montalcino.** This hill town has been inhabited since the Etruscans ruled it. For more information on the town, refer to p 117 in chapter 5.

Continue south along SS2 for 10km (6 miles), following the signs to:

❺ **Sant'Antimo.** Although it's in ruins, it remains one of the great Romanesque temples extant in Tuscany. For more details, see p 117 in chapter 5.

Continue southeast on the SS2 to the junction with SS323. Turn left onto this road, which climbs north. Bypass the hamlet of Castiglione d'Orcia until you approach Rocca d'Orcia. The distance between Sant'Antimo and Rocca d'Orcia is 19km (12 miles).

❻ **Rocca d'Orcia.** This town is a gem, from its medieval little village and stone houses, to its panoramic views—especially those of Monte Amiata and the Val d'Orcia. From the 11th to the 14th centuries, the **Rocca** (fortress) here was the center of power for the Aldobrandeschi clan, formidable toll collectors. The *castello* juts from its crag to the south and has a small church with 14th-century paintings.

A common sight throughout the region.

Continue along the SS323 as it winds north, and turn left at the signposts to Bagno Vignoni on Route SS2, a distance of 5km (3 miles) from Rocca d'Orcia.

❼ **Bagno Vignoni.** This curious village from medieval times has old houses that envelop a mammoth pool of steaming, sulphurous water. The Medici harnessed these springs percolating from the earth. In time, even St. Catherine of Siena came here for the cure.

Return to the SS2 and turn left for 6km (4 miles) on SR2 to:

❽ **San Quirico d'Orcia.** This farming community, with its 12th-century Romanesque **Collegiata,** was once an important stopover along the Via Franciegena linking Florence with Rome. Its tower-studded walls and 1580 Renaissance gardens can easily occupy 2 hours of your time.

Walk the SS146 10km (6 miles) to:

❾ **Pienza.** The model town created by native son Pope Pius II has been called utopian. Its attractions and service facilities are explored fully in chapter 6.

From Pienza, walk east along the SSW16 for 13km (8 miles) to:

❿ **Montepulciano.** Home to one of Tuscany's greatest wines, this town will be the highlight of this tour for many hikers. On the crest of a hill of volcanic rock, its *Città antica* (old town) is filled with Renaissance treasures. Its **Piazza Grande** is one of Tuscany's most elegant, dramatic squares. See chapter 6 for a full rundown of attractions, hotels, and restaurants.

From here, connections to public transportation links can be made to Siena, Florence, and even Rome. ●

5 The Best **Regional Tours of Tuscany**

Central **Tuscany**

Siena, Italy's epicenter of medieval art and architecture, makes the best base for exploring Chianti country, San Gimignano, and the western hill towns of Central Tuscany. But travelers who don't mind changing hotels nightly will also find many old-fashioned Tuscan inns, with excellent food and wine, in towns such as Etruscan Volterra, early Renaissance Massa Marittima, and medieval Colle di Val d'Elsa.

START: **The Chianti Road begins 17 miles south of Florence, along the Highway SS222. Trip Length: 7 days.**

A Note on Hotels & Restaurants

For hotels, restaurants, and detailed information on attractions in San Gimignano see p 156; in Siena see p 162; and in Volterra see p 174.

1 ★★ **The Chianti Road.** South of Florence, SS222 is called *La Chiantigiana* or "the Chianti Road." It winds and twists through the hills of Chianti country—a 167-sq.-km (65-sq.-mile) piece of land with 4,000 hectares (10,000 acres) of vineyards.

The unofficial capital of Chianti country is **Greve in Chianti,** 27km (17 miles) south of Florence on the SS222. **Piazza Matteotti,** the asymmetrical center square, is lined with porticoed 17th-century buildings, many with cafes and wine cellars.

Vinci: For Leonardo Fans

In 1452, amid olive trees and vineyards, Leonardo da Vinci was born in Vinci, this small town 9.6km (6 miles) north of Empoli. In a 13th-century castle of the Guidi counts, the **Museo Leonardino,** Piazza Guidi (☎ 0571-56055), displays reproductions of drawings and models of inventions from the *Codex Atlanticus* notebooks—from his flying machine to a spring-driven car and a device for walking on water. *Daily 9:30am–7pm (6pm in winter). 5€.*

Next door, in the church of **Santa Croce,** you can see the font in which the genius was baptized as a bambino. For a look at the farmhouse where he was born, take an idyllic walk (or drive) 3km (2 miles) southeast to **Archiano.** *Daily Mar–Oct 9:30am–7pm (Nov–Feb until 6pm). Free admission.*

It's best in September, when Greve hosts Chianti's annual wine fair.

The tourist office is at Viale Giovanni da Verrazano 33 (☎ 055-8546287). Also see the Chianti Road tour in "Tuscany for Food & Wine Lovers," p 82.

You could spend a week exploring wineries and just scratch the surface, but from Greve, you can visit two of the best.

Our favorite is south of Greve on the SS222, **Villa Vignamaggio,** Via Petriolo 5 (☎ 055-854661; www.vignamaggio.com). Its Renaissance villa once was home to Mona Lisa. In 1404, wine from this estate was the first red to be called "Chianti." *Mon, Thurs by reservation.*

Before hitting the second vineyard, stop by the agricultural hamlet of **Panzano,** 6km (3¾ miles) south of Greve on SS222. It's one of the loveliest stops along the wine route, with panoramic views. The focal point is the Santa Maria Assunta church, with its *Annunciation* by Michele di Ridolfo del Ghirlandaio (1503–77). *Daily 7am–noon, 4–6pm.*

Also, don't miss the medieval castle, once a witness to battles between Florence and Siena, and the embroidery made and sold by the village women.

Another favorite vineyard is **Fontodi,** Via San Leolino 89 (☎ 055-852005; www.fontodi.com), near Panzano, less than .8km (½ mile) southeast of Sant'Eufrosino. Vineyards radiate from an 18th-century

The Leonardo Museum in Vinci.

stone villa, with wine tastings and Chianti for sale. (Go for the Flaccianello della Pieve.) *Mon–Fri 8am–noon, 1:30–5:30pm, by reservation.*

In Greve, backtrack along the SS222 to the Firenze/Roma autostrada and cut west. Take the exit for Empoli north into town.

❷ **Empoli.** This glass-manufacturing town, 32km (20 miles) west of Florence, is home to the **Collegiata di Sant'Andrea,** Piazza della Prepositura 3 (☎ 0571-76284), an 8th-century church with a Romanesque green and white marble geometric facade (the lower portion is from 1093). Inside, the **Museo della Collegiata di Sant-Andrea** is filled with treasures: Masolino's *Pietà* fresco (1424), a 1447 Bernardo Rossellino font, and a Filippo Lippi *Madonna. Tues–Sun 9am–noon, 4–7pm. 3€.*

From Empoli, return south to the autostrada linking Florence and Livorno. Head west for 15km (9 miles) until the exit to San Miniato, south of the autostrada.

❸ **San Miniato.** This hilltop village is known for its kite-flying competitions, the weekend after Easter. In its heyday, it was an outpost for emperors from Otto I to Frederick II. The 1240 **Rocca,** or fortress, has views that stretch from Fiesole to the sea.

Ristorante Il Pozzo in Monteriggioni.

The **Duomo,** at the Prato del Duomo in the upper town, has a Romanesque facade and baroque interior. *Daily 8am–12:30pm, 3–6:30pm.*

Next door, the **Museo Diocesano** (☎ 0571-418071) has a Verrocchio terra-cotta bust of the *Redeemer,* Neri di Bicci's *Madonna con Bambino,* and a *Crucifixion* by Filippo Lippi. *2.50€.*

The tourist office is at Piazza del Popolo 3 (☎ 0571-42745).

After visiting San Miniato, return north to the autostrada and head east to Route 429. Then head south 23km (14 miles) to Castelfiorentino.

❹ **Castelfiorentino.** Stop in this hilltown to refuel and explore the bizarre 16th-century Franciscan **Monastery of San Vivaldo,** in the hamlet of San Vivaldo 17km (11 miles) southwest of Castelfiorentino. Its 17 remaining chapels (of 34) have re-creations of Jerusalem holy sites in miniature; painted terra cottas, some by della Robbia, depicting religious scenes nearly to scale; and frescoes depicting the life of Santa Verdiana, who walled herself into a cell here for nearly 35 years with only two snakes as companions. *Sun 9am–6pm; guided tours 5–6pm. Tours 5€. For more information, call the tourist office (☎ 0571-699255).*

Back on Route 429, continue southeast 11km (6½ miles) to Certaldo.

❺ **Certaldo.** This is the hometown of Giovanni Boccaccio (1313–75), the author of the *Decameron,* who is hailed today as one of the three great Italian writers. **Casi di Boccaccio,** Via Boccaccio 18 (☎ 0571-664208), is devoted to the author's writings and memorabilia. *Daily Apr–Sept 10am–7pm; Nov–Mar Tues–Sun 10:30am–4:30pm. 3€.*

Boccaccio is buried at the nearby **Church of San Jacopo** on Via Boccaccio (no phone), under an epitaph he wrote himself. ***Daily 9am–5pm.***

Palazzo Pretorio, Piazzetta del Vicariato 3 (☎ 0571-661219), a 14th-century palace rebuilt in the 16th century, bears the arms of the former vicars of Val d'Elsa. The museum is filled with frescoes and local Etruscan artifacts, and the adjacent church and cloisters boast Benozzo Gozzoli's *Tabernacle of the Punished.* ***Daily late Mar–Oct 10am–7pm; Nov–late Mar Tues–Sun 10:30am–4:30pm.***

The tourist office is at Via Boccaccio 16 (☎ 0571-665526).

From Certaldo a small road (signposted) leads 13km (8 miles) south to San Gimignano.

6 ★★ San Gimignano. After Siena (see below), medieval San Gimignano will be the highlight of any Central Tuscany tour. *If you have time for only 1 busy day here, see p 69 of "The Best of Tuscany in One Week." For complete coverage of San Gimignano—attractions, hotels, shops, restaurants, and nightlife—see p 156.*

To reach Siena from San Gimignano, drive 40km (24 miles) east on SS324 to Poggibonsi. Then take the Firenze/Siena autostrada south to the Siena exit.

7 ★★★ Siena. Writer Bernard Berenson likened Siena to a rare beast, "with heart, arteries, tail, paws, and teeth. Only the skeleton is left, intact, and it is enough to astound us." His words still ring true for this Gothic city whose monuments still slumber in the Middle Ages. We recommend spending 2 days here. *For what to see and do in 2 days, refer to Stop 4 of "The Best of Tuscany in One Week," p 70. For complete coverage of Siena—attractions, hotels, shops, restaurants, and nightlife—see p 162.*

The approach to Monteriggioni.

8 Monteriggioni. In the morning, depart for **Monteriggioni** (see "Italy's Most Perfectly Fortified Village," in chapter 6). This remarkable village, with 14 of its towers still intact, is 20km (12 miles) northeast of Siena along route SS2. *The tourist office is at Largo Fontebranda 5 (☎ 0577-304-810).*

From Monteriggioni, follow the small road northwest of town signposted Colle di Val d'Elsa for 10km (6 miles).

9 Colle di Val d'Elsa. Take in the panoramic view as you approach the birthplace of Arnolfo di Cambio, the master Gothic architect who designed Florence's Duomo (sans Brunelleschi's dome). Circle around town and enter from the west. You'll pass under the arch of Baccio d'Agnolo's Mannerist **Palazzo Campana** gate from 1539. Take **Via del Castello** to the old town and the **Piazza del Duomo,** dominated, of course, by the **Duomo.** Inside the baroque cathedral is a bronze 1619 *Crucifix* over the high altar (attributed to Giambologna). Next door is the **Palazzo Pretorio,** with its small archaeology museum (☎ 0577-922954) and collection of Etruscan artifacts and 14th-century frescoes. *Tues–Fri 10am–noon, 5–7pm; Sat, Sun 10am–noon, 5–7pm (closes 6pm off season). 1.55€.*

The tourist office is at Via Campana 43 (☎ 0577-922791).

From Colle di Val d'Elsa, continue west along Route 68 for 29km (18 miles) to Volterra.

⑩ ★ **Volterra.** You can take in Monteriggioni and Colle di Val d'Elsa in a partial day, with time for Volterra in the afternoon. For a preview of how to see Volterra in a nutshell, refer to Day 4 under "The Best of Tuscany in Ten Days," on p 73. For a complete list of hotels, attractions, nightlife, restaurants, and shops, see p 174.

From Volterra take Route 68 west out of town, following the signs to Saline di Volterra at which point you cut south along Route 439 for 70km (43 miles) south to:

⑪ **Massa Marittima.** Abandoned by the Middle Ages, this walled hilltop town at 356m (1,188 ft.) has two tiers: The Romanesque lower section **(Città Vecchia)** is linked by Via Moncini to the Gothic upper tier **(Città Nuova).** The second city of the Sienese Republic, the town once grew rich from silver and copper deposits nearby but declined when the mines gave out.

Most of the attractions are in Città Vecchia, around the triangular **Piazza Garibaldi.** The 11th-century **Duomo** (no phone) blends Romanesque and Gothic architecture. Its interior has massive columns capped by delicately carved capitals. Look for Duccio's luminous *Madonna* (1318) and Giovanni Pisano's wooden *Crucifix* over the main altar. *Daily 8am–noon, 3–6pm.*

Across the square, the **Palazzo del Podestà** houses the **Museo Archeologico e Pinacoteca** (☎ 0566-902289). Otherwise boring, it shelters Ambrogio Lorenzetti's *Virgin in Majesty,* a masterpiece painted in the late 1330s. *Tues–Sun 10am–12:30pm, 3:30–7pm (Nov–Feb until 5pm). 3€.*

In Città Nuova, climb **Torre del Candeliere** (☎ 0566-902289), a 1443 clock tower with views over the ramparts and countryside. *Daily 10am–1pm, 3–6pm (until 4:40pm in winter). 2.50€.*

The tourist office is at Via Parenti 22 (☎ 0566-902756).

Battistero Giovanni in Volterra.

Where to **Stay & Dine**

Tuscan crostini.

For other recommended hotels and restaurants in San Gimignano, Siena, and Volterra, refer to the expanded coverage of each town in chapter 6, "Charming Tuscan Towns & Villages."

★★ **Villa Belvedere** COLLE DI VAL D'ELSA European rulers once lodged in this villa, once the home of a Florentine nobleman. Spacious bedrooms have wrought-iron beds and antiques. Grounds have private gardens. *Via Senese-Località Belvedere. ☎ 0577-920966. www.villabelvedere.com. 15 units. Doubles 80€–120€ with breakfast. AE, DC, MC, V.*

★★★ **Arnolfo** COLLE DI VAL D'ELSA *CREATIVE TUSCAN* One of Tuscany's best restaurants serves regional fare in a 16th-century palace. Don't miss the pigeon with hazelnuts, figs, and a Vin Santo sauce. *Via XX Settembre 52. ☎ 0577-920549. Main courses 24€–35€. AE, DC, MC, V. Lunch, dinner Thurs–Mon. Closed Jan 17–Feb, July 28–Aug 10.*

★ **Cucina Sant'Andrea** EMPOLI *TUSCAN* Don't miss the Tuscan beef with mushrooms or the perfectly grilled fish, fresh harvested from the sea, served in an 18th-century decor in the historic center. *Via Salvagnoli 47. ☎ 0571-73657. Main courses 7€–18€. AE, DC, MC, V. Lunch, dinner Tues–Sun. Closed 2 weeks in Aug.*

Il Sole MASSA MARITTIMA In a stone medieval building near the Piazza Garibaldi, this is the best place to stay in town. Small to midsize rooms with white-tiled bathrooms offer simple elegance. *Via della Libertà 43. ☎ 0566-901971. 50 units. Doubles 95€; suites 130€–160€ with buffet breakfast. AE, DC, MC, V.*

★ **Taverna del Vecchio Borgo** MASSA MARITTIMA *MAREMMANA* The best choice in town serves Tuscan cowboy food from local ingredients in rustic surroundings. Try the juicy Florentine steaks or stewed wild boar with olives. *Via Parenti 12. ☎ 0566-903950. Main courses 6€–15€. AE, DC, MC, V. Dinner Tues–Sun (daily in summer). Closed Feb 15–Mar 15.*

★ **Miravelle** SAN MINIATO At the foot of a tower built by Frederick II, this hotel has the best atmosphere in the area. Large rooms have beamed ceilings with Tuscan furnishings. The covered veranda restaurant overlooks the Arno Valley. *Piazza del Castello 3. ☎ 0571-418075. www.albergomiravalle.com. 15 units. Doubles 85€. AE, MC, V.*

Tuscan boar chops.

Northwest **Tuscany**

Northwest Tuscany, land of Puccini, is best known for the ancient maritime republic of Pisa. But beyond the famous leaning tower, there's Lucca, with its Renaissance ramparts; the relatively forgotten art cities of Prato and Pistoia; and the Medicis great port city, Livorno, with the best seafood restaurants in Tuscany. Finally, when you've had enough of old churches and want your music loud, your beach crowd raucous, and your nightlife frantic, there is Viareggio, on the coast. START: **Prato is 17km (10 miles) west of Florence on the autostrada. Trip Length: 7 days.**

A Note on Hotels & Restaurants

For hotels, restaurants, and detailed information on attractions in Florence, see p 11; in Lucca, see p 134; in Pisa, see p 150.

1 ★★ **Prato.** Some observers have said that the historic city of Prato is often overlooked because it's "too close to Florence," a drive of only 17km (10 miles) west on the *autostrada.*

Known since the 13th century for its textiles, Prato has long lived in the shadow of Florence, but Florentines still claim "it is the tail that wags the dog." Iris Origo immortalized hometown boy Francesco di

A Filippo Lippi fresco in the Prato Duomo.

Marco Datini in literature as *The Merchant of Prato*.

Its Duomo alone is reason enough to visit. **Piazza del Duomo** (☎ 0574-26234) is famous for its *Pergamo del Sacro Cingolo* (chapel of the Holy Girdle), left of the cathedral entrance. It's reputed to enshrine the girdle of the Madonna, presented to the Apostle Thomas when she appeared to him after her Assumption. The actual girdle (actually a belt) is under lock and key, but visitors can view the frescoes by Agnolo Gaddi (1392–95) or the masterpiece Filippo Lippi (1452–66) frescoes, on the high altar, devoted to the lives of Saint Stephen and John the Baptist. *Wed–Mon 9:30am–12:30pm and Wed–Sat 3pm–6:30pm.*

A ticket for 5€ gets you into the **Museo dell'Opera del Duomo** (left of the Duomo entrance), with Donatello's dancing *putti* friezes and paintings by Filippino Lippi (1457–1504), Filippo's son. The same ticket is good for **Palazzo Pretorio,** Piazza del Comune (☎ 0574-616302), housing the **Galleria Comunale e Museo Civico.** Feast yourself to paintings by the 14th- and 15th-century Tuscan artists, highlighted by Bernardo Daddi's polyptychs. *Sun–Mon 9:30am–12:30pm, Wed–Sat 3–6:30pm.*

The tourist office is at Piazza della Carceri 15 (☎ 0574-24112).

From Prato, return to the autostrada and continue northwest to Pistoia, a distance of only 17km (10 miles) from Prato but 35km (21 miles) northwest of Florence.

2 ★★ **Pistoia.** Pistoia is an industrial town filled with art treasures from the Tuscan Renaissance in sculpture, evolving from 1250 to 1300. For centuries the Pistoiesi were known for rudeness and bellicosity. Machiavelli described them as "brought up to slaughter and war," and the first pistols made in Germany in the 1500s were named after the daggers *(pistolese)* worn by locals. The happy news: The Pistoiesi are friendly and welcoming today. The sad news: Most visitors skip their city, distracted by the glories of Lucca, Florence, and Pisa.

The core of town, **Piazza del Duomo,** contains most of the goodies, centering around the **Duomo** (☎ 0573-25095), rebuilt in the 12th

Detail of the Duomo balcony.

The Duomo in Prato.

and 13th centuries. Behind a harmonious Pisan-Romanesque facade, the church has a marble porch that makes it look as though it's crouching, ready to pounce. Inside the great treasure is the celebrated Altar of St. James, the work of an unknown silversmith from the 13th century. Close to a ton of partially gilded silver, remolded into medieval saints, rests in Capella di San Jacopo. *Daily 8:30am–12:30pm and 3:30–7pm. Cathedral free, Capella di San Jacopo 4€.*

Two other churches are among the architectural treasures of Tuscany—one, the Romanesque church of **San Andrea,** Via Sant'Andrea (☎ 0573-21912), with its famous pulpit (created 1298–1308) and beautiful gilded *Crucifix,* both by Giovanni Pisano. *Daily 8am–12:30pm, 3:30–6pm (7pm in summer). Free.*

The next most visited church, **San Giovanni Fuoricivitas,** Via Cavour (☎ 0573-24784), from the 12th to 14th centuries, is famous for its north facade in the Pisan-Romanesque style. Inside and on the right wall is a pulpit from 1270 by Gugliemo da Pisa, a polyptych by Taddeo Gaddi (left of the main altar), and glazed terra-cotta figures depicting the *Visitation,* by Luca della Robbia. *Daily 8am–noon, 5–6:30pm. Free.*

The glorious early-16th-century terra-cotta frieze on the **Osedale del Ceppo,** Piazza Giovanni XXIII, is the work of master Giovanni della Robbia (1469–1529). The hospital is a short way down Via Pacini from Piazza del Duomo.

The tourist office is at Piazza del Duomo in the Palazzo dei Vescovi (☎ 0573-21622).

From Pistoia drive south toward the autostrada but cut west onto A11 for 19km (12 miles), until you reach Montecatini Terme, 49km (30 miles) northwest of Florence.

❸ ★★ Montecatini Terme.

Immortalized in Fellini's *8½,* this is Tuscany's most celebrated and fashionable spa. Its waters have been known for centuries for their curative powers. The spa sprang up in

The gardens of Villa Real in Lucca.

Lucca's skyline.

the early 20th century, as suggested by its Art Nouveau buildings.

Come here for R&R and there's not much to do besides people-watch at **Piazza del Popolo** in the center of town. From Viale Diaz, a funicular railway ascends to the scenic old town, **Montecatini Alto.** Have an espresso on the main square in the path of summer mountain breezes. Most thermal houses are open from May to October, including the oldest, **Terme Tettuccio,** Viale Verdi 41 (☎ 0572-778501), where even the cocktails are reputedly healthy tonics. *The tourist office is at Viale Verdi 66–68 (☎ 0572-772244; www.turismo.toscana.it).*

From Montecatini Terme take the A11 west into Lucca, a distance of 30km (19 miles).

❹ ★★★ **Lucca.** The *Luccese* still say their city—with its 4km (2½ miles) of stone ramparts—is more impressive than Florence and Siena, its rivals from the Middle Ages. While they exaggerate, it's true that what they have is worth at least a day of your time. *For what to see and do in a day, refer to Stop 1 of "The Best of Tuscany in One Week," p 68. For complete coverage of Lucca—attractions, hotels, shops, restaurants, and nightlife—see p 134.*

Leave Lucca early and drive 22km (14 miles) southwest on SS12 to Pisa.

❺ ★★★ **Pisa.** The complex around the Duomo and the Leaning Tower in Pisa are triumphs of the Pisan-Romanesque style—and rightly one of Italy's top tourist magnets. *For how to see Pisa in 1 day, refer to Stop 1 of "The Best of Tuscany in Three Days," p 64. For a complete rundown of Pisan hotels, restaurants, attractions, shopping, and nightlife, see p 150.*

To reach our next stopover in Livorno, leave Pisa on the SS1 heading south to the port of Livorno, a distance of 22km (14 miles).

❻ **Livorno.** Short on attractions, Livorno is still Tuscany's "second city," outranked as a port only by Genoa. Since 1620, Livorno has been Florence's gateway to the world, teeming with sailors. Shelley wrote *To a Skylark* here and purchased the sailing boat that would lead to his death. Ferries depart from here to Elba, Corsica, and Sardinia.

A Montecatini Terme spa.

Piazza Grande, the main square, is dominated by a dull **Duomo,** designed by Inigo Jones in 1605. Pause at another square, **Piazza della Repubblica,** the most ghastly in Tuscany. One section of Livorno is riddled with canals. Locals refer to it as *Piccola Venezia* or Little Venice—a far stretch of the imagination.

The glory of Livorno is to stroll its streets, especially **Via Grande** lined with arcaded buildings. Along Via Grande is Livorno's prize sight, the Mannerist **Monumento dei Quattro Mori** (1623–26), the masterpiece of Pietro Tacca, crowned by a statue of Duke Ferdinand I (1595). Forget about the duke, though, and take in the celebrated manacled bronze slaves (1626) below. Walk along **Via Cairoli** or **Via Ricasoli** to soak up more flavor, pausing at **Piazza Micheli** for a view of **Fortezza Vecchia,** designed by Antonio da Sangallo (1521–34). The fort overlooks the water, naturally.

Museo Civico in Villa Mimbelli, in the public park along Via San Jacopo in Acquaviva (☎ 0586-808001), has a good collection by the Macchiaioli, a group of late-19th-century Italian impressionists. There's only one painting by Modigliani, but many works by native son, Giovanni Fattori, who worked from the 1860s to 1908. *Tues–Sun 10am–1pm, 4–7pm. 4€.*

The Livorno tourist office is at Piazza Cavour (☎ 0586-204611).

Fruits of the Sea. If you've made it to Livorno, don't leave without trying its seafood, Tuscany's best. Don't miss the local specialty, *cacciucco*—a spicy, tomato-based seafood stew. **La Chiave,** Scali delle Cantine 52 (off Piazza Garibaldi; ☎ 0586-888609), has the finest food in town, with an adventurous

The Livorno coast.

Revisiting Puccini

Music lovers flock to ❼ **Torre del Lago,** 6km (3½ miles) south of Viareggio along Via dei Tigli, to pay homage to the great composer, Giacomo Puccini (1858–1924). *Turandot,* his masterpiece and swan song, belongs among the great operas of all time.

The **Museo Pucciniano,** on the banks of Lake Massaciuccoli (☎ 0584-359322), holds mementos of the composer, autographed scores, and curios from the daily life of the Maestro. The surrounding garden is delightful, with fruit trees and bamboo thickets. *Apr–May Tues–Sun 10am–12:30pm, 3–6pm; June–Oct Tues–Sun 10am–12:30pm, 3–6:30pm; Dec–Mar Tues–Sun 10am–12:30pm, 2:30–5:30pm. 7€.*

menu that changes biweekly. **Antico Moro,** Via Bartelloni 59 (☎ 0586-884659), is humbler—with more basic, less expensive, nonetheless fresh dishes.

From Livorno, follow the autostrada north, bypassing Pisa and taking the exit west to Viareggio, a distance of 29 miles (46km).

❽ **Viareggio.** Opening onto the Tyrrhenian coast, this is the Biarritz of the Riviera della Versilia. Its heyday was the late 19th century and the 1920s, but it still attracts a well-heeled clientele. Its beaches, often private, are good, with rainbow-colored umbrellas. And its palm-shaded promenade, **Passeggiata Margherita,** is one of Italy's more elegant boardwalks—set against a backdrop of Art Deco and Art Nouveau villas, with expensive boutiques, cafes, and seafood restaurants.

Viareggio is the southern frontier of the Italian Riviera, at the foothills of the Apuan mountains. A lot of young Italians frequent the resort, mixing with European visitors, mostly from Germany. We often come here to escape the glories of the Renaissance with a beach-loving crowd of revelers.

The tourist office is at Viale Carducci 10 (☎ 0584-962233).

★★★ **L'Oca Bianca.** In the port area, Viareggio's best and most elegant restaurant has a panoramic view of the water. Prices are relatively low, and chefs add a special flair to each dish. Our favorite is homemade *bavettine* with baby squid, saffron, white beans, and black pepper. ***Via Coppino 409. ☎ 0584-388477. $$–$$$.***

Livorno's chief export.

Eastern **Tuscany**

You might call most of this offbeat tour a journey into "unknown Tuscany." Arezzo, the most landlocked of all municipalities in the region, is the only "city" represented; most other stopovers will be either small towns or hamlets. This tour takes in both the northeast of Tuscany and part of its southern rim. If you can't cover the entire route described here, you can easily take leave of it after spending the night in Pienza, and hit the nearby autostrada north to Florence or south to Rome, as your transportation arrangements dictate. START: **Arezzo is 81km (50 miles) southeast of Florence on the A1. Trip Length: 7 days.**

A Note on Hotels & Restaurants

For hotels, restaurants, and detailed information on attractions in Arezzo, see p 124; in Cortona, see p 128; in Montepulciano, see p 142; in Pienza, see p 146.

1 ★ **Arezzo.** One of the most important settlements of the Etruscan Federation, Arezzo will be the highlight of this tour for many art lovers. Besides being the city of Petrarch, it's the home of Piero della Francesca's masterful fresco cycle, the *Legend of the True Cross,* in the Basilica di San Francesco.

The Valdichiana.

Great artists of the Renaissance, including Michelangelo and Piero della Francesca, came from this region, which takes in the Chiana Valley, called the breadbasket of Italy. In the north are the thick forests of the Casentino mountains. The south is dominated by a landscape of grape vines and gnarled olive trees. At night you drink the two finest wines of the region—Brunello di Montalcino and Vino Nobile di Montepulciano. During the day, you discover walled medieval hill towns, forlorn monasteries, Renaissance *palazzo,* and fields of Etruscan tombs that predate the Roman empire. ***The Arezzo tourist office is Piazza della Repubblica 28 (☎ 0575-377-678).***

From Arezzo, drive south on SR71 for 19km (12 miles) until you come to the signposted turnoff for:

❷ Castiglion Fiorentino. To reach Castiglion Fiorentino and the neighboring town of Cortona, traverse the Valdichiana—a valley known for its snow-white cattle, from which comes the fabled *bistecca alla fiorentina.* Wandering into town, you pass through a medieval girdle of fortified walls, leading to the main square, **Piazza del Minicipio.** Dominating the square is the **Loggia del Vasari** designed by Giorgio Vasari in the 16th century. **Torre del Cassero,** a pronglike tower, presides over the skyline.

The chief attraction is **Palazzo Comunale/Pinacoteca** in the Piazza del Municipio 12 (☎ 0575-657466), a repository of precious goldsmithery and notable paintings including such works as Taddeo Gaddi's *Madonna and Child* and Bartolomeo della Gatta's bizarre *St. Francis Receiving the Stigmata.* ***Admission is 3€. Open Tues–Fri 10am–12:30pm, 4–6pm (7pm Sat–Sun).***

The tourist office is at Corso Italia 111 (☎ 0575-658278).

The Legend of the True Cross's *Virgin Mary.*

Leave Castiglion Fiorentino and continue south on SR71 for 12km (7 miles) to Cortona.

3 ★★ **Cortona.** This art city can be your stopover for the night. For a complete list of its attractions, hotels, restaurants, shops, and nightlife, see the Cortona section in chapter 6. To learn how to see Cortona in 1 day, check out Day 8 under "The Best of Tuscany in Ten Days," in chapter 3.

Leave Cortona and drive southwest for 32km (20 miles) to Montepulciano. From Cortona, follow the signposts southwest of town along a small secondary road leading to the village of Centoia. You'll reach an autostrada heading west from Perugia. Follow it west until you reach the Firenze/Roma autostrada. Follow the autostrada south toward Rome until you see the exit cutting west for Montepulciano.

4 & **5** **Montepulciano and Pienza.** Two of the great art cities of Tuscany—Montepulciano and Pienza—can be visited in a day. Both towns are covered in depth in chapter 6, which presents a complete range of hotels, restaurants, shops, attractions, and nightlife. For directions and what to see and do, refer to Day 6, "The Best of Tuscany in One Week," in chapter 3. You can overnight in either Montepulciano or Pienza.

From Montepulciano, follow SS146 into Chiusi. The distance between Montepulciano and Chiusi is 21km (13 miles).

6 **Chiusi.** If you're on the trail of the Etruscans, head here to see what's left of one of the most powerful cities in their 12-city confederation. Chiusi was then known as Camars, in the 7th to the 6th century B.C. So powerful was Camars, that its king, Lars Porsena, attacked Rome in 508 B.C. What's left of Camars is buried under the little town of Chiusi today. Many Etruscan tombs have been discovered in the area.

Museo Nazionale Etrusco, Via Porsenna (☎ 0578-20177), is one of Italy's most outstanding Etruscan museums. Wander back in time as you take in the alabaster and stone funerary urns (many shaped like heads), the clay ex-votos, the round tombstones *(cippi),* and other sarcophagi, including some stunning painted urns from the 2nd century B.C. The most famous sarcophagus depicts the Battle of the Gauls. *Admission is 4€. Open Mon–Sat 9am–2pm, Sun 9am–1pm.*

The tourist office is at Piazza Duomo 1 (☎ 0578-227667).

With time remaining you can make an excursion to the little town of Radicófani, reached by heading southwest along Route 573 a distance of 28km (18 miles).

7 **Radicófani.** You can spend 2 hours wandering this warren of streets and old houses from the Middle Ages. The little town is dominated by the **Rocca Fortezza** (☎ 0578-55867), which was constructed by

Poppies outside Radicófani.

Montalcino & Sant'Antimo

Visitors with more time can take in two attractions easily reached from Pienza. The first stop is the town of **Montalcino,** reached by heading 24km (15 miles) west along S146 from Pienza. As wine lovers well know, this hill town—left over from the Middle Ages—is the source of one of Europe's greatest red vintages, *Brunello di Montalcino*. The walled town stands on a hill, with the spires of its medieval buildings studding the air like an asparagus field. Its 14th century **Enoteca La Fortezza** in La Fortezza (☎ 0577-849211) is installed in the town's main attraction, a fortress Duke Cosimo I created in 1571. Within its vaults, built of ancient stone and brick, an abundance of Tuscan foodstuffs are for sale, including Pecorino cheese and the local regional Montalcino honey (famous among gourmands). Of course, most visitors come here to stock up on bottles of Brunello di Montalcino. At the fortress, mount the ramparts for one of the great views in Tuscany, a wide sweep from Val d'Orcia to Vallombrone. *Entrance 3.50€.* Daily Apr–Oct 9am–8pm; Nov–Mar Tues–Sun 9am–6pm. The town gathering place is **Caffè Fiaschetteria Italiana,** Piazza del Popolo 6 (☎ 0557-849043), an Art Nouveau cafe that has served the celebrated local wine since 1888. With its Thonet chairs, mirrored walls, red-velvet banquettes, and marble tables, this is one of only five *fiaschetteria* left in Italy. *Closed Feb.*

At this point, you can easily cut short the tour and head home—or continue for more fun. If you spent the night in Pienza (see above), return to Montepulciano. From here your next stop is a town in the south, Chiusi, on the road to Orvieto.

Hadrian IV, and was the home of the "gentle outlaw" that Dante immortalized in his *Inferno* and Boccaccio in his *Decameron*. ***Admission is 3€. Daily Apr–Oct 10am–7pm.***

Although its attractions are a bit lean, the town used to be on the grand tour, attracting such intrepid travelers as Dickens and Montaigne. The tourist office is at Renato Magi 25 (☎ 0578-55-684).

Return to Chiusi for an overnight stopover.

From Chiusi, follow the signs west to the autostrada bound for Florence. Travel for 47km (28 miles) until you see the exit for Lucignano.

8 ★ **Lucignano.** Lucignano along with Monte San Savino (see below) might be called "the lost towns" of the Valdichiana. They both lie in this beautiful valley, the largest and broadest in the Apennines. Both can be visited in 1 day. They're approached through a countryside that was the breadbasket for Hannibal and his troops, including elephants, before their descent upon Rome.

The ideal way to see this town is from the air because it's elliptical, its street plan unique in the annals of Tuscan city planning. Like a simplified maze, the village is laid out in four concentric ellipses with four quaint little squares in the center.

One is dominated by the **Collegiata,** with its lovely oval staircase; another by the **Palazzo Comunale** (☎ 0575-836128), with its artwork from the Siena school, which flourished from the 13th to the 15th centuries. The big names here include Signorelli and Bartolo di Fredi; the masterpiece is a delicate reliquary, *Albero di Lucignano,* the work of Aretine goldsmiths.

After a morning visit, drive another 8km (5 miles) north along a signposted byroad to:

9 ★ Monte San Savino. This Valdichiana village is one of the most beautiful in Tuscany, yet it remains relatively undiscovered. The High Renaissance sculptor Andrea Sansovino (1460–1529) is from here, as his name suggests. Filled with medieval and Renaissance *palazzo,* the scenic walled town invites an afternoon of exploration and makes a good place to stop for the night.

As you hoof it around the town, you can see some of Sansovino's works, notably his altarpiece at the little church of **Santa Chiara.** The Della Robbia brothers are believed to have glazed this altarpiece for him, depicting *Madonna and Child with Saints.* **The Loggia dei Mercanti,** with its early Corinthian capitals, is also attributed to Sansovino. It's along the Corso Sangallo. At the Piazza di Monte, check out the church, **Sant'Agostino.** Sansovino designed the double loggia against the front wall of this building. He also created the cloister in 1528.

From Monte San Savino take the Firenze/Roma *autostrada* north and exit just south of Arezzo. Follow SS73 east into Monterchi for 47km (30 miles).

10 Monterchi. A visit to Monterchi combines well with a visit to Sansepolcro, with an overnight there. Art lovers visit Monterchi for one reason: to see the world-famous *Madonna del Parto* by Piero della Francesca. One of his greatest masterpieces, it rests in a small

Val D'Orcia, outside Pienza.

Monterchi.

museum built especially for it at Via della Relgia 1 (☎ 0575-70713). It's extremely rare in that it depicts the Virgin Mary 9 months pregnant. In its day, the work caused a scandal and protests of outrage. One of Mary's eyelids droops, and her hand rests on her swollen belly. Painted in 1467, it's one of the most psychologically penetrating paintings of the *quattrocentro*. ***Admission 3.10€. Open Tues–Sun 9am–1pm, 2–7pm (until 6pm Oct–Mar).***

After viewing the Madonna, stroll this medieval town with its mysterious underground passageway around the apse of the parish church.

From Monterchi, continue northeast on 21 for 16km (10 miles) to:

⓫ ★ Sansepolcro. Art lovers make a pilgrimage to this medieval walled town, far off the beaten path, to pay homage to Early Renaissance master Piero della Francesca, born here in 1420. (Sansepolcro is also home to the Buitoni pasta empire.)

Della Francesca was a visionary who imbued his art with an ethereal quality. A master of perspective, he created very humanlike figures that seemed to have souls, surviving centuries after he died, in 1492.

Visitors head for the **Museo Civico,** Via Aggiunti 65, off Piazza Garibaldi (☎ 0575-732218), to see the della Francesca masterpieces—notably the *Madonna della Misericordia* (1445) in room 3. The "Mary of Mercy" spreads her cloak around kneeling donors. Room 4 has other masterful della Francesca works: *San Ludovico da Tolosa* (1460), *San Giuliano* (1455–58), and *Resurrection of Christ* (1463), one of the most

Sunflowers outside Monterchi.

Lucignano, in the Valdichiana.

famous works of the Renaissance. Aldous Huxley called it "the best picture in the world." *Admission 6.20€. Daily June–Sept 9am–1:30pm, 2:30–7:30pm; Oct–May 9:30am–1pm, 2:30–6pm.*

From Sansepolcro, take the *autostrada* north to the intersection with a secondary route, cutting west along Route 208 and following the signs into La Verna, a distance of 28km (18 miles).

Travel Tip

La Verna, Poppi, and Camáldoli can be visited in 1 relatively easy day, with an overnight in Poppi.

⓬ **La Verna.** Count Orlando Cattani presented this rocky outcropping to St. Francis of Assisi (1182–1226), who received history's first reported case of stigmata while praying here in 1224. Today the **Cappella della Stimmate** is constructed over the site. Tours are conducted daily of the saint's cell and the spot where the miracle took place. *Free admission. Daily 6:30am–9:30pm (7:30pm in winter).*

The main church, **Santuario della Verna** (☎ 0575-599356), open 7am to 7pm (free), shelters glazed terra-cotta masterpieces by Andrea della Robbia. These terra cottas in blue, green, and white are the most transcendently beautiful the artist ever created.

To climax your tour, climb to **La Penna,** at 1,283m (4,209 ft.), for an evocative view of the Arno and Tiber valleys.

Leave La Verna and head west along Route 208, bypassing the town of Bibblena and following the road into Poppi, a distance of 28km (18 miles).

⓭ ★ **Poppi.** Crowned by a castle visible for miles around—once the seat of the powerful Counts of Guidi, who ruled the area until 1440—our favorite Casentino hilltown overlooks the Arno Valley. Dating to 1274,

Romanesque Ruin

Devotees of Romanesque architecture should take the southern road out of Montalcino and follow signs for Sant'Antimo for 10km (6 miles), until they come upon the **Abbazia di Sant'Antimo,** Castelnuovo dell'Abate (☎ 0577-835659). In the 12th century, it became a Cistercian abbey, and French monks still sound their Gregorian chants here. Although it's mostly in ruins, it's one of Tuscany's best examples of Romanesque architecture, in the Lombard French style, with a 30m (100-ft.) bell tower. *Free admission. Open Mon–Sat 10:30am–12:30pm and 3–6:30pm, Sun 9:15–10:30am and 3–6pm.*

A chapel near Pienza.

Palazzo Pretorio, Piazza Grande (☎ 0575-520516), resembles the Palazzo Vecchio in Florence, and you'll immediately detect the handiwork of Arnolfo di Cambio. Its magnificent courtyard, with zigzagging stairs, is emblazoned with coats-of-arms. The Grand Hall is decorated with 15th-century Florentine frescoes. Taddeo Gaddi created the beautiful chapel in 1330. The tower yields panoramic views of the countryside. *Admission 4€. Daily Mar–Oct 10am–7pm; winter Thurs–Sun 9:30am–1pm, 2:30–5:30pm.*

You can wander Poppi's narrow, arcaded old streets. Walk the main street, Via Cavour, until you reach the Romanesque church of **San Fedele** and hope that it's open (it keeps irregular hours). If you get in, seek out a 13th-century Madonna and Child in the right transept, the work of an artist known as "Maestro della Maddalena." Shops throughout the town sell a locally made copperware.

The Poppi tourist office is at Via Cavour 11 (☎ 0575-5021).

From Poppi, head north and follow signs to Camáldoli for 13km (8 miles) on Route 71.

⓮ **Camáldoli.** Some intrepid visitors come here to view the religious complexes. We visit this sylvan region for its cool mountain breezes in summer and beautiful walks in almost any direction. With its forested hills, streams, and waterfalls, Camáldoli is one of the most beautiful, yet undiscovered, regions of Tuscany.

St. Romauld founded an ascetic Order of Benedictines here in 1046. Little remains of the original monastery except for an 11th-century cloister and a 16th-century pharmacy where the on-site monks still sell their herbal remedies, liqueurs, and balsams.

Since the monastery became overrun with visitors, the saint erected the **Monasterio di Camáldoli,** about an hour's walk up the hill at 1,104m (335 ft.). The hike is beautiful, but only men are allowed in past the gate (fortunately, there isn't anything much worth seeing). All vegetarians, the monks eat only what they can grow, and they plant 5,000 new trees in the region every year. The little baroque church of Il Salvatore here, decorated by Vasari, has two marble tabernacles by Desiderio da Settignano.

Where to **Stay & Dine**

For other recommended hotels and restaurants in Arezzo, Cortona, Montepulciano, and Pienza, refer to the expanded coverage of each town in chapter 6, "Charming Tuscan Towns & Villages."

Albergo La Sfinge CHIUSI Of a lackluster lot, this emerges as the winner, thanks to the friendly owners and the simple but tidy, spacious bedrooms. Some units open onto panoramic views of valley and mountain landscapes. *Via Marconi 2. ☎ 0578-20157. www.albergolasfinge.com. 14 units. Doubles 77€. Triples 100€. MC, V. Closed Jan 30–Mar 8.*

★★ Borgo Palace Hotel SANSEPOLCRO The best game in town, this hotel is elegantly furnished and refined, yet affordable, with a first-class restaurant serving Tuscan regional cuisine. *Via Senese Aretina 80. ☎ 0575-73650. 75 units. Doubles 95€–125€. AE, DC, MC, V.*

★ La Solita Zuppa CHIUSI *SOUTHERN TUSCAN* In the historic core, Roberto and Luana Pacchieri welcome you to their friendly precincts, under vaulted ceilings, then ply you with regional dishes made from old recipes with a modern twist. They serve a wide variety of soups, Chiana beef, free-range chickens and rabbits, and wild game, seasoned with fresh herbs. *Via Porsenna 21. ☎ 0578-21006. Main courses 5.90€–8.80€. Fixed-price menu 20€. AE, DC, MC, V. Open Wed–Mon for lunch and dinner. Closed Jan 15–Feb.*

★★ Ristorante Fiorentino SANSEPOLCRO This 190-year-old trattoria in the Hotel Fiorentino serves handmade pastas, pappardelle with fresh rabbit, and other Tuscan staples from antique recipes. Don't miss the ricotta- and vegetable-stuffed spinach ravioli. *Via L. Pacioli 60. ☎ 0575-742033. Main courses 9€–13€. DC, MC, V. Thurs–Tues 12:30–3pm and 7:30–10:30pm. Closed Jan 20–30 and last 2 weeks of July.* ●

Tuscan veal.

6 Charming Tuscan Towns & Villages

Arezzo

Young Aretines are proud and prosperous, racing their Vespas through the Etruscan-era streets of this bustling town amid the fertile Valdarno and Valdichiana farmlands. Famous native sons include the poet Petrarch (1304–74); architect and author Giorgio Vasari (1512–74); and Roberto Benigni, who brought Arezzo to a world audience as director and star of *Life Is Beautiful.* Time here is best spent strolling the medieval core and Piazza Grande, but don't miss the frescoes of Piero della Francesca in Basilica di San Francesco. START: **Arezzo is southeast of Florence on the A1. Just follow the directional signs to the city. Trip length: 81km (50 miles).**

1 ★★★ Basilica di San Francesco. Between 1452 and 1466, Piero della Francesca painted *The Legend of the True Cross*—a series of frescoes that proved to be an art-historical milestone. Each is remarkable for its grace, ascetic severity, brilliant colors, and dramatic light effects—"the most perfect morning light in all Renaissance painting," said Sir Kenneth Clark. The rose window from 1520, by Guillaume de Marcillat, is also worth a look. *30 min. Piazza San Francesco. 0575-20630 or 0575-900404 for reservations (25 people admitted every 30 min.). Admission 6€. Daily 8:30am–noon and 2–6pm.*

2 Casa di Vasari. The first art historian—who chronicled the lives of Michelangelo, da Vinci, and others—Vasari bought this house in 1540. He decorated it with semi-Mannerist art works, often by his students, and executed the frescoes himself—the most ingenuous and charming of all his creations. *Via XX Settembre 55. ☎ 0575-40901. 2€ adults, 1€ ages 17 and under. Wed–Mon 9am–7pm; Sun 9am–1pm.*

3 Duomo. At the highest point in town, the 13th-century cathedral of Arezzo is a rare Tuscan Gothic–style construction. Don't miss Della Francesca's *Mary Magdalene* and the stained-glass windows (1519–23) by Guillaume de Marcillat. *Piazza del Duomo. ☎ 0575-23991. Free. 5€ panoramic terrace by elevator; 3.50€ terrace by stairs. Daily 7am–12:30pm, 3–6:30pm.*

4 ★ Museo Statale d'Arte Medievale e Moderna. Arezzo's art museum, in the Palazzo Bruni-Ciocchi, has an impressive collection of paintings (some from the 11th c.). Our favorites are Vasari's *Esther's Wedding Banquet* and the frescoes by Spinello Aretino. But the 13th- to 18th-century *majolicas* overshadow the art. *Via San Lorentino 8. ☎ 0575-409050. 4.90€ adults, 2.90€ ages 18–25; free 17 and under. Tues–Sun 9am–6pm.*

5 San Domenico. There is one reason to visit this church, begun in 1275: young Cimabue's painted Crucifix (ca. 1260) over the high altar. The stone Gothic chapel on the right wall is also fine. *Piazza San Domenico. ☎ 0575-22906. Free. Mar 23–Nov 2 daily 9am–7pm, Nov 3–Mar 22 daily 9am–6:30pm.*

6 ★ Santa Maria della Pieve. This 12th-century church on the Piazza Grande is a stellar example of the Pisan-Romanesque style. Its chief treasure is Pietro Lorenzetti's polyptych *Madonna and Child with Saints,* on the high altar above the raised crypt. *30 min. Corso Italia 7. ☎ 0575-377678. Free. Daily 8am–7pm May–Sept; 8am–noon and 3–6pm Oct–Apr.*

Ceiling frescoes from the Duomo.

Shopping Tip

Diehard shoppers time their visit to coincide with the **Arezzo Flea Market**—which sprawls across the Piazza Grande the first Sunday of each month. Bargains and rare finds usually disappear by 10am. Antiques and crafts are among the items for sale.

A detail from the Piero della Francesco frescoes in Arezzo's Duomo.

7 **Borghini.** Arezzo is a world-class center for gold production. This outlet sells one of the finest collections of gold jewelry set with precious and semi-precious stones. *Corso Italia 126. ☎ 0575-24678. AE, DC, MC, V.*

8 ★★★ **Busatti.** Since 1842, the Busatti-Sassolini family has been selling exquisite textiles and handmade fabrics—including sumptuous linens, and hemp, cotton, and wool items such as curtains, towels, cushions, tablecloths, and rugs in many colors. You'll also find lace, earthenware, and glassware. *Corso Italia 48. ☎ 0575-355295; www.busatti.com. AE, DC, MC, V.*

9 ★ **Prosperi.** This is one of Tuscany's finest jewelry stores, since 1816, with an impressive collection of silver, gold, and platinum jewelry. Prosperi is also an authorized Rolex dealer. *Corso Italia 76. ☎ 0575-20746. AE, DC, MC, V.*

10 **Discoteca Grace.** Arezzo's best dance club, with live and recorded disco, hip-hop, garage, house, and techno music. Open from midnight to dawn, on Friday and Saturday, from September to May. *Via Madonna del Prato 125. ☎ 0575-403669. 10€ cover.*

11 **Narciso.** This dance club sometimes features live music, but it's less lively than Grace. The schedule is irregular, so call first. *Via Isonzo 58. ☎ 0575-907867. 10€ cover.*

Arezzo's Piazza della Liberte.

Where to Stay

★ Cavaliere Palace Hotel CENTRO STORICO This patrician mansion from 1600 is now a modern hotel. Midsize to large rooms are soundproof, half with showers, half with tubs. Eat breakfast on the terrace in good weather. *Via Madonna del Prato 83.* ☎ *0575-26836. www.cavalierehotels.com. 29 units. Doubles 135€ w/breakfast. AE, DC, MC, V.*

★ Etrusco Palace Hotel WEST AREZZO This dull modern structure, 2km (1¼ miles) west of the old town, is Arezzo's best hotel for comfort. The interior is warmer, with midsize to large generic rooms. Many guests are Italian businessmen. *Via Fleming 39 (on the road to Firenze).* ☎ *0575-984066. www.etruscohotel.it. 80 units. Doubles 135€. AE, DC, MC, V.*

★ Minerva CENTRO STORICO This postwar structure is a bastion of modern comfort inside, with a touch of Italian style and elegance. Midsize rooms are soundproof with large windows. The town's best fitness center is free to guests. *Via Fiorentina 4.* ☎ *0575-370390. www.hotel-minerva.it. 130 units. Doubles 135€ w/breakfast. AE, DC, MC, V.*

★★ Patio CENTRO STORICO For atmosphere, this ambitious hotel in the 18th-century Palazzo de' Giudici is our local favorite. Each of the large units is dedicated to one of Bruce Chatwin's travel books, with furniture from the country it represents—say, Emperor Wu-Ti–style from China. *Via Cavour 23.* ☎ *0575-401962. www.hotelpatio. 7 units. Doubles 155€–176€; suite 224€ w/breakfast. AE, DC, MC, V.*

Where to Dine

Antica Osteria l'Agania CENTRO STORICO *TUSCAN* Locals pack this place for rib-sticking *ribollita,* hand-rolled pasta, and robust local fare such as *fegatelli* (pig liver). The waiter plops down a bottle of Chianti, and you pay for what you drink. *Via Mazzini 10.* ☎ *0575-295381. Entrees 7€–15€. AE, DC, MC, V. Lunch, dinner Tues–Sun.*

★ Buca di San Francesco CENTRO STORICO *TUSCAN/ARETINE* Arezzo's finest restaurant is in the frescoed cellar of a *palazzo* from the 1300s. In its 7th decade, it's still keeping alive "the memory of the old Tuscan flavors." Opt for *la saporita di bonconte,* a platter including baked rabbit, sausages, and tripe. *Via Francesco 1.* ☎ *0575-23271. Entrees 8€–15€. AE, DC, MC, V. Lunch, dinner Wed–Mon. Closed 2 weeks in Aug.*

★ La Torre di Gnicche CENTRO STORICO *TUSCAN* This overly decorated little dive is a Tuscan tavern with a vengeance—the kind from the 1950s, when the region was being discovered by the post-war generation. The cookery is fresh but unrefined. Try the local cheese and cold cuts, onion soup, or tripe. *Piagga San Martino 8.* ☎ *0575-352035. Entrees 5€–10€. AE, DC, MC, V. Lunch, dinner Thurs–Tues.*

★ Trattoria il Saraceno CENTRO STORICO *TUSCAN* This restaurant serves consistently good, cheap, regional food, with an excellent wine list, and friendly service. Specialties include wild boar with polenta and Tuscan lamb in fresh rosemary sauce. *Via Mazzini 6A.* ☎ *0575-27. Entrees 7.50€–15€. AE, DC, MC, V. Open Thurs–Tues lunch and dinner. Closed 3 weeks Jan.*

Cortona

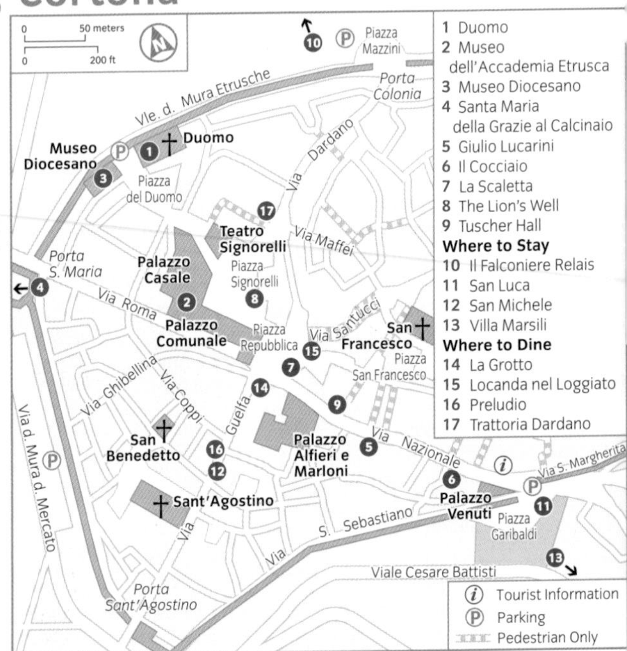

Medieval Cortona, known as the "city of art," is most often visited as a day trip from Arezzo (see above). The town's medieval ramparts cling to the slopes of a hill planted with olive groves, opening onto views of Lake Trasimeno. At its peak Cortona rivaled Arezzo and Perugia, almost Florence itself, in power. Memories of its heyday linger in its art collections and in its architecture, making it one of Tuscany's most romantic hill towns. The great Fra Angelico lived here for a decade, and Cortona's native son, Luca Signorelli (1450–1523), was the art historical precursor to Michelangelo. Despite its wealth of art, it was a book that placed Cortona on the tourist circuit: Frances Mayes' *Under the Tuscan Sun.* START: **Cortona is southeast of Florence on the SS69 to the SS71. From Arezzo, take the SS71 and turn off for Cortona at Il Sodo or Camucia and follow the signs. Trip length: From Florence 105km (63 miles); from Arezzo 34km (22miles).**

❶ **Duomo.** If you're rushed, skip the town cathedral at Piazza del Duomo, at the end of Via Casali. It was built unimaginatively in 1560, and it's filled with mediocre paintings. *Free admission. Daily 8am–12:30pm, 3–5:30pm.*

❷ ★ **Museo dell'Accademia Etrusca.** Cortona's Etruscan

A typical cobblestone street in medieval Cortona.

collection, housed in a 13th-century mansion, Palazzo Casali, includes an oil lamp chandelier from the late 4th century B.C. Works from other periods are also here—from Greek vases to Egyptian mummies, 15th-century ivories, Renaissance and baroque-era paintings (including works by Pietro Berrettini and Luca Signorelli). ⏲ ***40 min. Piazza Signorelli 9.*** ☎ ***0575-637235. www.accademia-etrusca.org/museo. 4.20€ adults, 2.50€ ages 17 and under. Apr–Sept daily 10am–7pm; Oct–Mar Tues–Sun 10am–5pm.***

3 ★★ Museo Diocesano. This museum is Cortona's chief attraction, with a splendid array of paintings from the Florentine and Sienese schools in a deconsecrated church. The best is Luca Signorelli's *Deposition* with background scenes of the Crucifixion and Resurrection. *The Ecstasy of St. Margaret,* by the 17th-century Bolognese artist G. M. Crespi, is also impressive. Two Fra Angelicos are worth the visit: the still-bright *Madonna Enthroned with Four Saints* (1437) and an *Annunciation* (1436) over the main altar. Other works include masterpieces by Pietro Lorenzetti and Bartolomeo della Gatta and a fine Roman sarcophagus from the 2nd century A.D. ⏲ ***1 hr. Piazza del Duomo 1.*** ☎ ***0575-62830. Admission 5€, 3€ ages 14 and under. Daily 9:30am–1pm and 3:30–7pm (closes at 5pm in winter).***

4 ★ Santa Maria della Grazie al Calcinaio. Three kilometers (2 miles) west of the town center, this monument to High Renaissance architecture was built by Francesco di Giorgio Martini from 1485 to 1513 (but you might swear the architect was Brunelleschi). Laid out on the Latin cross plan, the church enjoys a bucolic setting in olive groves below the ancient town walls. The 1516 rose window by Guillaume de Marcillat is remarkable, as is the late 16th-century *Madonna and Saints,* by Alessandro Allori, in the right transept. ⏲ ***30 min. Via del Calcinaio. No phone (call tourist office at 0575-630352 for information). Free. Mon–Sat 3–7pm. Sun Mass at 11am.***

A view of the countryside around Cortona.

Farmers Market

Saturday is **Market Day.** Head to Palazzo Casali (home of the Museo dell'Accademia Etrusca) in the morning, when local farmers start hawking fresh produce. You'll also find regional crafts and an annual Antiques Fair in late August and early September (dates vary). ☎ *0575-630610.*

Tuscan produce for sale at the farmers market outside Palazzo Casali.

5 Giulio Lucarini. CENTRO STORICO We infinitely prefer shopping at Il Cocciaio (see below), but the serious pottery shopper will also consider its major rival. At this address you will also find a wide array of terra-cotta ceramics in the traditional Cortonese patterns of field green, cream, and dark yellow, along with many old-fashioned blue-on-white designs. These local ceramics are designed and manufactured in Giulio Lucarini's own workshops. *Via Nazionale 54 (off Piazza della Repubblica).* ☎ *0575-604405. AE, DC, MC, V.*

Santa Maria della Grazie al Calcinaio

6 ★ Il Cocciaio. CENTRO STORICO Cortona is known for its distinctive ceramics, and Il Cocciaio is the oldest and best of the ceramic shops. Cortona is famous for its ceramic patterns of green, cream, and dark yellow, and this shop carries a large selection in these colors. Look for the symbolic daisy on the patterns, a design created by Gino Severini. This shop is unbelievably stuffed—don't bring your pet bull. You'll find not only traditional earthenware, but ovenware pots (note the special chicken casserole dish), along with a wide assortment of beautiful medieval Tuscan reproductions such as wall plates and jars. *Via Nazionale 69 (off Piazza della Repubblica).* ☎ *0575-601246. AE, DC, MC, V.*

Where to Stay

★★★ Il Falconiere Relais SAN MARTINO In San Martino, 4.5km (3 miles) north of Cortona, one of Tuscany's best country inns also runs the finest dining room in the area, with Tuscan cuisine. A restored series of 17th-century buildings have the feeling of a family house in the Valdichiana country-side, with original furnishings, four-poster iron beds, and a large pool amid an olive grove. *Località San Martino.* ☎ *0575-612679. www.ilfalconiere.it. 19 units. Doubles 260€–320€; suite 420€–560€ w/buffet breakfast. AE, DC, MC, V.*

San Luca CENTRO STORICO If you'll settle for standard, yet comfortable, bedrooms, San Luca will put you in the heart of Cortona for an affordable price. This government-rated, four-star hotel also offers great views. The on-site restaurant serves market-fresh food with a view of the valley. *Piazza Garibaldi 2.* ☎ *0575-630460. www.sanlucacortona.com. 60 units. Doubles 100€; 136€ triples w/breakfast. AE, DC, MC, V.*

Frescoes from the Museo Diocesano, Cortona's chief attraction.

★★ San Michele CENTRO STORICO This government-rated, 4-star hotel in an 11th-century palace has vaulted ceilings with *pietra serena* arches, small to mid-size rooms under wood-beamed ceilings, and

Palazzo Communale at night.

Guest quarters at the San Michele Hotel.

antique furnishings. The tower rooms are ideal for lovers. Opt for a suite with a terrace. *Via Guelfa 15.* ☎ *0575-604348. www.hotelsanmichele.net. 50 units. Doubles 134€–150€; junior suite 165€; suite 250€ w/breakfast. AE, DC, MC, V.*

★★ **Villa Marsili** CENTRO STORICO With dignified lounges and finely furnished, frescoed bedrooms, this former gentleman's residence from 1786 is the coziest nest in town, with outdoor gardens. Most rooms are elaborately furnished (bordering on campy) with views of the Valdichiana. *Via Cesare Battisti 13.* ☎ *0575-605252. www.vilamarsili.net. 27 units. Doubles 132€–217€; suite 260€–310€ w/buffet breakfast. AE, DC, MC, V.*

Cortona After Dark

La Saletta is the best cafe and wine bar in town *(open daily from 7pm–2am)* with live jazz on Saturday nights in winter. Patrons of all ages come for excellent Tuscan wines by the glass and elegant surroundings. *Via Nazionale 26–28 (off Piazza della Repubblica).* ☎ *0575-603366.* Unlikely as it seems, **The Lion's Well** is Cortona's traditional Irish-style pub. Attracting a young crowd in their 20s and 30s, it is a hard-drinking place with some wines available by the glass. *Piazza Signorelli 28.* ☎ *0575-604918.* Centrally located, **Tuscher Hall** is Cortona's most elegant bar, with an attractive mix of visitors and locals in their 20s and 30s. Excellent pastries, snacks, coffee, and tea are available Tuesday to Sunday from 9:30am to midnight. *Via Nazionale 43.* ☎ *0575-62053.*

Where to Dine

★★★ Il Falconiere SAN MARTINO *TUSCAN* This 17th-century *limonaia* affords one of Tuscany's grand dining experiences. Make a detour just to dine at this two-story glass and wrought-iron conservatory with an outdoor terrace. Silvia Baracchi, the owner, supervises every detail, and her well-trained staff will dazzle your palate with innovations on old recipes. Many ingredients come from the hotel garden. Wines are chosen to complement the menu. *Località San Martino.* ☎ *0575-612679. Entrees 18€–28€. AE, MC, V. Lunch, dinner daily. Closed Jan 10–Feb10 and Mon–Tues for lunch in Nov.*

Wine Tip

The local wine to order is the very distinguished white **Vergine di Valdichiana.** We'd avoid the sugary, harsh reds; leave that to the hard-drinking and robust tavern regulars.

La Grotta CENTRO STORICO *TUSCAN* Come to this trattoria on a dead-end alley for tasty *casalinga* (home-cooking) and grotto-style dining, at tables in cozy chambers lined with stone and brick. Don't miss the thick *ribollita* and tender, flavorful Florentine steaks—the most affordable in town. *Piazza Baldelli 3.* ☎ *0575-630271. Entrees 5.50€–8€. AE, DC, MC, V. Open Wed–Mon for lunch and dinner.*

★ Locanda nel Loggiato CENTRO STORICO *TUSCAN* Dine under wood-beamed ceilings, in rooms separated by stone arches, at this trattoria under the 16th-century Palazzo Pocetti. Good food at bargain prices is the rule: "We feed you well for not much lire," the owner said. The red turnip gnocchi with goat cheese is our favorite. *Piazza di Pescheria 3.* ☎ *0575-630575. Entrees 5€–13€. AE, DC, MC, V. Lunch, dinner Thurs–Tues. Closed Jan.*

★ Preludio CENTRO STORICO *TUSCAN* Your best bet in the historic core, this casual spot draws many regulars for savory, fresh food, great service, and cozy surrounds. Try the *pici* (homemade local pasta) with a ragout and game sauce. Menu varies seasonally. *Via Guelfa 11.* ☎ *0575-630104. Entrees 9€–18€. AE, DC, MC, V. Lunch, dinner Tues–Sun. Closed Jan 7–15.*

Trattoria Dardano CENTRO STORICO *TUSCAN* Visitors often overlook this modest, family-owned, budget trattoria with Tuscan fare made with market-fresh bounty from the Cortonese countryside. The cooks are known for their roast specialties—duck, chicken, and guinea hen (our favorite). In winter, Mr. Castelli hunts game for the menu. *Via Dardano 26.* ☎ *0575-601944. Entrees 5€–9€. No credit cards. Lunch, dinner Thurs–Tues. Closed Jan–Feb.*

A table at Il Falconiere, one of Tuscany's finest restaurants.

Lucca

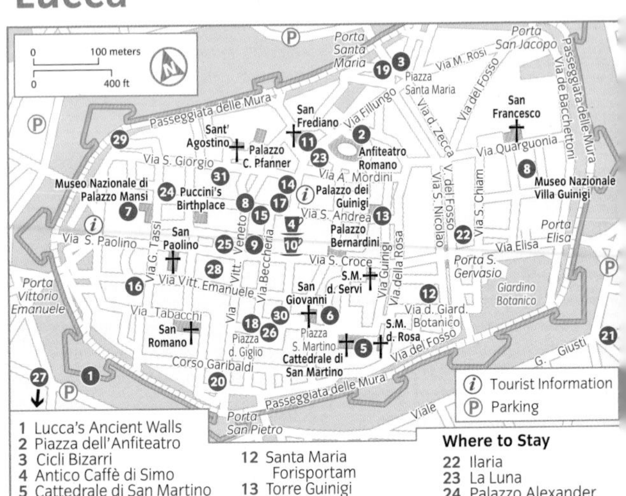

1 Lucca's Ancient Walls
2 Piazza dell'Anfiteatro
3 Cicli Bizarri
4 Antico Caffè di Simo
5 Cattedrale di San Martino & Museo della Cattedrale
6 Chiesa e Battistero di S.Giovanni e S. Reparata
7 Museo Nazionale di Palazzo Mansi
8 Museo Nazionale di Villa Guinigi
9 San Michele in Foro
10 Pasticceria Taddeucci
11 San Frediano
12 Santa Maria Forisportam
13 Torre Guinigi
14 Carli
15 Enoteca Vanni
16 Insieme
17 L'incontro
18 Teatro del Giglio

Nightlife

19 Betty Blu American Bar
20 Gelateria Veneta
21 Happy Days

Where to Stay

22 Ilaria
23 La Luna
24 Palazzo Alexander
25 Piccolo Hotel Puccini
26 Universo
27 Villa La Principessa

Where to Dine

28 Buca di Sant'Antonio
29 Da Giulio Pelleria
30 Giglio
31 Trattoria da Leo

Lucca is the most graceful provincial city of Tuscany, set within massive medieval and Renaissance walls. At the heart of one of Europe's richest agricultural regions, locals eat well and can boast about their outstanding art and architecture. Hometown to Puccini, the entire city is dotted with grand *palazzi* and churches. We like to wander for hours through the streets and historic squares of the **Città Vecchia** (old city). Music events at various churches begin in spring and continue through September; the tourist office has a complete schedule of events. START: **Lucca is west of Florence on the A11, past Prato, Pistoia, and Montecatini. It's east of Pisa on the SS12. Trip length: from Florence 72km (45 miles); from Pisa 21km (13 miles).**

1 Lucca's Ancient Walls. Planted with plane, chestnut, and ilex trees, Lucca's ramparts make for one of Tuscany's great city walks. Now a city park stretching for 4.9km (2⅔ miles), the **Passeggiata delle Mura** gives Lucca its special charm. Our favorite entry point is Piazzale Verdi. You can also explore the ramparts by bike (see below).

2 Piazza dell' Anfiteatro. If you want to hang out at a local cafe, make it one near the lovely Piazza dell' Anfiteatro, near the northern end of the main shopping street, Via Fillungo. A Roman amphitheater stood here until its destruction in the 1100s. Locals used the theater as a quarry for the stones to construct many of Lucca's palaces and churches. The foundations of what were the grandstands today support an ellipse of attractive medieval houses. The piazza is always open.

3 **Cicli Bizzarri.** Rent your own wheels here at Piazza Santa Maria 31 (☎ 0583-496031), near the tourist office. The basic cost is 2.10€ per hour or 9.30€ per day. Open daily 9am to 8pm. Another outfitter is **Antonio Poli,** Piazza Santa Maria 42 (☎ 0583-493787), which offers the same types of bikes and charges identical prices. *Daily 8:30am–8pm.*

4 **Antico Caffè di Simo.** On a pedestrian-only shopping street, this is the most famous cafe in town. Even Puccini came here for a drink, perhaps contemplating his next opera. The historic cafe serves the best gelato in town against an antique backdrop of faded mirrors, brass, and marble. *Via Villungo 58. ☎ 0583-496234. $.*

A cyclist on Lucca's massive ramparts.

5 ★★ **Cattedrale di San Martino.** Pope Alexander II consecrated the Duomo in 1070, but it took 4 centuries to finish. This ornate, asymmetrical structure was constructed around its *campanile* or bell tower with an arched facade in the Pisan-Lucchese Romanesque style. This facade was never completed; the top-most loggia and tympanum have yet to be built. Look for the reliefs under the portico, a stellar example of 13th-century stonework, some of them carved by Guido da Como. The interior was

A sidewalk cafe in Lucca.

given a Gothic dress in the 14th to 15th centuries. In the left transept is Jacopo della Quercia's tomb of Ilaria del Carretto (ca. 1406), his earliest surviving masterpiece and the first sculptural creation of the Renaissance to use Roman decorative motifs. Author John Ruskin called it "the loveliest Christian tomb in Italy." The Duomo is also filled with great art by Italian masters including a *Last Supper* by Tintoretto (third altar on the right). Adjacent to the cathedral is the **Museo della Cattedrale,** exhibiting minor works and some major ones, including Jacopo della Quercia's majestic early-15th-century sculpture, *St. John the Evangelist.* ⏲ ***40 min. Piazza San Martino.*** ☎ ***0583-957068. Cathedral free; 3.50€ to sacristy, inner sanctum, and Duomo Museum. Apr–Oct daily 10am–6pm; Nov–Mar Mon–Fri 10am–2pm, Sat–Sun 10am–5pm.***

6 Chiesa e Battistero di San Giovanni e Santa Reparata. The main structure of the present church dates from the 1100s, although the facade is largely from the 1500s. The three aisles are divided by columns, many of them recycled from Roman days. On the north side of the church, a baroque chapel honors Saint Ignazio. For a part of the 19th century, the church served as a mausoleum, as dozens of tombs and memorials testify to this day. ⏲ ***30 min. Piazza San Giovanni (off Via del Duomo).*** ☎ ***0583-490530. Admission 2.50€. May–Oct daily 10am–6pm; Nov–Apr Mon–Fri 10am–3pm and Sat–Sun 10am–6pm.***

7 Museo Nazionale di Palazzo Mansi. One of the grandest palaces in town, dating from the 16th century, now houses an art gallery (upstairs) enriched by acquisitions from private collections. Frankly, the lavishly decorated palace competes with the exhibits—a case of the frame outshining the painting. There are some important paintings, however, notably *Portrait of a Youth* by Pontormo; Medici portraits by Agnolo Bronzino; Correggio's *Madonna and Child;* Il Sodoma's *Christ with the Cross,* and Luca Giordano's *St. Sebastian.* ⏲ ***45 min. Via Galli Tassi 43 (at Via del Toro).*** ☎ ***0583-55570. Admission 4€ adults, 2€ 17 and under.***

Maionchi Fattoria, open for lunch.

Flower vendors in the Piazza dell' Anfiteatro.

June–Sept Tues–Sat 8:30am–7pm, Sun 8:30am–1pm. Off-season Tues–Sat 9am–7pm, Sun 9am–2pm.

8 **Museo Nazionale di Villa Guinigi.** This 15th-century palace is the one to see. Once owned by the powerful ruler, Paolo Guinigi, it displays the best of archaeological digs as well as Romanesque, Gothic, and Renaissance sculpture. Its painting collection is strong on works by regional artists. Highlights include a tomb slab by Jacopo della Quercia, and Zainobi Machiavelli's *Madonna and Child with Saints*. Some of the oversized 16th-century canvases are by Vasari. ⌚ ***30 min. Via della Quarquonia (at Via del Bastardo).*** ☎ ***0583-496033. June–Sept Tues–Sat 8:30am–7:30pm, Sun 8:30am–1:30pm. Off-season Tues–Sat 8:30am–7:30pm, Sun 8:30am–1:30pm. Admission 4€ adults, 2€ 17 and under.***

9 ★ **San Michele in Foro.** The *foro* in the name of this 12th-century Romanesque monument comes from the fact that it was built atop a Roman forum. The facade, with its four galleries, blind arches, and imaginative columns, is its main attraction. Inside is a three-aisled basilica whose nave is supported by arches resting on monolithic columns. Of the many paintings, the most brilliant is Andrea della Robbia's *Madonna* in the south transept. ⌚ ***30 min. Piazza San Michele (off Via Caldera).*** ☎ ***0583-48459. Free. Daily 9am–noon and 3–5:30pm.***

10 **Pasticceria Taddeucci.** This shop, founded in 1881, created a legendary confection called *Buccellato Taddeucci,* that is still sold today. Even Prince Charles dropped in for a taste of this anise-flavored cake studded with raisins. ***Piazza San Michele 34. Via S. Giustina.*** ☎ ***0583-494933. $.***

A detail of San Michele in Foro.

⓫ **San Frediano.** The original 6th-century basilica was reconstructed in the 12th century in the Lucchese-Romanesque style, using white marble from the ancient Roman amphitheater. The golden mosaic of the Ascension on the facade, possibly by Berlinghieri, was restored in the 1800s. Like an early Christian basilica, the interior consists of a nave and two aisles, flanked by chapels. Just inside the entrance is the church's most dazzling treasure, a 12th-century Romanesque baptismal font depicting the story of Moses. Also seek out a fresco cycle painted by Amico Aspertini (1508-09), depicting the *Miracles of St. Frediano.* ***25 min. Piazza San Frediano (off Via Cesare Battisti). ☎ 0583-493627. Free admission. Apr to mid-Nov Mon–Sat 7:30am–noon and 3–5pm, Sun 10:30am–5pm.***

⓬ **Santa Maria Forisportam.** This church was constructed in the late 12th century in the Pisan-Romanesque style, with a plain nave and two aisles. There are only a few treasures: a 5th-century A.D. Roman sarcophagus used as a baptismal font, two late-17th-century Guercino paintings (*St. Lucia* and the *Assumption*), and the main altar by Matteo Civitali. ***20 min. Via Santa Croce (at Via della Rosa). ☎ 0583-467769. Free admission. Mon–Sat 9am–noon and 3:15–6:30pm.***

Lucca's medieval city gate.

⓭ ★ **Torre Guinigi.** This tower, rising 44m (146 ft.), was built by the powerful ruling family of Lucca in the 15th century. Climb its 230 steps and you'll be rewarded with one of the great panoramas of Tuscany. ***20***

Lucca After Dark

Lucca is a drowsy Tuscan town after dark, with only a few nightspots. Strolling floodlit Centro Storico with a gelato is the best way to spend a warm evening here. In business since 1927, **Gelateria Veneta** (Via Vittorio Veneto 74; ☎ 0583-467037) makes the city's finest. Also in Centro Storico is **Betty Blu American Bar** (Via Gonfalone 16–18; ☎ 0583-492166; no cover; Thurs–Tues until 1am), popular with young locals for its live music (most often Italian rock groups). **Happy Days** (Via del Antonio Cantore 91; ☎ 0583-440264) attracts a youthful crowd with its 1960s retro atmosphere. The owners serve focaccia with savory toppings, bruschette, salads, and antipasti, with beer and wine by the glass.

min. Via Sant'Andrea (at Via Chiave d'Oro). ☎ 0583-48524. Admission 3.50€, Mar–May daily 9am–7:30pm; June–Sept 15 daily 9am–midnight. Sept 16–Oct daily 9:30am–8pm; Nov–Feb daily 9:30am–5:30pm.

⑭ ★★ **Carli.** On the pedestrian shopping street is one of the oldest jewelry stores in Tuscany, from 1655. It specializes in the finest antique jewelry, silver, and watches. *Via Fillungo 95 (off Piazza Santa Maria). ☎ 0583-491119. AE, DC, MC, V.*

⑮ ★ **Enoteca Vanni.** CENTRO STORICO Lucca has long been acclaimed for manufacturing the greatest extra virgin olive oils in Italy. Founded in 1965 in the historical center, this shop has the best of the lot. It also has the best wine cellar. *Piazza S. Salvatore 7 (off Via Buia). ☎ 0583-491902. AE, DC, MC, V.*

⑯ **Insieme.** CENTRO STORICO If you're looking for a gift or souvenir, this central shop has the best selection. Check out the Swarovski crystal. *Via Vittorio Emanuele II 70 (off Piazza Napoleone). ☎ 0583-419649. AE, DC, MC, V.*

⑰ **L'incontro.** CENTRO STORICO This shop is a grab bag of delights. It has one of the best selections of Lucca's rustically appealing porcelain, pottery, and tiles. Everyone from decorators to "homebodies" patronizes this overstuffed store. *Via Buia 9 (off Via Fillungo). ☎ 0583-491225. AE, DC, MC, V.*

⑱ ★★ **Teatro del Giglio.** This is the cultural center of Lucca, and one of the major 19th-century opera houses in Tuscany. Rossini premiered *William Tell* here in 1831. Concerts are presented year-round. Music of hometown artist Puccini remains the eternal favorite. The theater season lasts from mid-November to mid-March. *Piazza del Giglio. ☎ 0583-467521. Tickets 14€–26€.*

The rooftops of Lucca and the surrounding countryside.

Where to Stay

★ **Ilaria** CENTRO STORICO This hotel, within the city walls, is flanked by the ancient gardens of Villa Bottini and a medieval city gate. The hotel itself was just built, in 2000, on the site of the villa stables. The comfortable, well-furnished rooms are spread across three floors. Bikes are free. *Via del Fosso 25 (off Via Elisa).* ☎ *0583-47615. www.hotellilaria.com. 41 units. Doubles 200€–230€; suites 300€–450€ w/buffet breakfast.*

La Luna CENTRO STORICO You'll find problems here if you look for them, but no one complains about the price. In the historic center, La Luna faces Via Fillungo, the famous pedestrian shopping street. Rooms come in all sizes—from spacious to tiny; ditto for the bathrooms. Still, the hotel offers a warm and welcoming atmosphere. *Corte Compagni 12 (off Via Fillungo).* ☎ *0583-493634. www.hotellaluna.com. 29 units. Doubles 110€; suites 175€. AE, DC, MC, V.*

★★ **Palazzo Alexander** CENTRO STORICO In the historic center, this is Lucca's top boutique hotel. The 12th-century building became a girls' boarding school in the 1800s. Closed for years, it was restored and reopened as a hotel in 2000. Timbered ceilings were left intact. Modern conveniences such as whirlpool baths and computer hookups have been installed discreetly. *Via S. Giustina 48 (off Via Gialli Tassi). 12 units. Doubles 190€; suites 270€ w/buffet breakfast. AE, DC, MC, V.*

Piccolo Hotel Puccini CENTRO STORICO The city's best value and most conveniently located hotel takes its name from the composer, who was born across the street. Small and friendly, the hotel offers clean, cozy bedrooms with modern furnishings. Some bedrooms open onto the small square in front. *Via Di Poggio 9 (off Piazza San Michele).* ☎ *0583-55421. www.hotelpuccini.com. 14 units. Doubles 85€. AE, DC, MC, V.*

Villa La Principessa, Lucca's finest hotel.

Universo CENTRO STORICO This landmark 1857 hotel is housed in a 15th-century palace across the square from the city's opera house. Each of the attractively furnished rooms is individually decorated. The hotel has a wide range of public lounges, a bar, and a first-class restaurant serving Tuscan cuisine. *Piazza del Giglio 1 (off Piazza Napoleone).* ☎ *0583-493678. www.universolucca.com. 60 units. Doubles 120€–170€; suites 190€–260€ w/breakfast. MC, V.*

★★★ **Villa la Principessa** MASSA PISANA Lucca's poshest digs are in a luxurious building with roots that date to 1320. The location is 3km (2 miles) south of the city walls on the road to Pisa. There's nothing in the historic core as elegant as this private villa. The present building dates largely from an 18th-century reconstruction, complete with gardens and swimming pool. The formal restaurant serves sublime Italian and Tuscan cuisine. *Via Nuova per Pisa 1616, Massa Pisana.* ☎ *0583-370037. www.hotelprincipessa.com. 41 units. Doubles 200€–290€; suites 395€–450€. AE, DC, MC, V. Closed Nov–Mar. Bus: 54.*

Where to Dine

★★ **Buca di Sant'Antonio** CENTRO STORICO *TUSCAN* The finest, most reliable cuisine in Lucca is served in a 1782 building where Puccini used to dine. The regional dishes are market fresh and prepared with flavor, flair, and superb simplicity. Try the roast Tuscan goat or meat-filled ravioli in a scrumptious ragout. ***Via della Cervia 3 (off Piazza San Michele). ☎ 0583-55881. Entrees 7€–13€. AE, DC, MC, V. Tues–Sun 12:30–3pm and 7:30–10:30pm.***

★ **Da Giulio Pelleria** CENTRO STORICO *LUCCHESE* There's no more authentic Luccese dining within the city walls. Local specialties include horse tartar, veal snout, and tripe. For less adventurous diners, there's stewed beef with olives or Tuscan sausages with white beans. ***Via della Conce 45 (off Via S. Giorgio). ☎ 0583-55948. Entrees 4.50€–7.50€. AE, MC, V. Closed Aug 1–21.***

★ **Giglio** CENTRO STORICO *TUSCAN/LUCCHESE* Time-honored recipes are prepared authentically here, using farm products from the surrounding region. This much-frequented trattoria is a local favorite because the cooks are not timid when it comes to seasonings. Meals begin with steaming bowls of minestrone and proceed to entrees such as stewed rabbit with olives. Don't miss the homemade torte of the day. ***Piazza del Giglio 2 (off Piazza Napoleone). ☎ 0583-494058. Entrees 6.50€–13€. AE, DC, MC, V. Thurs–Mon 12:15–3pm and 7–10pm; Tues 12:15–3pm. Closed 2 weeks in Nov.***

Trattoria da Leo CENTRO STORICO *TUSCAN/LUCCHESE* The Buralli family will make you feel welcome at their unpretentious tavern in a 16th-century building. Guests come not for the 1930s decor but for the affordable regional menu, including homemade pastas prepared fresh daily, served with succulent sauces. In autumn we opt for the game dishes. Otherwise, we order such regional fare as calf's liver with wild fennel or one of the roasted meats seasoned with fresh rosemary. ***Via Tegrimi 1 (off Piazza San Michele). ☎ 0583-492236. Entrees 5€–11€. Mon–Sat daily noon–2:30pm and 7:30–10:30pm. July–Aug Sun 7:30–10:30pm; Sept–June Sun noon–2:30pm. No credit cards.***

Cyclists and cafes are equally common sites in Lucca.

Montepulciano

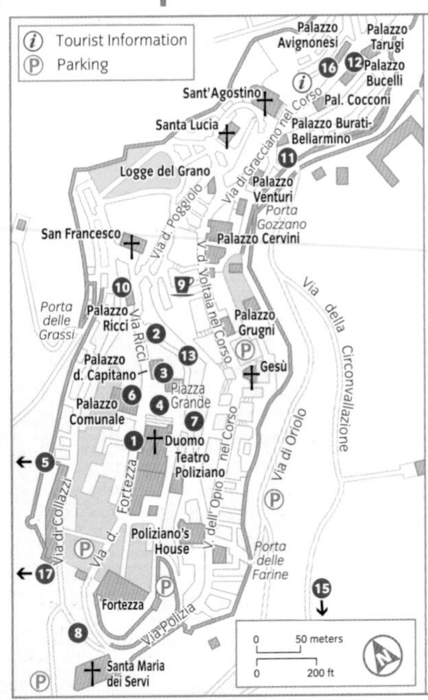

1 Duomo
2 Palazzo Neri Orselli (Museo Civico)
3 Palazzo Nobili-Tarugi
4 Piazza Grande
5 Tempio di San Biagio
6 Conforzio del Vino Nobile di Montepulciano
7 Contucci
8 Gattavecchi
9 Antico Caffé Poliziano

Where to Stay
10 Albergo Duomo
11 Il Borghetto
12 Il Marzocco
13 Mueble Il Riccio
14 San Biagio

Where to Dine
15 Fattoria Pulcino
16 Il Cantuccio
17 La Grotta

The garnet colored Vino Nobile, beloved by epicures, put the medieval hamlet of Montepulciano on the map. At an altitude of 605m (1,985 ft.), Montepulciano is also Tuscany's loftiest hill town, with remarkable views over the nearby vineyards. Surrounded by fortifications from 1511, the town prohibits cars inside the old walls. Before checking out individual sites, climb its steeply graded, serpentine main street—it has many names, but locals simply call it "Corso." Piazza Grande is at the summit of Corso, where you can begin your tour of the individual attractions. The town has fine hotels, but it's also an easy day trip from Pienza. START: **From Florence, take the A1 south to the Chianciano Terme exit, then SS146 toward Chianciano for 18km (11 miles). From Siena, head south on the SS2 to San Quírico d'Orcia, then follow SS146 through Pienza to Montepulciano. Trip length: 124km (74miles) from Florence; 67km (40 miles) from Siena.**

1 Duomo. To the world, this uncompleted Duomo presents a stark facade, but the sparse interior is not without its treasures. We visit just to gaze at Taddeo di Bartolo's triptych, *Assumption of the Virgin,* above the high altar. It glows, with the artist's use of subtle pinks, blood

Montepulciano's Piazza Grande.

orange, eggplant purple, and amber gold. The monumental altarpiece dates to 1401, and there are scattered sculptures by Michelozzo too. *20 min. Piazza Grande (off Via Ricci). No phone. Free admission. Daily 9am–12:30pm, 3:15–7pm.*

2 Palazzo Neri-Orselli (Museo Civico). This Sienese-Gothic *palazzo* houses most of Montepulciano's art treasures. Its collection of some 200 Tuscan paintings include works from the 13th to 17th centuries. The two most important are *St. Francis* by Margaritone da Arezzo and the lush *Coronation of the Virgin* by Jacopo de Mino. Other gems include 15th-century illuminated choir books, enameled terra cottas by della Robbia, Etruscan funerary urns, and other booty. *45 min. Via Ricci 10 (off Piazza Grande). 0578-17300. Admission 4.15€ or 2.60€ ages 17 and under. Tues–Sun 10am–1pm and 3–7pm.*

3 ★ Palazzo Nobili-Tarugi. Facing the Duomo, this *palazzo*—with its half-moon arches, Ionic columns, great portico, and entryway with pilasters—is attributed to Antonio da Sangallo the Elder. The open loggia on the ground floor is a masterpiece. The much-photographed 1520 fountain out front incorporates two Etruscan columns, topped by two griffins and two lions bearing the Medici coat of arms. The interior isn't open to the public. *15 min. Piazza Grande (off Via Ricci).*

4 ★ Piazza Grande. At the highest point in town, this square is known as Piazza Grande, though its official name is Piazza Vittorio Emanuele. Home to the Duomo, it's enveloped with Renaissance *palazzo*, including the Gothic town hall and the austere, 15th-century Palazzo Comunale, the work of Michelozzo, who was clearly inspired by the Palazzo Vecchio in Florence. The view from the Town Hall clock tower is one of the most magnificent vistas in Tuscany. *20 min. Piazza Grande (off Via Ricci). 0578-7121. Admission to tower 1.55€. Mon–Sat 10am–5pm.*

5 ★★ Tempio di San Biagio. This masterpiece of High Renaissance architecture was the greatest achievement of architect Antonio da Sangallo, who finished it in 1529. He was obviously inspired by Bramante's design for St. Peter's in Rome. Built on a Greek cross plan, it

Another view of Piazza Grande.

was built to house a statue of the Madonna. Crowned by its dome, the church has two *campaniles* or bell towers—one left unfinished. In the right light, the golden yellow travertine structure shines like gold. ⏱ *20 min. Via di San Giagio (1km/¾ mile) west of city via Porta al Prato, below the town walls). No phone. Free admission. Daily 9am–12:30pm, 3:30–7:30pm.*

Vino Nobile

Montepulciano's vintners have organized a consortium-cum-showroom, **Conforzio del Vino Nobile di Montepulciano** (www.consorziovino nobile.it). The public can visit, at the Palazzo del Capitano on Piazza Grande, and sample members' wines. *Mon–Fri 10am–1pm, 4–7pm; Sat 11am–3pm.* Montepulciano is riddled with *enteche* and *cantine* (wine cellars) where you can sample or purchase Vino Nobile wines and other local products. Our favorites follow below.

❻ ★★ **Contucci.** In the heart of town on the main square, this 13th-century winery occupies the ancient cellars of the Palazzo Contucci, occupied by popes and grand dukes over the years. This establishment was one of the first makers of Vino Nobile, a strong tradition today. Epicures have deemed the wine here "perfect," but the family owners keep trying to improve it. *Palazzo Contucci (at Piazza Grande).* ☎ *0578-757006. AE, DC, MC, V.*

❼ ★★ **Gattavecchi.** This historic winery with underground grottos and caves once belonged to a 12th-century convent. In the adjacent vaults of the church of Santa Maria dei Servi, wines rest for 2 years before they're sent out to world markets. *Via Collazzi 74 (località Santa Maria).* ☎ *0578-757110. AE, DC, MC, V.*

❽ ★★ **Antico Caffè Poliziano.** CENTRO STORICO *TUSCAN* This cafe, which opened in 1868, has bounced back after decades of slumber, since the days when Pirandello and Fellini quaffed here. Restored to some of its former glory, it is the center of sleepy Montepulciano's cultural life and nighttime activities. You can sip Nobile wines here and enjoy such Tuscan fare as pigeon with black truffles. In summer there is an outdoor terrace; in off-season there's a winter garden dining room. Many dishes are based on medieval recipes. *Via Voltaia nel Corso (off Via di San Donato).* ☎ *0578-758615. Closed Nov 15–30 and Feb.*

San Biagio and the surrounding farmland.

Where to Stay

Albergo Duomo. CENTRO STORICO Small to midsize rooms at this family-run favorite, named for the adjacent Duomo, are decorated in Tuscan *arte povera* style. All have private baths. ***Via San Donato 14. ☎ 0578-757473. www.albergo duomo.it. 13 units. Doubles 100€; triples 129€ w/breakfast. AE, DC, MC, V.***

★ **Il Borghetto.** CENTRO STORICO This rustic hostelry in a 16th-century building has small to midsize rooms with panoramic views, old brick floors, Tuscan antiques, and modern amenities. ***Via Borgo Buio 7. ☎ 0578-757535. www.ilborghetto.it. 17 units. Doubles 105€; suites 152€. AE, DC, MC, V.***

Il Marzocco. CENTRO STORICO Most rooms are spacious with Victorian and modern furnishings; the best have terraces. It's renovated but retains the patina of another era. ***Piazza Savonarola 18. ☎ 0578-757262. www.albergoilmarzocco.it. Doubles 90€; triples 120€ w/buffet breakfast. AE, DC, MC, V.***

Mueble Il Riccio. CENTRO STORICO In a 1280 palace, this walk-up hotel has a rooftop terrace overlooking the Valdichiana Valley. Comfortable midsize rooms have small baths. ***Via Talosa 21. ☎ 0578-757713. www.ilriccio.net. 6 units. Doubles 85€. AE, DC, MC, V.***

★ **San Biagio.** SAN BIAGIO The town's leading inn is a restored nobleman's house near San Biagio outside the city walls. Rooms have Tuscan decor and balconies with postcard views. The indoor pool evokes Pompei. ***Via San Bartolomeo 2. ☎ 0578-717233. www.albergosanbiagio.it. 27 units. Doubles 95€–105€, triples 135€ w/buffet breakfast. MC, V.***

Where to Dine

★ **Fattoria Pulcino.** TOWARD CHIANCIANO *TUSCAN* Southwest of town, this restaurant serves the area's best food and wine at communal tables in a 16th-century farmhouse. The owners sell their own extra virgin olive oil and wine. Try the grilled free-range chicken and Florentine steaks. ***SS146 per Chianciano 35 (on the road to Chianciano). ☎ 0578-758711. Entrees 12€–22€. AE, DC, MC, V. Lunch, dinner daily. Closed Jan–Easter.***

Il Cantuccio. CENTRO STORICO *TUSCAN* Many dishes here, such as the chicken and rabbit platter, are based on Etruscan recipes; all are Poliziana, the local cuisine. Try the tagliatelle in duck ragout or grilled Florentine steak with Tuscan white beans and roast potatoes, finished with the ricotta torte. ***Via delle Cantine 1–2. ☎ 0578-757870. Entrees 8€–24€. AE, DC, MC, V. Lunch, dinner Tues–Sun. Closed 2 weeks in early Nov, first 2 weeks of July.***

★ **La Grotta.** SAN BIAGIO *ITALIAN* Across the street from San Biagio, this old–fashioned tavern with arched brick ceilings serves tasty specialties, most of it recently harvested from the countryside. We return again and again for pasta with guinea fowl ragout and pork filet flavored with coffee beans and served with carrot-and-onion flan. ***Località San Biagio 15 (1km/⅔ miles west of center). ☎ 0578-757479. Entrees 12€–19€. AE, MC, V. Lunch, dinner Thurs–Tues. Closed Jan 10–Mar 10.***

Pienza

This model Renaissance town was the creation of Pope Pius II, who wanted to transform the modest village of Corsignano where he was born into a town that would glorify his name. He was born here as Enea Silvio Piccolomini, in an impoverished branch of a noble Sienese family, and reigned as pope from 1458 to 1464. At astronomical expense, Pienza emerged in just 3 years, with a new Duomo, and several palaces. The pope's envisioned city never grew beyond a few blocks, but what a masterpiece it remains! Zeffirelli recognized it for the stage setting it was, deserting Verona to film his *Romeo and Juliet* here. Give it at least a morning or afternoon. It has a few good hotels and restaurants, so you can use it as a base for your travels, or come just for the day from Siena. **START: From Siena, take the SS2 south to SS146 and follow the signs. Trip length: from Siena 55km (33 miles).**

1 Piazza Pio II. Begin in the center of town at Piazza Pio II. Virtually all the sights are here or nearby. The square is flanked by the Duomo, Palazzo Piccolomini (papal palace), and the Palazzo Vescovile. Palazzo Vescovile houses the Museo Diocesano.

The Palazzo Comunale, home to the town hall and municipal offices, was begun in 1462. The bell tower, added later, was made lower than the Duomo's to emphasize the power of the church over civil authority.

2 ★★ **Duomo.** The Renaissance facade (1462) conceals a restored Gothic interior influenced by the German churches Pius II saw on his travels. The pope's family is honored with a coat-of-arms above the rose window and in hundreds of family crests with five moons. The Duomo is built on clay and sandstone, and may one day collapse unless it's properly buttressed. The single-most acclaimed painting is the *Assumption of Il Vecchietta.* ⌚ ***30 min. Piazza Pio II (off Corso Rossellino). No phone. Free admission. Daily 7am–1pm and 2:30–7pm.***

3 **Museo Diocesano.** This museum looted local churches for a remarkable array of 14th- and 15th-century Sienese school paintings and an early-14th-century cape of Pius II. Il Vecchietta is the star here with his altarpiece of the *Virgin and Bambino with Saints*. Bartolo di Fredi dazzles us with his 1364 *Madonna della Misericordia.* ⌚ ***45 min. Corso Rossellino 30 (off Piazza Pio II).*** ☎ ***0578-749905. Admission 4.10€ or 2.60€ ages 6–12. Mar 15–Oct Wed–Mon 10am–1pm and 3–6:30pm. Off-season Sat–Sun 10am–1pm and 3–6pm.***

Virgin and Child fresco.

The Pienza Cathedral on the Piazza Pio.

4 ★ **Palazzo Piccolomini.** The papal home of Pius II is the masterpiece of Rossellino (1409-64), although he was obviously influenced by Alberti's Palazzo Rucellai in Florence. In Tuscany most facades are the star attraction. Not here. Go to the rear to admire a three-story loggia overlooking a hanging garden on the edge of a cliff. The interior courtyard with its thin Corinthian columns is a work of great beauty. In the pope's private apartments is his original baroque bed. Descendants of Pius II lived here until 1968. ⌚ ***40 min. Piazza Pio II (off Corso Rossellino).*** ☎ ***0578-748503. Admission 3€ adults, 2€ ages 17 and under. Tues–Sun 10am–12:30pm and 3–6pm.***

Pecorino is Pienza's most famous export.

A Local Treat

Italy's best Pecorino, a sheep's-milk cheese, is sold in shops along the **Corso Rossellino.** Fancier varieties are soaked in wine or dusted with truffles. Take a wedge along on a picnic.

5 ★ **Biagiotti Frattelli.** Come for quality wrought-iron handcrafts, based on ancient designs. The products are made by an ancient technique, using fire, anvil, and hammer. *Corso Rossellini 67 (off Piazza Pio II).* ☎ *0578-748666. AE, MC, V.*

6 **Calzoleria Pientina.** This shop, a real discovery, sells beautifully crafted handmade shoes and a tasteful array of leather accessories. *Via Gozzante 22 (at Via di Circonvallazione).* ☎ *0578-749040. AE, MC, V.*

Nightlife is virtually nonexistent in Pienza, so do as the locals do and end your day at a local cafe.

7 **Bar Il Casello,** in the Centro Storico, minutes from the Duomo, is the social center of town—a sleek, modern cafe with snacks during the day and excellent regional wines. It's open daily until midnight, shockingly late by local standards. *Via del Casello 3 (off Piazza Pio II).* ☎ *0578-749105.$–$$$.*

Pienza's Via dell'Amore.

Where to Stay

★★ Castello di Ripa d'Orcia RIPA D'ORCIA Huge rooms with stone walls, beamed ceilings, and plush beds in a medieval castle. A 10-minute walk outside Centro Storico. The owners run a restaurant and enoteca on the premises and require a 2-night stay. *Loc. Ripa d'Orcia (signposted from San Quirico). ☎ 0577-897376. www.castelloripadorcia.com. 6 units, 8 apts (sleep 2–4). Doubles 99€–130€ w/breakfast (2-night min.); apt 490€–575€ per week for 2. MC, V.*

★★ Hotel Residence San Gregorio CENTRO STORICO Our second choice opened in 1997 in a former cultural center bombed in World War II. Standard doubles and suites are elegant and comfortable. With an outdoor pool and restaurant serving traditional Tuscan fare. *Via della Madonnina 4. ☎ 0578-748175. 19 units. Doubles 80€–120€ w/breakfast. AE, MC, V.*

★★ Il Chiostro di Pienza CENTRO STORICO Converted to a hotel in 2005, this 15th-century convent is the best choice within city walls, with a pool overlooking the lush Val d'Orcia. Spacious rooms have frescoes; those in the wing are best. *Corso Rossellino 26. ☎ 0578-748400. www.relaisilchiostrodipienza.com. 37 units. Doubles 120€–220€; suites 220€–280€ w/buffet breakfast. AE, DC, MC, V.*

Piccolo Hotel la Valle CENTRO STORICO Our third choice hotel has spacious rooms, comfortably furnished, with fridges and safes. In good weather ask for breakfast on the terrace overlooking the Orchia Valley. *Via di Circonvallazione 7. ☎ 0578-749402. www.piccolohotellavalle.it. 15 units. Doubles 80€–125€ w/buffet breakfast. AE, MC, V.*

Where to Dine

La Chiocciola CENTRO STORICO *TUSCAN* Dishes at this rustic tavern with outdoor tables have stood the test of time. Try the pappardelle with wild boar or rabbit sauce or the ravioli stuffed with local pecorino. The cuisine, with its abundant use of regional produce, is never mannered. *Viale Mencattelli 4. ☎ 0578-748683. Entrees 7€–15€. AE, MC, V. Lunch, dinner Thurs–Tues. Closed 2 weeks in Jan.*

★ La Porta MONTICCHIELLO *TUSCAN* For a special treat, drive 6km (3¾ miles) southeast to the medieval village of Montichiello for this osteria-wine bar. The restaurant is at the main town gate, in an elegant room furnished in typical Tuscan style. There's terrace dining in fair weather, with tables opening onto views of Val d'Orcia. Regional fare includes such favorites as wild boar carpaccio and ravioli stuffed with spinach and ricotta, served with a truffle sauce. *Via del Piano 3, Monticchiello. ☎ 0578-755163. Entrees 7€–14€. MC, V. Lunch, dinner Fri–Wed. Closed last 3 weeks of June and 3 weeks starting Jan 10.*

★ kids Trattoria Latte di Luna CENTRO STORICO This laid-back trattoria, serving Southern Tuscan cuisine, draws a diverse regular crowd—from foreign exchange students to local *carabinieri*. Don't miss the house specials—roast suckling pig and homemade *semifreddi*. *Via San Carlo 2–4. ☎ 0578-748606. Main courses 6€–13€. MC, V. Wed–Mon 12:20–2:20 and 7:30–9:20. Closed Feb–Mar 15 and July.*

Pisa

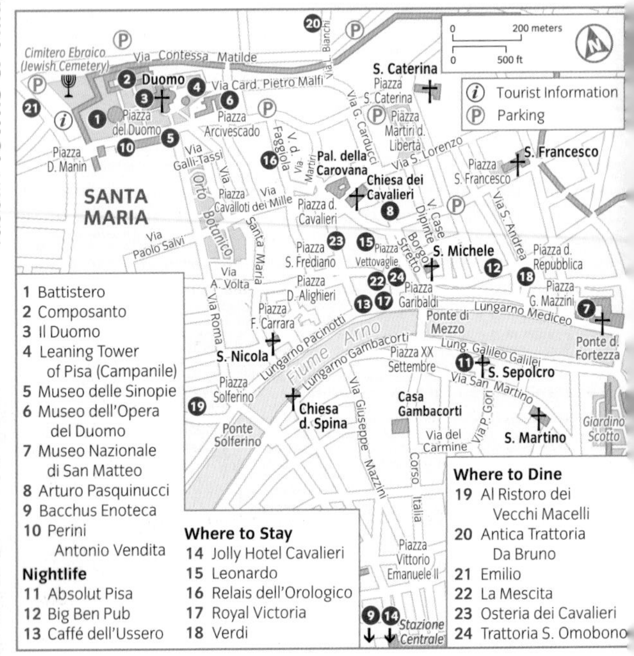

When Pisans talk of the good old days, they're talking about the 12th century—the apogee of their power. Their great buildings, such as the Duomo and the Leaning Tower were created in those heady days. Pisa enjoyed great maritime influence because of its harbor at the mouth of the Arno River, but the Pisan-Romanesque architecture that developed through the 13th century is the reason most outsiders pass through today. With Nicola Pisano and his son, Giovanni, Pisa became the center of Gothic sculpture in Italy. The city began to decline following its defeat at sea by the Genovese in 1285 and the silting up of its vital harbor. We suggest you spend the night in Pisa, and enjoy a free summer concert on the Duomo steps. (Nearly all of Pisa's major sites are nearby, on the Piazza del Duomo, also known as Campo dei Miracoli.) Many visitors, however, prefer to make the 1-hour drive back to Florence for the night. START: **From Florence, take the A11 and A12 west and follow signs; 76km (47 miles).**

1 ★★★ **Battistero.** This stunning example of the Pisan-Romanesque style was begun in 1153 and crowned by a Gothic dome in the 14th century. Don't miss the pulpit (1260) by Nicola Pisano; it's supported by pillars

Pisa's oft-photographed 12th-century tower.

resting on the backs of three marble lions. ⏲ ***30 min. Piazza del Duomo.*** ☎ ***050-560547. Admission 5€. Nov–Feb daily 9am–4:20pm; Mar and Oct daily 9am–5:30pm; Apr–Sept daily 8am–7:30pm.***

❷ **Camposanto.** In 1278, Giovanni di Simone designed this cemetery, allegedly using dirt from the Holy Land, which was shipped to Pisa by the Crusaders. In time, some 600 members of Pisan nobility were interred here. On view today are some 84 Roman sarcophagi and the celebrated fresco cycles, *The Triumph of Death*, the *Last Judgment*, and *Hell*. ⏲ ***30 min. Piazza del Duomo.*** ☎ ***050-560547. Admission 5€. Nov–Feb daily 9am–4:30pm; Oct and Mar daily 9am–5:30pm; Apr–Sept daily 8am–7:30pm.***

❸ ★★ **Il Duomo.** This cathedral, designed by Buschetto in 1063, is perhaps the most influential Romanesque building in Tuscany. The facade was erected by Rainaldo in the 1200s, with arches that diminish in size as they ascend. The interior has a nave and four aisles. The pulpit of Giovanni Pisano (1302–11) is among the most beautiful in the world. Galileo's lamp hangs near the pulpit. ⏲ ***40 min. Piazza del Duomo 17.*** ☎ ***050-560547. Admission 2€. Nov–Feb Mon–Sat 10am–12:45pm, 3–4:30pm, Sun 3–6:30pm; Oct, Mar Mon–Sat 10am–5:30pm, Sun 1–5:30pm; Apr–Sept Mon–Sat 10am–7:30pm.***

Pisa's Battistero.

The Battistero is a prime example of the Pisan-Romanesque architectural style.

❹ ★★★ **Leaning Tower of Pisa (Campanile).** The bell tower of the cathedral was begun in 1173. Construction continued, with two long interruptions, until 1350. It was designed to be vertical and started to lean during construction. The problem was that you couldn't stack that much heavy marble on sinking subsoil. In December 2001, it was righted to lean a mere 4m (14 ft.), as it did in 1838. It was here that Galileo dropped balls of different masses, disproving Aristotle's theories about the acceleration of falling bodies. *30 min. Piazza del Duomo 17. 050-560547. www.duomo.pisa.it. Admission 15€. Winter daily 9am–5:50pm, summer 8am–8pm. Maximum of 40 visitors admitted at one time.*

❺ ★ **Museo delle Sinopie.** The sketches displayed here were unearthed beneath the Camposanto's ruined frescoes in the 1944 bombardment. The red-brown pigment (or *sinopia*) came from Sinope on the Black Sea. The restored sketches are the work of 13th- to 15th-century painters. *30 min. Piazza del Duomo. 050-560547. Admission 5€. Nov–Feb daily 9am–4:30pm; Oct, Mar daily 9am–5:30pm; Apr–Sept daily 8am–7:30pm.*

❻ ★★ **Museo dell'Opera del Duomo.** Romanesque, Gothic, and Renaissance art removed from the grand monuments on the Piazza del Duomo are showcased here. Such masterpieces as Giovanni Pisano's ivory *Madonna and Child* are on display. The courtyard has a unique view of the leaning tower. *30 min. Piazza Arcives-covado 6. 050-560547. Admission 5€. Nov–Feb daily 9am–4:20pm; Mar, Oct daily 9am–5:20pm; Apr–Sept daily 8am–7:20pm.*

Bustling, modern shopping amid medieval architecture.

Santa Maria della Spina, on the quay.

7 ★★ **Museo Nazionale di San Matteo.** An old convent that once was a prison today houses the best collection of Pisan art and sculpture from medieval times to the Renaissance. Masterpieces include Simone Martini's polyptych of the *Virgin and Child with Saints,* Nino Pisano's *Madonna del Latte,* and statues by Giovanni Pisano. *40 min. Piazzetta San Matteo 1. ☎ 050-541865. Admission 4€. Tues–Sat 8:30am–7pm, Sun 8:30am–1pm.*

8 **Arturo Pasquinucci.** This kitchenware outlet, dating from 1870, offers crystal, glass, and ceramics. *Via Oberdan 22. ☎ 050-580140. AE, DC, MC, V.*

9 ★ **Bacchus Enoteca.** This is the best wine shop in Pisa, especially strong on Tuscan vintages. Wines can be shipped anywhere. *Via Mascagni 1. ☎ 050-500560. AE, MC, V.*

10 **Perini Antonio Vendita.** Pisa abounds in gift shops, hawking junk. If you'd like to purchase typical Pisan arts and crafts, try this outlet. It's next door to the Duomo. *Piazza del Duomo. ☎ 050-554579. AE, MC, V.*

Pisa After Dark

★ **Caffè dell'Ussero** is one of Italy's oldest literary cafes, founded in 1775. Many famous young men of the *Risorgimento* drank and plotted here as students. Ice creams, pastries, and cafe-style fare are served daily. The cafe lies on the ground floor of the historic 15th-century Palazzo Agostini. *Lungarno Pacinotti 27. ☎ 050-581100.* The sedate, English-style **Big Ben Pub** is the oldest in town. Popular with visitors and locals alike, it serves a vast selection of beers and plates of bar food. And it's open daily until 2am—*late* for Pisan standards. *Via Palestro 11. ☎ 050-581158.* Many nights at **Absolut Pisa,** a gay and lesbian bar in Centro Storico, are devoted to drag. Live music and campy cabaret shows are staples, and broadband computers are available. *Via Mossotti 10. ☎ 050-500248. 14€* membership. Closed Mon.

Where to Stay

★★ **Jolly Hotel Cavalieri.** STAZIONE CENTRALE Knocked off its pedestal by the new Relais dell'Orologio, this is still Pisa's largest, best full-service hotel, with seven floors. Rooms are stylish—the best of them on the fifth floor. *Piazza della Stazione 2.* ☎ *050-43290. www.jollyhotels.it. 100 units. Doubles 180€–249€ w/breakfast. AE, DC, MC, V.*

Leonardo. CENTRO STORICO The best budget hotel in town, in the traffic-free historic center. Rooms are simply furnished but comfortable. Ask for an upper-floor room. *Via Tavoleria 17.* ☎ *050-579946. www.hotelleonardopisa.it. 27 units. Doubles 85€–115€ w/breakfast. AE, DC, MC, V.*

★★★ **Relais dell'Orologico.** CENTRO STORICO This former private home of a noble family is the best, most intimate hotel in town. In the rear is a romantic garden for breakfast. *Via della Faggiola Uguccione 12.* ☎ *050-551869. www.hotelrelaisorologio.com. 21 units. Doubles 350€. AE, DC, MC, V.*

★ **Royal Victoria.** CENTRO STORICO In business since 1839, this traditional hotel's medieval towers and antique houses blend harmoniously. Opt for a room overlooking the Arno—or, best, a room in the 10th-century tower. *Lungarno Pacio Pacinotti 12.* ☎ *050-940111. 48 units. Doubles without bath 77€; doubles with bath 128€ w/buffet breakfast. AE, DC, MC, V.*

Verdi. CENTRO STORICO This outwardly plain former *palazzo* and convent has a warm heart. It was fully reconstructed after World War II, with respect to its old charm. *Piazza della Repubblica.* ☎ *050-598947. www.verdihotel.it. 32 units. Doubles 85€–115€ w/buffet breakfast. AE, DC, MC, V.*

The facade of the traditional Royal Victoria.

Where to Dine

★ Al Ristoro dei Vecchi Macelli *SEAFOOD PISAN* Pisa's finest restaurant specializes in Tuscan meat and fish dishes. Try the "surf" or "turf" antipasto samplers or any of the handmade pastas, such as pork ravioli in broccoli sauce. *Via Volturno 49. ☎ 050-20-424. Main courses 16€–18€. AE, DC, MC, V. Thurs–Tues 12:30–3pm and 7:30–10pm; Sun 8–10pm.*

Antica Trattoria Da Bruno. *CASALINGA PISANA* Near the Leaning Tower, this popular trattoria has been feeding visitors for half a century. Market-fresh ingredients are used in time-tested recipes. Baked rabbit, roast garlic-studded lamb, and salt cod with leeks and tomatoes are a few of the specials here. *Via Luigi Bianchi 12 (outside Porta Lucca; north end of Pisa). ☎ 050-560818. Entrees 10€–16€. AE, DC, MC, V. Lunch Wed–Mon, dinner Wed–Sun.*

Emilio. *TUSCAN* A favorite with locals, Emilio serves the best spaghetti and clams in Pisa. Also good are the tender, Florentine beefsteaks and the fresh fish, cooked to perfection. *Via Cammero 44. ☎ 050-562141. Entrees 5€–15€. Fixed-price 9.50€–22€. AE, DC, MC. Lunch Sat–Thurs. Closed Nov.*

La Mescita CENTRO STORICO *TUSCAN* Simple, fine cuisine near the Piazza Vettovaglie marketplace. The menu changes monthly. After hours, the place becomes an enoteca with a long wine list. *Via D. Cavalca 2. ☎ 050-544294. Entrees 15€–16€. AE, DC, MC, V. Tues–Sun 8–11pm, Sat–Sun 1–2:30pm. Closed 20 days in Aug. Bus: 1, 2, or 4.*

★ Osteria dei Cavalieri. *TUSCAN* This is a temple of Tuscan cuisine:

Traditional crostini.

The menu is traditional, but skilled chefs manage to lighten and modernize many of the region's robust specialties. Try the grilled fish and such unusual pastas as *tagliata* with thin slivers of rare beef. *Via San Frediano 16, Santa Maria. ☎ 050-580858. Entrees 13€–15€. AE, DC, MC, V. Lunch Mon–Fri, dinner Mon–Sat. Closed July 25–Aug 25 and Dec 29–Jan 7.*

★ Trattoria S. Omobono *CASALINGA PISANA* A full, home-cooked meal, including wine, can run less than $25 here. Dine among locals on Pisan classics such as *brochette alla renaiaola* (pasta squares in a puree of turnip greens and smoked fish) or *baccala alla livornese* (salt cod with tomatoes). *Piazza S. Omobono 6. ☎ 050-540847. Main courses 8€. DC, MC, V. Mon–Sat 12:30–2:30pm and 7:30–10pm. Closed Aug 8–20.*

San Gimignano

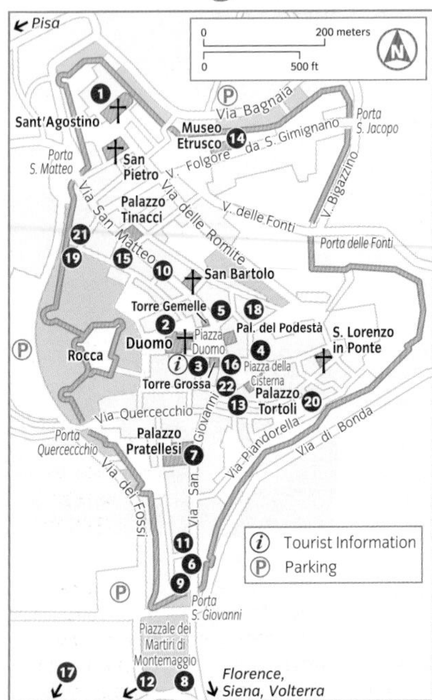

1 Chiesa di Sant'Agostino
2 Collegiata
3 Museo Civico & Torre Grossa
4 Museo della Tortura
5 I Ninnoli
6 La Bottega di San Gimignano
7 Tinacci Tito & Martia Maria Grazia
8 Avalon Pub
9 Bar I Combattenti
10 Da Gustavo

Where to Stay
11 Bel Soggiorno
12 Hotel Pescille
13 La Cisterna
14 La Collegiata
15 L'Antico Pozzo
16 Leon Bianco
17 Relais Santa Chiara

Where to Dine
18 Dorandó
19 La Mangiatoia
20 Le Vecchie Mura
21 Osteria delle Catene
22 Ristorante Le Terrazze

Tuscany's best-preserved medieval town, San Gimignano once had a defense system encompassing more than 70 towers, and no fewer than 13 of them survive. The painter Benozzo Gozzoli was born here, and many novelists and film directors have used it as a setting (E. M. Forster in *Where Angels Fear to Tread* and Franco Zeffirelli in *Tea with Mussolini*). In summer, it's the real-life setting for open-air operas, in the Piazza del Duomo. START: **San Gimignano is northwest of Siena and southwest of Florence. From either city take the Florence/Siena autostrada to Poggibonsi, and cut west for 12km (8m) on S324 into San Gimignano. Parking lots are outside city walls. Trip length: 40km (24 miles) from Siena, 52km (32 miles) from Florence.**

1 ★ Chiesa di Sant'Agostino. This Romanesque-Gothic church from 1290, on the north side of town, houses 17 famous frescoes by Benozzo Gozzoli from 1464, Piero del Pollaiuolo's 1483 *Coronation of the Virgin*, and Benedetto di Maiano's 1494 marble altar. In 1464, a plague swept the town and the citizens prayed to Saint Gimignano to end it. When the sickness passed, they dutifully hired Gozzoli to paint a thankful scene on the nave's left wall showing the patron

Two Beautiful Squares & Market Days

Two of Tuscany's loveliest town squares, **Piazza del Duomo** and **Piazza della Cisterna,** stand side by side in the heart of town. On Thursday and Saturday mornings, country vendors hawk their wares along the ancient town streets and disappear by afternoon. Pre-15th-century palaces and seven towers envelop Piazza del Duomo. Piazza della Cisterna, named for its 13th-century cistern, is lined with 13th- and 14th-century buildings. Sit, sip, and people-watch at the gift shops, churches, and cafes in these public spaces.

saint and his cloak full of angels stopping and breaking the plague arrows being thrown down by a vengeful God and his angelic hosts. The city liked the results, so they commissioned Gozzoli to spend the next 2 years frescoing the choir behind the main altar with scenes from the *Life of St. Augustine.* ⌚ *20 min. Piazza Sant'Agostino (north of Via 20 Settembre).* ☎ *0577-907012. Free. Daily 7am–noon, 3–7pm (6pm Oct–Apr).*

❷ ★★ **Collegiata.** The city's main church dates from the 11th century, but its present look is mostly from the 1400s. Inside, it's among Tuscany's most richly decorated churches, with 14th- and 15th-century frescoes by Barolo di Fredi and Domenico Ghirlandaio, and Giuliano da Maiano's Cappella di Santa Fina, a highlight of Renaissance architecture. ⌚ *30 min. Piazza del Duomo.* ☎ *0577-940316. Free admission to church; 3.50€ to chapel. Mar–Oct daily 9:30am–7pm; Nov–Feb Mon–Sat 9:30am–5pm, Sun 1–5pm.*

❸ ★ **Museo Civico & Torre Grossa.** Climb 54m (175 ft.) for one of Tuscany's best panoramic views. Post-descent, take in the art at the 13th-century Palazzo del Popolo (town hall). In the Council Chamber, Lippo Memmi's impressive *Madonna and Child* dates from 1317. The second floor museum of paintings mostly shows the 12th- to

With its dramatic skyline, San Gimignano has been called the medieval Manhattan.

15th-century Florentine and Sienese schools, including Pinturicchio's 1511 *Madonna in Glory* and the matching tondos of the *Annunciation* by a young (25-year-old) Filippo Lippi. *40 min. Piazza del Duomo 1 (off Vicolo Santa). 0577-990312. Admission 5€. Nov–Feb daily 10am–6pm; Mar–Oct daily 9:30am–7:30pm.*

4 Museo della Tortura. Housed in the Torre del Diavolo (Devil's Tower), this museum of medieval torture devices features cast-iron chastity belts, bone-crunching manacles, breast rippers, the garrote (that horror of the Inquisition), and other gruesome implements. Commentary in English explains how each tool was employed. Most grim: the fact that some of these devices are still in use around the world today. *30 min. Via del Castello 1. 0577-942243. Admission 8€. Apr–Oct daily 10am–8pm; Nov–Mar daily 10am–6pm.*

A typical street in San Gimignano.

La Bottega di San Gimignano has a diverse selection of high-quality ceramics.

5 I Ninnoli. Portable home goods include Florentine boxes inlaid with gold, reproductions of famous paintings, and an array of mirrors, lamps, plaster bas-reliefs, and chandeliers. Merchandise is mostly high quality, handmade by skilled artisans. *Via San Matteo 3. 0577-943011. AE, MC, V.*

6 La Bottega di San Gimignano. This the best outlet for high-quality ceramics, with one of the greatest selections and many items of artistic quality, entirely handmade and decorated in limited number. *Via San Giovanni 108. 0577-940205. AE, DC, MC, V.*

7 Tinacci Tito & Martia Maria Grazia. Three generations of the Tinacci family have sold high-quality local artisania—leather goods, ceramics, pottery, terra cottas, wooden trays, sacred art images, and carnival masks—from these ancient cellars. *Via San Giovanni 41A. 0577-940345. AE, DC, MC, V.*

Where to Stay

Bel Soggiorno CENTRO STORICO Family-run since 1886, this hotel is a fine choice near the major sites, with grand public areas and comfy, basic rooms; three open onto a terrace. *Via San Giovanni 91 (at Via Piandorella). ☎ 0577-940375. www.belsoggiorno.com. 22 units. Doubles 95€–120€; triples 120€–170€. AE, DC, MC, V. Closed Jan–Feb.*

★ **Hotel Pescille** PESCILLE This country hotel has a garden, pool, tennis court, and some rooms with balconies (our favorite is the Tower). Poolside brunch in summer and cold buffet dinner Tuesday to Sunday. *Località Pescille. ☎ 0577-940186. www.pescille.it. 50 units. Doubles 100€–130€; triples 150€–170€. AE, DC, MC, V.*

San Gimignano After Dark

Avalon Pub is one of the town's most popular, with restaurant meals, the best selection of national wines, and international beers (from 3€ per glass), live music, Internet access, and a terrace. *Viale Roma 1 (at Porta San Giovanni). ☎ 0577-940023. Closed Mon.* **Bar I Combattenti** has served the town's best ice cream since 1924 (made from award-winning family recipes), as well as sweets from Siena—and Chianti and Vernaccia from the cellar. *Via San Giovanni 124. ☎ 0577-940391. Closed Tues.* **Da Gustavo,** one of the town's best bars, draws a young crowd of visitors and locals. The Vernaccias and Chiantis are especially good, often sold by the glass, with snacks such as crostini and bruschette. *Via San Matteo 29. ☎ 0577-940057. Daily 8am–8pm. Closed Nov and Feb.*

The Piazza del Duomo takes on added drama at night.

Guest quarters at the Bel Soggiorno.

★ **La Cisterna** CENTRO STORICO Rooms vary—from spacious with views to small and cramped—at this 18th-century palace on a hill above the Elsa Valley. *Piazza della Cisterna 24. ☎ 0577-940328. 50 units. Doubles 82€–120€; junior suites 112€–135€ w/breakfast. AE, DC, MC, V.*

★★★ **La Collegiata** NORTH SAN GIMIGNANO One of the town's top two hotels, this Relais & Châteaux property in a 16th-century convent amid centuries-old cypresses has tapestries, frescoes, and tasteful rooms. *Località Strada 27. ☎ 0577-943201. www.lacollegiata.it/indexe.html. 19 units. Doubles 210€–520€; suites 600€–1,050€. AE, MC, V.*

★★ **L'Antico Pozzo** CENTRO STORICO Dante slept in this 15th-century *palazzo* (old town's best) with rooms of varying size, many with antiques and some with frescoes. *Via San Matteo 87. ☎ 0577-942014. www.anticopozzo.com. 18 units. Doubles 110€–135€; triples 150€–180€ w/breakfast. AE, DC, MC, V.*

Ceiling detail from the Bel Soggiorno hotel.

★ **Leon Bianco** CENTRO STORICO This 11th-century, family-run villa has many original features, views of the Elsa Valley, and medium to large rooms, most with beamed ceilings. *Piazza della Cisterna 8. ☎ 0577-941294. www.leonbianco.com. 26 units. Doubles 90€–130€; triples 145€. AE, DC, MC, V*

★★ **Relais Santa Chiara** SOUTH SAN GIMIGNANO This government-rated four-star hotel, near the old ramparts, is one of the city's top two, with terra-cotta floors, marble mosaics, and large rooms, many with balconies or terraces; superior doubles have hydro-massage tubs. *Via San Matteotti 15. ☎ 0577-940701. www.tuscany.net/santachiara. Doubles 150€–225€; suites 205€–270€ w/breakfast. AE, DC, MC, V.*

Where to Dine

★★★ **Dorandó** CENTRO STORICO *TUSCAN* The city's top restaurant, with stone walls and vaulted roof, serves creative, light seasonal dishes from medieval and Etruscan recipes. *Vicolo dell'Oro 2. ☎ 0577-941862. Entrees 12€–23€; fixed-price menu 47€. AE, DC, MC, V. Lunch, dinner daily; Nov–Easter closed Mon.*

★★ **La Mangiatoia** CENTRO STORICO *TUSCAN* Many dishes at this fine old-town restaurant—like venison with pine nuts, raisins, vinegar, and chocolate—derive from old Sangimignanese recipes. *Via Mainardi 5. ☎ 0577-941528. Entrees 8.50€–18€. MC, V. Lunch, dinner Wed–Mon. Nov, Jan, and June–Sept closed Sun.*

Le Vecchie Mura CENTRO STORICO *TUSCAN* Seasonal, quintessentially Tuscan dishes—*ribollita,* wild boar in Vernaccia wine—are served in a cavernous 18th-century interior with vaulted ceilings. *Via Piandornella 15. ☎ 0577-940270. Entrees 8€–15€. AE, DC, MC, V. Dinner Wed–Mon. Closed Nov, Jan–Feb.*

★ **Osteria delle Catene** CENTRO STORICO *TUSCAN* Tuscan wines and food—saffron soup from a medieval recipe, tagliatelle with wild boar sauce—reign in this medieval setting with modern lighting. *Via Mainardi 18. ☎ 0577-941966. Entrees 7€–14€. AE, DC, MC, V. Lunch, dinner Thurs–Tues. Closed Jan 6–Feb 28.*

Ristorante Le Terrazze CENTRO STORICO *TUSCAN* Large windows open onto old town and Val d'Elsa at this first-rate, family-run, seasonal Tuscan restaurant. *Piazza della Cisterna 24. ☎ 0577-940328. Entrees 8.60€–15€. AE, DC, MC, V. Thurs–Mon Lunch 12:30–2:30pm, Dinner 7:30–9:30; Wed Dinner 7:30–10pm).*

La Mangiatoia ("the Eating Trough").

Siena

1 Piazza del Campo
2 Battistero
3 Il Duomo
4 Museo Civico
5 Museo dell'Opera Metropolitana
6 Palazzo Pubblico
7 Torre del Mangia
8 Casa di Santa Caterina
9 Chiesa di San Domenico
10 Chiesa di San Francesco
11 Oratorio di San Bernardino e Museo Diocesano
12 Ospedale di Santa Maria della Scala
13 Pinacoteca Nazionale
14 Antichita Sena Vetus
15 Ceramiche Artistiche Santa Caterina
16 Cortecci
17 Enoteca San Domenico
18 Il Telaio
19 Martini Marisa
20 Mercatissimo della Calzature e Pelletteria
21 Zina Provedi

Nightlife

22 Concha d'Oro
23 Enoteca Italiana
24 Enoteca I Terzi
25 The Dublin Post
26 Kroeg
27 Essenza

Where to Stay

28 Antica Torre
29 Certosa di Maggiano
30 Chiusarelli
31 Duomo
32 Garden Hotel
33 Grand Hotel Continental
34 Palazzo Ravizza
35 Park Hotel Siena
36 Piccolo Hotel Etruria
37 Santa Caterina
38 Villa Scacciapensieri

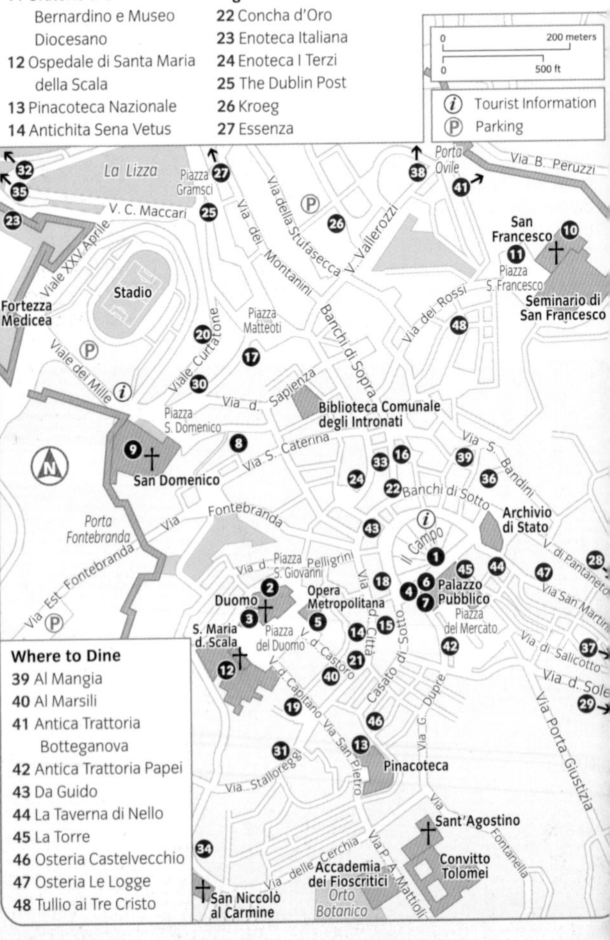

Where to Dine

39 Al Mangia
40 Al Marsili
41 Antica Trattoria Botteganova
42 Antica Trattoria Papei
43 Da Guido
44 La Taverna di Nello
45 La Torre
46 Osteria Castelvecchio
47 Osteria Le Logge
48 Tullio ai Tre Cristo

If you have time for only one Tuscan town besides Florence, make it Siena. Dominating the medieval trade routes between France and Rome, the city in its day had Italy's richest banks, Gothic architecture, a quasi-democratic government, and its own constitution. Once Florence's rival in might and arts patronage, Siena never fully recovered from the Black Death, which mowed down the population from 100,000 to 30,000 in 1348. Now, the medieval character of its public features is frozen in time—a sort of living museum for art, architecture, and history buffs. START: **From Florence, Siena is southeast along the Firenze-Siena autostrada. Trip length: From Florence 70km (43 miles).**

❶ **Piazza del Campo.** The most beautiful piazza in Italy is Siena's. First laid out in the early 12th century on the site of a Roman forum, it is dramatically shaped like a sloping scallop shell or fan.

By 1340, the town leaders had paved the square in brick and divided it into nine sections in honor of the Council of Nine, who ruled Siena during its golden age. Today the most major festival in Italy, the **Palio,** takes place here (see below).

At the upper end of the square stands the **Fonte Gaia** (fountain of joy), created from 1408 to 1419 by Jacopo della Quercia, Siena's greatest sculptor. Regrettably, what you see today is an inferior copy from 1868. The eroded remains of the original panels for the fountain can be seen on the loggia of the Palazzo Pubblico (see below).

❷ ★ **Battistero.** The 14th-century Baptistery stands on its own little square on top of a steep flight of steps, hiding behind a Gothic facade. It contains some remarkable art, its crown jewel being a baptismal font embellished with some of the finest sculpture of the quattrocento. The hexagonal marble font (1411–30) is a masterpiece by Jacopo della Quercia in the Gothic-Renaissance style. The two statues around the basin, *Faith* and *Hope,* are by Donatello. Panels on the font

Siena's medieval Piazza del Campo.

Palio, Siena's annual horse race and medieval pageant.

include Ghiberti's *Baptism of Christ* and *John in Prison,* and the even greater *Herod's Feast* by Donatello. *30 min. Piazza San Giovanni (off Piazza del Duomo). ☎ 0577-283048. Admission 3€. Apr–Sept daily 9am–7:30pm; Oct daily 9am–6pm; Nov–Mar daily 10:30am–1pm and 2–5pm.*

❸ ★★★ **Il Duomo.** The architectural highlight of Siena's golden age is the cathedral of Santa Maria dell'Assunta (its formal name). Beginning in the 12th century, architects set out to create a dramatic facade with colored bands of marble in a Romanesque and Italian Gothic style. Between 1369 and 1547, some 40 leading Sienese artists created the 56 designs on the floor. The sober *campanile* (bell tower) dates from 1513. In the chancel are richly decorated choir stalls from the 14th to the

Bareback Anarchy & Royal Pomp

Two times a year, on July 2 and August 16, Europe's most daring horse race takes place on Siena's main square. Jockeys fly around the dirt-filled square three times with one aim: winning. Forget sportsmanship. "The rule of the barbarian prevails," says a parade marshal. The single rule is that no jockey can grab another horse's reins. But you *can* drug an opponent the morning of the race, kidnap him the night before or, as he rides by, "whip him with a leather belt made from the skin of the bull's penis, which leaves the deepest welts and lasting scars," as recounted by a parade marshal.

All this is in tribute to the Virgin Mary, in whose honor the Palio has taken place since 1310.

16th centuries. The 13th-century pulpit is the creation of Nicola Pisano (Giovanni's father). The architectural highlight is the Libreria Piccolomini, constructed in 1485 by Cardinal Francesco Piccolomini (later Pope Pius III), to house the library of his more famous uncle, Pope Pius II. Art lovers flock here to see the remarkable early-16th-century frescoes by the Umbrian master Pinturicchio. *45 min. Piazza del Duomo (off Piazza del Campo). ☎ 0577-283048. Free admission to Duomo; 3€ library. Duomo: Mar 16–Oct daily 8am–1pm and 2:30–7:30pm. Off-season daily 8am–1pm and 2:30–5pm. Library: Mar 15–Oct daily 9am–7:30pm; Nov–Mar 14 daily 10am–1pm and 2:30–5pm.*

4 ★★★ Museo Civico. The major rooms of Palazzo Pubblico have been frescoed with themes of secular life in medieval Siena, creating one of Tuscany's grandest and most unusual museums. The Sala dei Priori was frescoed by Spinello

Siena's 12th-century Duomo is the city's great architectural triumph.

The Casa di Santa Caterina, devoted to Italy's patron saint, Catherine of Siena.

Aretino in 1476 with episodes from the life of Pope Alexander III. The Sala del Risorgimento boasts 19 murals illustrating the life of Vittorio Emanuele, who unified the country.

In Room 10, Sala del Mappamondo, don't miss the stunning *Maestà* (Virgin in Majesty) of Simone Martini. Painted in 1315, it is Martini's earliest known work, and perhaps his best. Hanging opposite it is his equally famous equestrian portrait of *Guidoriccio da Fogliano,* the Sienese general.

In the Sala della Pace or "peace room" are the badly damaged but celebrated frescoes (1335–40) of *The Effects of Good and Bad Government* by Ambrogio Lorenzetti. This is the greatest secular medieval fresco cycle in Europe. *1½ hr. In the Palazzo Pubblico, Piazza del Campo. ☎ 0577-292263. Admission 6.50€; 4€ students; free ages 10 and under. Mar–Oct daily 10am–7pm; Nov–Feb daily 10am–5:30pm.*

5 ★★ Museo dell'Opera Metropolitana. This art museum is housed in a 14th-century building originally designed to be the transept of a grand new cathedral until the plague of 1348 descended. Many of the cathedral's masterpieces are now sheltered here, including Giovanni Pisano's statues that originally adorned the facade of the Duomo. The museum's greatest treasure is Duccio's *Maestà* (Virgin in Majesty) on the second floor. This double-sided altarpiece (1311) is hailed as one of the greatest late medieval paintings in Europe. Nearby is Pietro Lorenzetti's majestic *Birth of the Virgin,* which, fortunately for us, he managed to finish before the plague finished him. Climb up to the walkway for Siena's grandest panorama. ⌚ *1 hr. Piazza del Duomo 8 (off Piazza del Campo).* ☎ *0577-42309. Admission 6€. Mar 16–Sept daily 9am–7:30pm; Oct daily 9am–6pm; Nov–Mar 15 daily 9am–1:30pm.*

6 ★★ **Palazzo Pubblico.** This Gothic *palazzo,* the finest in Siena, was constructed in a crenellated Gothic style from 1297 to 1310. The faithful built the loggia chapel, **Cappella della Piazza,** to thank God for delivering them from the plague. The chapel was begun in 1352 and not completed until the mid-1400s. The cafes along the square outside are great for cappuccinos and people-watching.

7 ★★ **Torre del Mangia.** The 14th-century tower at the Palazzo Pubblico (see above) was named for a gluttonous bell-ringer, Giovanni di Duccio. At 102m (336 ft.), it is the tallest secular monument from the Middle Ages remaining in Tuscany. Climb the tower for one of the grandest views in Tuscany. ⌚ *20 min. At the Palazzo Pubblico, Piazza del Campo.* ☎ *0577-292262. Admission 6€. Mar 16–Oct daily 10am–7pm; Nov–Mar 15 daily 10am–4pm.*

8 ★ **Casa di Santa Caterina.** Who would have thought that Caterina Benincasa, daughter of a Sienese dyer, would grow up to become the patron saint of Italy? After the first of many visions of Christ at the age of 8, she took a nun's veil in 1355. The house where she lived as a Dominican nun still stands today, except it now has a Renaissance loggia and a series of baroque oratories, the small Oratorio della Cucina being the most beautiful. Her greatest accomplishment was persuading Pope Gregory XI to return to Rome from Avignon. She died in 1380 at age 33, and was the first woman to be canonized, 81 years later. ⌚ *40 min. Costa di San Antonio (between Via Santa Caterina and Via della Sapienza).* ☎ *0577-247393. www.caterinati.org. Free admission. Easter–Oct daily 9am–12:30pm and 3–6pm. Off season daily 9am–12:30pm and 3:30–6pm.*

9 ★ **Chiesa di San Domenico.** This severe-looking church in the monastic Gothic style was founded

Casa di Santa Caterina.

The Siena skyline and surrounding countryside.

in 1125 and closely linked with St. Catherine, who is said to have had her visions here. Inside you can see a portrait of her by her contemporary, Andrea Vanni. This is the only known portrait by someone who actually knew her. Frescoed scenes from Catherine's life are found in the Cappella di Santa Caterina. Scenes of the saint swooning in ecstasy (1526) represent some of Il Sodoma's finest achievements. Ask a church official for the exact spot where Catherine is said to have received her stigmata. ◷ *20 min. Piazza San Domenico (off Via Curtatone). No phone. Free admission. Apr–Oct 7am–1pm and 3–6:30pm. Nov–Mar 9am–1pm and 3–6pm.*

⑩ Chiesa di San Francesco. This late Gothic church was begun in 1326 and reconstructed in the 1880s. The cavernous interior has frescoes from the 1330s by the brothers Ambrogio and Pietro Lorenzetti. Time has been cruel to these works, but their beauty survives. ◷ *20 min. Piazza San Francesco (off Via dei Baroncelli). No phone. Daily 7:30am–noon and 3:30–7pm.*

⑪ Oratorio di San Bernardino e Museo Diocesano. St. Bernadine became a monk at the church of San Francesco (see above), but she prayed and preached at the late 15th-century Oratorio. The frescoes on the lower level are by some of Siena's greatest 17th-century artists. Don't miss the 16th-century frescoes on the upper level including works by Il Sodoma, so named because of his sexual practices. If time is limited, skip the Diocesian Museum. ◷ *20 min. Piazza San Francesco 18 (off Via dei Baroncelli). ☎ 0577-283048. Admission 2.50€. Mar 15–Oct daily 10:30am–1:30pm and 3–5:30pm. Closed Nov–Mar 14.*

⑫ ★ Ospedale di Santa Maria della Scale. This 14th-century hospital, one of Europe's oldest, is slowly being turned into a museum and cultural complex displaying a wealth of art and archaeological treasures. The frescoes of Domenico di Bartolo (1440–41) are richly colored. Don't miss the vast Pilgrims Hall with its cycle of 14th-century frescoes. ◷ *40 min. Piazza del Duomo 2. ☎ 0577-49153. www.santamaria.comune.siena.it. Admission 6€ without reservations, 5.50€ with reservations. Children 10 and under free. Daily 10:30am–4:30pm.*

⑬ ★ Pinacoteca Nazionale. Regrettably, the greatest works by Sienese masters are found elsewhere, often in Florence, but this is still an impressive and representative showcase of the city's greatest artists including Duccio's *Madonna of the Franciscans;* Simone Martini's *Virgin and Child,* Giovanni di Paolo's *Virgin of Humility,* and the almond-eyed *Madonna and Bambino* by Ambrogio Lorenzetti. Of exceptional interest are the cartoons of the Mannerist master Beccafumi, from which many of the panels in the Duomo floor were created. *1½ hr. Via San Pietro 29 (off Via del Capitano). ☎ 0577-281161. Admission 4€ Sun–Mon 8:30am–1:30pm, Tues–Sat 8:30am–7pm.*

⑭ Antichita Sena Vetus. CENTRO STORICO The staff could be more helpful, but serious collectors may want to storm the gates anyway to see the stunning antique furniture and jewelry. *Via di Città 53 (at Via dei Pellegrini). ☎ 0577-42395. AE, MC, V.*

Al Mangia's sidewalk tables on the Piazza del Campo.

Siena After Dark

Sienese line up at **Gelateria Brivido** from March through October for the best homemade ice cream in town—it's a virtual tradition on summer nights. *Via dei Pellegrini 1–3 (at Via di Città). ☎ 0577-280058.* **Concha d'Oro** is the Siena's most popular cafe, with their own roast and the most delectable pastries and cookies around. *Via Banchi di Sopra 24 (at Via Rinuccini). ☎ 0577-236009.* ★★ **Enoteca Italiana** is the only state-sponsored wine bar in Italy, with vaults that were constructed for Cosimo de' Medici in 1560. *In the Fortezza Medicea (at Viale Cesare Maccari). ☎ 0577-236012.* **Enoteca I Terzi** is under the vaulted ceiling of a 12th-century tower. A glass of wine averages 3.50€. *Via dei Termini 7 (at Vicolo de la Macina). ☎ 0577-44329.* **The Dublin Post** is Siena's liveliest bar—with Harp, Kilkenny, Guinness, and a small menu. Rock, pop, and traditional Irish music set the mood. *Piazza Gramsci 20–21 (at Via del Cavallerizzo). ☎ 0577-289089.* Belgian beer and french fries are the star attractions at **Kroeg.** *Via del Pian D'Ovile 70 (at Piazza del Sale). ☎ 0577-223256.* Siena has no dance clubs within its walls, but at **Essenza,** 15km (9⅓ miles) east in the village of Casetta, you can dance the night away with Tuscan youth. Bus service from Statua di Santa Caterina (Uscita Stadio) in Siena is free Saturday at 11:15pm, midnight, and 12:45am, with free returns at 2:30am and 3:30pm. *Casetta. ☎ 0339-719914. Cover 15€. Fri–Sun 11pm until very late; closed May–Sept.*

Shopping Tip

Market Day in Siena is every Wednesday at La Lizza from 8:30am to 1:30pm. The streets around the Fortezza bustle with street vendors, many of who come in from the neighboring countryside. Everything's for sale—not just fresh fruits, vegetables, and flowers, but shoes, crafts, and leather handbags too. **The Antique Market** also takes place at Piazza del Mercato on the third Sunday of every month.

⑮ ★★ Ceramiche Artistiche Santa Caterine. CENTRO STORICO This is the best outlet for Sienese ceramics in the classic black, white, and burnt sienna motif, based on floor panels in the Duomo. *Via di Città 51 (at Via dei Pellegrini). ☎ 0577-283098. AE, DC, MC, V.*

⑯ Cortecci. CENTRO STORICO The city's best designer clothing is sold in this house of fashion, going strong since 1935. You get better prices than in Florence on designer names from Gucci to Giorgio Armani and Fendi. *Banchi di Sopra 27 (at Piazza Tolomei). ☎ 0577-280984. AE, DC, MC, V.*

⑰ Enoteca San Domenico. CENTRO STORICO This shop sells gourmet products for which Tuscany is famous. There's a wide selection of Tuscan wines, virgin olive oils, liqueurs, unusual pasta products, bottled sauces, jams, and sweets. *Via del Paradise 56 (at Piazza Matteotti). ☎ 0577-271181. AE, MC, V.*

The medieval fortifications of Monteriggioni, outside Siena.

18 Il Telaio. CENTRO STORICO We shop here often for a wide selection of handcrafted leather accessories, including belts and scarves, as well as for classic and trendy clothing for men and women. Check out the pullovers for men. ***Chiasso del Bargello 2 (at Piazza Bonelli).*** ☎ *0577-47065. AE, DC, MC, V.*

19 ★ Martini Marisa. CENTRO STORICO This is a top purveyor of hand-painted Sienese *majolica* (ceramics), the designs based on traditional motifs. The ceramics are as functional as they are beautiful. ***Via del Capitano 5 (at Piazza del Duomo).*** ☎ *0577-288177. AE, MC, V.*

20 Mercatissimo della Calzature e Pelletteria. CENTRO STORICO Bargain hunters descend on this store, which hawks high-quality leather goods, including shoes of famous Italian designers at discounted prices. ***Viale Curtatone 1 (at Piazza San Domenico).*** ☎ *0577-45310. AE, DC, MC, V.*

21 Zina Provedi. CENTRO STORICO This shop doesn't have the selection of Martini Marisa (see above), but what it has is choice. The focus is on rustic, handmade pottery as well as painted tiles set into wood. ***Via di Città 96 (at Via del Castoro).*** ☎ *0577-286078. AE, MC, V.*

Italy's Most Perfectly Preserved Fortified Village

Dante compared the towers of the village of **Monteriggioni** to giants. High above the Firenze-Siena autostrada, the tiny fortress village looms like a spillover from the Middle Ages. Its walls are still intact. Throughout Tuscany, vendors sell aerial photos of this remarkably well-preserved village. All 14 of the town's towers are still here, more or less, and still looking like that "circle of titans" guarding the lowest level of Hell in Dante's view.

Monteriggioni is panoramically situated on a hill above the Val d'Elsa. With its 13th-century walls and 14 square towers, it is camera ready. In the fading glow of a dying day, it appears (if the weather holds) a red gold set against the deep amber green of the surrounding vegetation.

There's just enough room inside this hamlet for two oversize piazzas along with some medieval stone houses and their gardens. Since Monteriggioni has only two streets, lined with handcraft shops, chances are you won't get lost.

Monteriggioni makes an easy day trip from Siena. You need allow no more than 1½ hours to see everything. It lies 20km (12 miles) northwest of Siena and is reached along the SS2.

Where to Stay

★ **Antica Torre** CENTRO STORICO The rooms in this 16th-century tower are midsize with stone floors, antique prints, and wrought-iron beds. The top level has panoramic views. *Via di Fieravecchia 7. ☎ 0577-222244. 8 units. Doubles 80€–110€. AE, DC, MC, V.*

★★ **Certosa di Maggiano** PORTA ROMANA Siena's most luxurious hotel is in a 14th-century monastery rife with antiques. Half board required in summer. No kids under 12. *Strada di Certosa 82. ☎ 0577-288180. www.certosadimaggiano.com. 17 units. Doubles 400€–620€; suites from 680€ w/breakfast. AE, MC, V.*

Chiusarelli CENTRO STORICO Five minutes from Piazza del Campo, this 1870 building with columns and caryatids has midsize to large neoclassical rooms, many with views (quietest in the rear). *Viale Curtatone. ☎ 0577-280562. www.chiusarelli.com. 49 units. Doubles 95€–119€; triples 135€–161€ w/breakfast. AE, DC, MC, V.*

Duomo CENTRO STORICO This restored 12th-century *palazzo* lacks character unless you get a room with a cathedral view; units 61 and 62 have terraces overlooking the Duomo. *Via Stagoreggi 38. ☎ 0577-289088. www.hotelduomo.it. 23 units. Doubles 100€–130€ w/breakfast. AE, DC, MC, V.*

The dining room at Certosa di Maggiano.

Guest quarters at Certosa di Maggiano, in a converted 14th-century monastery.

★ **Garden Hotel** NORTH SIENA This 18th-century villa is one of Siena's best moderately priced hotels, with a garden and pool. Rooms in the main building have the most character and space; all have panoramic views. *Via Custoza 2. ☎ 0577-47056. www.gardenhotel.it. 122 units. Doubles 100€–200€ w/breakfast. AE, DC, MC, V.*

★★ **Grand Hotel Continental** CENTRO STORICO This government-rated five-star hotel has 15th-century architecture and frescoes, medium to large rooms with deluxe tiled baths, and junior suites with terraces. *Banchi di Sopra 85. ☎ 0577-56011. www.grandhotelcontinentalsienna.com. 51 units. Doubles 310€–540€; suites from 720€. AE, DC, MC, V.*

★★ **Palazzo Ravizza** CENTRO STORICO Siena's best *pensione* since the 1920s, this Renaissance *palazzo* has antiques, frescoes, large, high-ceilinged rooms, and fine dining. *Pian dei Mantellini 34. ☎ 0577-280462. www.palazzoravizza.it. 38 units. Doubles 130€–180€; suites 220€–270€ w/breakfast. AE, DC, MC, V.*

★★ **Park Hotel Siena** MARCIANO In terms of size, facilities, and services, this modern hotel in 16th-century digs is Siena's grandest, with a golf course and large rooms and baths—lacking only antique charm. *Via di Marciano 18. ☎ 0577-290290. www.parkhotelsienna.it. 69 units. Doubles 256€–405€; suites 524€–939€. AE, DC, MC, V. Closed Nov 16–Mar 14.*

Piccolo Hotel Eturia CENTRO STORICO Rooms in the main building of this small, immaculate, welcoming family-run hotel are largest, with the most character. *Via Donzelle 3. ☎ 0577-288088. www.hoteletruria.com. 13 units. Doubles 80€; triples 105€. AE, DC, MC, V.*

★ **Santa Caterina** CENTRO STORICO With Siena's most hospitable owners, this 18th-century villa with midsize rooms and antiques is surrounded by a terraced garden overlooking the southern valley. *Via Enea Silvio Piccolomini). ☎ 0577-280462. www.hscsiena.com. 22 units. Doubles 130€–180€ w/breakfast. AE, DC, MC, V.*

★ **Villa Scacciapensieri** NORTH SIENA Amid a large park, with a pool, tennis court, and terraces, this 19th-century villa has medium to large rooms; some face the Chianti hills. *Via di Scacciapensieri 10. ☎ 0577-41441. www.villascacciapensieri.it. 31 units. Doubles 185€–245€; suites 305€ w/breakfast. AE, DC, MC, V.*

Where to **Dine**

★ **Al Mangia** CENTRO STORICO *TUSCAN/INTERNATIONAL* On the Piazza del Campo in 12th-century quarters, one of Siena's finest restaurants makes dishes such as *pici alla Sienese* (handmade pasta with fresh tomatoes, tarragon, and cheese) from the best local stuff. *Piazza del Campo 43 (off Via della Galluzza). ☎ 0577-281121. Entrees 15€–25€. AE, DC, MC, V. Lunch, dinner daily.*

★ **Al Marsili** CENTRO STORICO *SIENESE/ITALIAN* A mass of cross-vaulted ceilings, old bricks, and stones, Siena's most elegant restaurant serves wild boar and goose pâté alongside Tuscan classics. *Via Del Castoro 3. ☎ 0577-47154. Entrees 12€–18€. AE, DC, MC, V. Lunch, dinner Tues–Sun.*

★★★ **Antica Trattoria Botteganova** NORTH SIENA *TUSCAN*

Traditional Tuscan bean soup.

Michel Sonentino's restaurant is Siena's finest, with light innovations on Tuscan standards and 400 local vintages. ***Strada Chiantigiana 408.*** ☎ ***0577-284230. Entrees 22€–24€; tasting menu 44€–50€. AE, DC, MC, V. Lunch, dinner Mon–Sat. Closed Jan and 10 days between July and Aug. Bus: 3 or 8.***

★ **Antica Trattoria Papei** CENTRO STORICO *SIENESE* This family-run trattoria serves simple but well-prepared Sienese fare such as rabbit in white wine with rosemary and sage or wide noodles in wild boar sauce. ***Piazza del Mercato 6.*** ☎ ***0577-280894. Entrees 6.50€–11€. AE, MC, V. Lunch, dinner Tues–Sun.***

Da Guido CENTRO STORICO *SIENESE/INTERNATIONAL* Modern cuisine—among Siena's best grilled meats and antipasti tables—is served under old beams, arched ceilings, and brick walls. ***Vicolo Pier Pettinaio 7 (Via della Galluzza).*** ☎ ***0577-280042. Entrees 7€–17€. AE, DC, MC, V. Lunch, dinner daily.***

La Taverna di Nello CENTRO STORICO *TUSCAN/VEGETARIAN* This 1930s-style restaurant is another good choice on the periphery of Piazza del Campo. Pasta is made fresh daily, served with light or heavy sauces and a choice of more than 150 Tuscan wines. ***Via del Porrione (off Via della Galluzza).*** ☎ ***0577-289043. Entrees 9€–18€. AE, DC, MC, V. Lunch, dinner Mon–Sat.***

La Torre CENTRO STORICO *TUSCAN* This mamma and poppa operation enjoys a loyal clientele. Try the delectable homemade pastas, the perfectly cooked meats, and a few exotic dishes such as *piccione al forno* (oven-baked pigeon). ***Via Salicotto 7–9 (off Piazza del Campo).*** ☎ ***0577-287548. Entrees 6€–11€. AE. Lunch, dinner Fri–Wed. Closed Aug 17–Sept 1.***

Pastry lovers at Nannini cafe.

★ **Osteria Castelvecchio** CENTRO STORICO *TUSCAN/VEGETARIAN* This ancient building, convenient to all the major monuments, including the Duomo, is the best place in town for fresh vegetables. You can order meat and poultry dishes, but the rich harvest of the Tuscan countryside is given special attention. The menu changes daily. ***Via Castelvecchio 65 (off Via San Pietro).*** ☎ ***0577-49586. Entrees 7.50€–12€. AE, DC, MC, V. Lunch, dinner Mon–Sat.***

★★ **Osteria Le Logge** CENTRO STORICO *SIENESE/TUSCAN* This tranquil trattoria serves the freshest cuisine in a refined but old-fashioned atmosphere. The menu changes with the seasons. The tender veal steaks are the best in town, and the delicate black truffle is used to enhance many dishes such as taglierini pasta. ***Via del Porrione 33 (off Via del Rialto).*** ☎ ***0577-48013. Entrees 16€–18€. AE, DC, MC, V. Lunch, dinner Mon–Sat.***

Tullio ai Tre Cristo CENTRO STORICO *SIENESE* Wander back in time to this hidden, mid-19th-century trattoria off the tourist trail. Expect pure, bold flavors from dishes such as "fat" spaghetti with porcini mushrooms, or noodles in hare ragout. ***Vicolo di Provenzano (off Via del Giglio).*** ☎ ***0577-280608. Entrees 9€–16€. Fixed-price menu of 5 courses 58€. MC, V. Lunch, dinner Thurs–Tues. Closed Dec 15–31.***

Volterra

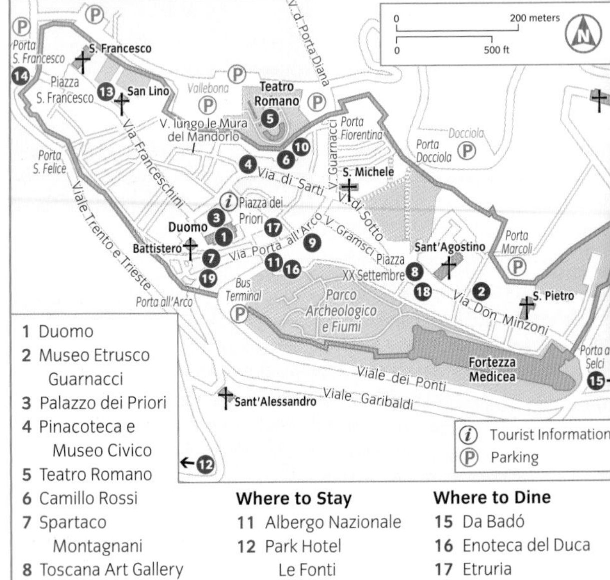

Volterra still rises like a fortress, 540m (1,800 ft.) above a desolate terrain. The Etruscans who settled here in the 9th century B.C. made thousands of alabaster funerary urns from local stone, many of which are preserved in the Museo Etrusco Guarnacci (see below). Volterra still has a medieval appearance, with foreboding *palazzi*, walled gateways, cobblestone streets (some mere alleyways), and dozens of shops hawking alabaster wares. Come for the alabaster, the panoramic views, numerous walks, and a major Etruscan museum.

START: **Volterra is easily accessible from San Gimignano, Siena, and Florence. It's on the SS68 route 30km (19 miles) from where it branches off the Colle di Val d'Elsa exit on the Firenze-Siena autostrada. Trip length: 28km (18 miles) from San Gimignano, 50km (31 miles) from Siena, and 72km (45 miles) from Florence.**

❶ ★ **Duomo.** A simple facade hides a lush interior with a carved and gold-embossed wooden ceiling. The best baroque painting is Francesco Curradi's *Crucifixion*. Our favorite chapel is the *Cappella dell'Addolorata*, with frescoes by Benozzo Gozzoli, and 15th-century terra-cotta sculptures. The octagonal baptistery, from 1283, has a

The Etruscan town of Volterra was settled in the 9th century.

baptismal font (1502) by Andrea Sansovino. *30 min. Piazza San Giovanni. No phone. Free admission. Daily 8am–12:30pm and 3–7pm (closes 6pm in winter).*

2 ★★ Museo Etrusco Guarnacci. This gem has one of the best (and most poorly displayed) Etruscan collections in Italy. Some 600 cinerary urns, dating from the 6th to the 1st century B.C., are made of alabaster, tufa, or terra cotta. The most celebrated piece is in Room XIV: an elongated bronze called *The Shadow of the Evening,* an early-3rd-century B.C. votive figure of a young boy. One of the most famous urns, *Urna degli Sposi,* depicts an unhappy couple. *45 min. Via Minzoni 15. 0588-86347. Mid–Mar to Oct daily 9am–7pm; off-season daily 9am–2pm.*

3 ★ Palazzo dei Priori. Built between 1208 and 1257, this is the oldest Gothic town hall in Tuscany. Florence's more famous Palazzo Vecchio was modeled after it. The council hall and antechamber are open to the public. On view is the masterful but damaged *Annunciation with Four Saints* by Jacopo di Cione from 1383. Off the same square is the Palazzo **Pretorio,** with its **Torre del Porcellino,** a tower named for the wild boar that peers out near the top window. The nearby public park is an idyllic spot for a picnic. *20 min. Piazza dei Priori. 0588-86050. Free. June–Sept Mon–Sat 10am–1pm and 3–4pm; off-season Mon–Sat 10am–1pm.*

The plain facade of Volterra's Duomo belies its lush interior.

Alabaster wares by local artists for sale.

4 ★ **Pinacoteca e Museo Civico.** This combined picture gallery and museum of regional artifacts is acclaimed for its religious art—mostly the work of Tuscan artists from the 14th to the 17th century. Taddeo di Bartolo's altarpiece from 1411 is glorious. Room 12 houses the treasures, including a *Deposition* painted by the young Rosso Fiorentino in 1521, and two large 1491 Luca Signorelli paintings, a *Madonna and Saints* and an *Annunciation*. The latter is a seminal work that bridged the gap between the Renaissance and Mannerism; art scholars flock here to see it. ⏱ *45 min. Via dei Sartiri 1.* ☎ *0588-87580. Mar 16–Nov 2 daily 9am–7pm; off-season daily 9am–2pm.*

Alabaster or Pietra Candida

Volterra is called "the town of alabaster." Since the days of the Etruscans, locals have shaped objects both practical and artistic from this semi-precious stone found in the region. Revived in the late 19th century, the industry has been going strong since, turning out lampshades, sculptures, jewel boxes, even elegant sinks. For more than a souvenir, visit the **Società Cooperative Artieri Alabastro,** Piazza dei Priori (tel 0588-87590), a sales outlet for work by regional artists. It has been in business since 1895.

Crumbling Etruria

Northwest of the city center (3.5km), **Le Balze** is one of Italy's more quietly frightening scenes—a bowl-shaped ravine where fast-paced erosion is devouring the edges of Etruscan Volterra. Aided by periodic earthquakes, erosion has already exposed and then destroyed much of the Etruscan necropolis at this end of town. Now it threatens the medieval Badia church, abandoned after an 1846 quake brought the erosion to its doorstep, leaving it to teeter on the precipice.

5 ★ Teatro Romano. You can stand atop medieval ramparts and look down upon the remains of a Roman theater and baths, among the best preserved in Italy, from the 1st century B.C. You can also wander down among the ruins, from the entrance on Viale Francesco Ferrucci. *20 min. Viale Francesco Ferrucci. ☎ 0588-87850. Admission 2€. Open daily 10am–1pm and 2–6pm.*

6 ★★ Camillo Rossi. This workshop, founded in 1912, is the best outlet for alabaster objects. *Via lungo le Mura del Mandorlo 7. ☎ 0588-86133. AE, DC, MC, V.*

7 ★★ Spartaco Montagnani. The town's most distinguished alabaster sculptor has been turning out fused bronze statuettes since 1978, most of them inspired by Etruscan originals. Look for the seal of *Bronzo garantito,* which distinguishes these hand-finished objects from others. *Via Porta dell'Arco 6. ☎ 0588-86184. AE, MC, V.*

8 Toscana Art Gallery. This gallery displays the works of established artists and emerging ones. Tuscan landscapes are a specialty. *Piazza XX Settembre 3. ☎ 0588-86868. AE, MC, V.*

9 L'incontro. Our favorite wine bar and cafe lies in the historic center. Some of the finest Tuscan wines begin at only 2.50€ per glass. The cafe also has the most delectable pastries and cakes in town. *Via Matteoti 18. Daily until 1am (closed Wed in winter).*

10 Quo Vadis? The town's only bar is Irish-inspired, hawking Guinness on tap. Near the ancient Roman theater, it's the most popular place in town for the under-30 crowd. *Via lungo le Mura del Mandorlo 18. ☎ 0588-80033.*

Etruscan ruins.

Where to Stay

Volterra's medieval city gate.

Albergo Nazionale CENTRO STORICO This *palazzo* in the historic center became a hotel in 1890. Ask for a room with a view. The restaurants serve tasty regional dishes with fine wines. *Via dei Marchesi 11. ☎ 0588-86284. www.albergonazionalevolterra.it. 36 units. Doubles 64€–69€; triples 76€–80€. AE, DC, MC, V.*

★★ **Park Hotel Le Fonti** SOUTH VOLTERRA The town's best hotel is in the Tuscan hills, a 10-minute walk south of the center. The hotel achieves a delicate balance between modern amenities (two outdoor swimming pools) and an old Tuscan ambience. Our favorite nest is a suite lodged in an old tower. *Via di Fontecorrenti. ☎ 0588-92728. www.parkhotellefonti.com. 67 units. Doubles 110€–165€; suites 185€–330€ w/buffet breakfast. AE, DC, MC, V.*

★ **San Lino** CENTRO STORICO This is the best choice for those who want to be within the medieval walls. It was built as a convent in 1480, and converted to a hotel in 1982. Ignore the timeworn rooms on the first floor, used mainly by backpackers, and head for the rooms upstairs. *Via Lino 26. ☎ 0588-85250. www.hotelsanlino.com. 44 units. Doubles 77€–100€; triples 90€–115€ w/buffet breakfast. AE, DC, MC, V.*

★ **Villa Nencini** WEST VOLTERRA This cozy inn, a 10-minute walk west of the center, was converted from a 17th-century villa, with panoramic views. Rooms in the older building, more antique in style, are preferred by traditionalists; the newer wing offers larger rooms and wraps around an outdoor pool. *Borgo Santo Stefano 55. ☎ 0588-86571. www.villanencini.it. 36 units. Doubles 68€–83€; triples 88€–112€ w/buffet breakfast. AE, DC, MC, V.*

Piazza dei Priori, Tuscany's oldest town hall.

Where to Dine

Boar meat is the staple of Tuscany's old Etruscan recipes.

★ **Da Badò** SAN LAZZERO *VOLTERRANA* In the district of San Lazzero, east of Volterra, Da Bado is a mecca for devotees of regional cuisine. The chef places his personal stamp on traditional recipes, using vegetables from the restaurant garden. Stewed rabbit is the specialty. *Borgo San Lazzero. ☎ 0588-86477. 2km (1¼ miles) east of the center along SS68. ☎ 0588-86477. Entrees 8€–12€. MC, V. Lunch, dinner Thurs–Tues. MC, V.*

★★ **Enoteca del Duca** CENTRO STORICO *TUSCAN* The town's finest restaurant is installed in a restored, 16th-century building with high ceilings and terra-cotta floors. Try the *lavagnette* (homemade egg pasta) with porcini mushrooms or the pigeon breast. *Via di Castello 2. ☎ 0588-91510. Entrees 6€–15€. AE, DC, MC, V. Lunch, dinner Wed–Mon. Closed Jan 23–Feb 6, Nov 13–26.*

Etruria CENTRO STORICO *TUSCAN* This could be a tourist trap because of its location on the main square, but locals will tell you it serves the best food within the town's walls. In an elegant 19th-century setting, feast on stewed wild boar with olives or filet of beef with truffles and arugula. *Piazza dei Priori 6–8. ☎ 0588-86064. Entrees 4€–16€. AE, DC, MC, V. Lunch, dinner daily May–Sept; Thurs–Tues Oct–April.*

★ **Il Sacco Fiorentino** CENTRO STORICO *TUSCAN* Visit this popular neighborhood tavern not for its decor but for its tasty menu and its market-fresh ingredients, prepared with Tuscan flair. We like to visit in autumn for the game dishes such as *pappardelle* (wide noodles) in a wild boar sauce or pan-fried pigeon with radicchio. The tender Tuscan beef filet with black truffles is a year-round treat. *Piazza XX Settembre 18. ☎ 0588-88537. Entrees 6.50€–11€. AE, DC, MC, V. Lunch, dinner Thurs–Tues. Closed 1 week in late June.*

Web & Wine. Volterra has entered the 21st century with this Internet cafe and wine bar. You can sit at worm-holed tables and sip some of the best Tuscan vintages, such as Sassicala, Solaia, and Tignanello. *Via Porta all'Arco. ☎ 0588-81531. Daily until 1am (closed Thurs in winter).* ●

Volterra's Internet cafe cum wine bar.

Volterra

The **Savvy Traveler**

Before You Go

Government Tourist Offices

In the U.S.: 630 Fifth Ave., Suite 1565, New York, NY 10111 ☎ 212/245-4822; 500 N. Michigan Ave., Suite 2240, Chicago, IL 60611 ☎ 312/644-0996; and 12400 Wilshire Blvd., Suite 550, Los Angeles, CA 90025 ☎ 310/820-1898.
In Canada: 175 Bloor St. E., South Tower, Suite 907, Toronto, ONT, M4W 3R8 ☎ 020/7408-1254.
In the U.K. & Ireland: 1 Princes St., London, W1B 2AY ☎ 020/7408-1254; www.italiantouristboard.co.uk.
In Australia: Level 4, 46 Market St., Sydney, NSW 2000 ☎ 02/9262-1666.

Entry Requirements

U.S., Canadian, U.K., Irish, Australian, and New Zealand citizens with a **valid passport** don't need a visa to enter Italy if they don't expect to stay more than 90 days and don't expect to work there. If after entering Italy you find you want to stay more than 90 days, you can apply for a permit for an extra 90 days, which as a rule is granted immediately. Go to the nearest *questura* (police headquarters) or your home country's consulate.

For passport information and applications in the **U.S.,** call ☎ **202/647-0518** or check http://travel.state.gov; in **Canada,** call ☎ **800/567-6868** or check www.dfait-maeci.gc.ca/passport; in the **U.K.,** call ☎ **0870/521-0410** or visit www.passports.gov.uk; in **Ireland,** call ☎ **01/671-1633** or check www.irlgov.ie/iveagh; in **Australia,** call ☎ **131-232** or visit www.passports.gov.au; and in **New Zealand,** call ☎ **0800/225-050** or check www.passports.govt.nz. Allow plenty of time before your trip to apply for a passport; processing usually takes 3 weeks but can take longer during busy periods (especially spring). When traveling, safeguard your passport and keep a copy of the critical pages with your passport number in a separate place. If you lose your passport, visit the nearest consulate of your native country as soon as possible for a replacement.

The Best Times to Go

April to June and late September to October are the best months to visit Tuscany.

From mid-June through mid-September, when the summer rush season is full-blown, Florence, Siena, and other Tuscan towns teem with visitors. August is the worst month, when it's uncomfortably hot, muggy, and crowded. And from August 15 to the end of the month, the entire region goes on vacation, and many hotels, restaurants, and shops are closed (except at the spas, beaches, and islands—where 70% of the Italians head).

From late October to Easter, most attractions go on shorter winter hours or close for renovation. Many hotels and restaurants take a month or two off between November and February, spa and beach destinations such as Viareggio become padlocked ghost towns, and it can get much colder than you'd expect; it might even snow.

Festivals & Special Events

SPRING. **Easter** is always a big event in Tuscany, especially in Florence at the **Scoppia del Carro** (Explosion of the Cart), with its Renaissance pyrotechnics on Easter Sunday. An 18th-century cart, pulled by two snowy white oxen loaded with fireworks, arrives at the Piazza del Duomo, where it's ignited.

More cultural, Florence's **Maggio Musicale Fiorentino** (Musical May) features a month's worth of concerts and dance recitals in *Palazzi* and churches around town; sometimes it stretches into June. ☎ 0935-564767.

A wacky festival called **Festa del Grillo** (Cricket Festival) takes place in mid- to late May, the First Sunday after Ascension Day. In Florence's Cascine Park, vendors sell crickets in decorated cages. After a parade along the Arno, participants release the crickets into the grass.

The first week of May, Cortona hosts a crossbow competition, **Giostro dell'Archidado,** in which participants dress in 14th-century costumes. ☎ 0575-630352. The first Sunday in June (in Pisa in 2006), the **Regatta of the Great Maritime Republics** takes place—a competition among the four medieval maritime republics—Venice, Amalfi, Genoa, and Pisa.

Also in Pisa, the **Festa di San Ranieri** celebrates that city's patron saint by lining the Arno with flickering torches, usually in mid-June. ☎ 060-42291.

SUMMER. During the last Sunday in June, Pisa stages **Gioco del Ponte** (War of the Bridge) when teams in Renaissance costumes on opposite banks of the river have a push-of-war with a seven-ton cart. ☎ 050-42291.

From late June to August, Fiesole hosts **Estate Fiesolana,** a summertime festival of music, ballet, film, and theater. Most performances take place in the ruins of the ancient Roman theater. ☎ 055-210804.

The biggest event on the Tuscan calendar is the **Palio della Contrade,** the famous bareback horse race among the districts of Siena. The race occurs around the dirt-packed main square, with parades and heavy partying. The first event occurs July 2; the second on August 16. ☎ 0577-280551.

The **Gistra del Orso** (Joust of the Bear) takes place in Pistoia on July 25. The jousting match pits mounted knights in medieval costume against targets shaped like bears. ☎ 0573-34326.

In San Gimignano, **Sangimignanese Summer** is a festival of concerts, opera, and film staged from late June to early September. ☎ 0577-940008. For 1 week in either July or August, **Settimana Musicale Senese,** in Siena, presents Italy's best concerts and opera programs. ☎ 0577-22091.

The first Sunday in September in Arezzo, the **Giostra del Saracino** (Saracen Joust) takes place—a tournament between mounted knights in 13th-century armor and the effigy of a Saracen warrior. ☎ 0575-377678.

During the second week of September, the **Rassegna del Chianti** or wine festival takes place in Greve in Chianti.

AUTUMN. In Montalcino, residents present the **Sagra del Tordo** or "Feast of the Thrush." Locals in medieval costume stage archery tournaments and parades. ☎ 0577-849331.

In November the opera, concert, and ballet season opens in Florence at the **Teatro Comunale.** ☎ 055-211158.

WINTER. On December 25, the famous **Display of the Virgin's Girdle** takes place in Prato. The belt that the Virgin handed to Thomas upon her Assumption is displayed to the people massed inside the Duomo. Plenty of Renaissance-styled drummers and fifers are in attendance. The pomp is repeated on Easter, May 1, August 15, and September 8. ☎ 0574-24112.

Useful Websites

- www.yourwaytoflorence.com: Information on accommodations, shopping, tourism, art, history, wines—a general catchall.

- **www.italiantourism.com:** This is the site of the Italian government's official tourist board.
- **www.pisa-airport.com:** Information about the Pisa International Airport (Galileo Galilei), Tuscany's largest.
- **www.aboutflorence.com:** Data on history, museums, and tourism, and useful phone numbers.
- **www.firenze.net:** Data on accommodations, museums, entertainment, and dining in Florence.
- **www.sangimignano.toscana.it:** Information on the town of San Gimignano, including accommodations and events.
- **www.pisaonline.it:** Data about the city of Pisa.
- **www.comune.siena.it:** Information about the city of Siena.
- **www.comune.lucca.it:** Information about Lucca.
- **www.greve-in-chianti.com:** Information about the Chianti wine country south of Florence.
- **www.chiantiturismo.it:** More data about the Chianti wine country.

Cellphones (Mobiles)

World phones are the only U.S. phones that can be used in Tuscany. Italy (like most of the world) is on the GSM (Global System for Mobiles) wireless network. GSM phones function with a removable plastic SIM card, encoded with your phone number and account information. In Italy, you can purchase a phone and SIM card for about 100€ and buy prepaid minutes in increments of 5€ to 20€.

We recommend you rent a cell phone before leaving home from **InTouch USA** ☎ 800/872-7262 (www.intouchglobal.com), **Road-Post** ☎ 888/290-1606 or 905/272-5665 (www.roadpost.com), or **Cellhire** (www.cellhire.com, www.cellhire.co.uk, www.cellhire.com.au).

If you didn't make arrangements to lease a cellphone before leaving home, you can lease one at major car-rental firms (see below). **Auto Europe** ☎ 800/223-5555 (www.autoeurope.com) usually offers cheaper rentals than major competitors such as Hertz or Avis.

U.K. mobiles all work in Italy; call your service provider before departing your home country to ensure that the international call bar has been switched off, and to check call charges, which can be extremely high. Remember that you are also charged for calls you *receive* on a U.K. mobile used abroad.

Money

Italy falls somewhere in the middle of pricing in Europe—not as expensive as, say, London, Switzerland, or Scandinavia, but not as cheap as Spain and Greece. Popular central Italy, especially Tuscany, comes just behind Venice in terms of costliest bit of Italy to travel through, but the advice in this book should help guide you to the best options to fit any budget.

Luckily, ATMs (automated teller machines) are now to be found just about everywhere, even in the smallest towns, so cash is readily available. And as luck would have it, banks in Italy do not (as of yet) charge you a fee for using their bank—though your home bank probably will for using an out-of-network ATM, and these days often a premium for withdrawing foreign currency.

It's a good idea to exchange at least some money—just enough to cover airport incidentals and transportation to your hotel—before you leave home, so you can avoid lines at airport ATMs. You can exchange money at your local American Express or Thomas Cook office or your bank (often, though, only at the major branches). If you're far away from a bank with currency-exchange services, American Express offers travelers checks and foreign currency—though with a $15 order fee and additional shipping costs—at www.americanexpress.com or ☎ **800/807-6233.**

Currency

In January 2002, Italy retired the lira and joined most of Western Europe in switching to the euro. Coins are issued in denominations of .01€, .02€, .05€, .10€, .20€, and .50€, as well as 1€ and 2€; bills come in denominations of 5€, 10€, 20€, 50€, 100€, 200€, and 500€.

Exchange rates are established daily and listed in most international newspapers. To get a transaction as close to this rate as possible, pay for as much as possible with credit cards and get cash out of ATMs.

Travelers checks, while still the safest way to carry money, are going the way of the dinosaur. The aggressive evolution of international computerized banking and consolidated ATM networks has led to the triumph of plastic throughout the Italian peninsula—even if cold cash is still the most trusted currency, especially in smaller towns or cheaper mom-and-pop joints, where credit cards may not be accepted.

You'll get the best rate if you **exchange money** at a bank or one of its ATMs. The rates at "Cambio/change/wechsel" exchange booths are invariably less favorable but still a good deal better than what you'd get exchanging money at a hotel or shop (a last-resort tactic only). The bill-to-bill changers you'll see in some touristy places exist solely to rip you off.

ATMs

The ability to access your personal checking account through the **Cirrus** (☎ **800/424-7787;** www.mastercard.com) or **PLUS** (☎ **800/843-7587;** www.visa.com) network of ATMs—or get a cash advance on an enabled Visa or MasterCard—has grown by leaps and bounds in Italy in the last few years. It works just like at home. All you need to do is search out a machine that has your network's symbol displayed, pop in your card, and punch in your PIN (make sure it's four digits; six-digit PINs won't work). It'll spit out local currency drawn directly from your home checking account (and at a more favorable rate than converting traveler's checks or cash). Also keep in mind that many banks impose a fee every time a card is used at a different bank's ATM, and that fee can be higher for international transactions (up to $5 or more) than for domestic ones (where they're rarely more than $1.50). However, as I mentioned above, banks in Italy do not (at least yet) charge you a second fee to use their ATMs. To compare banks' ATM fees within the U.S., use www.bankrate.com. For international withdrawal fees, ask your bank.

An ATM in Italian is a ***Bancomat*** (though Bancomat is a private company, its name has become the generic word for ATMs). Increased internationalism has been slowly doing away with the old worry that your card's PIN, be it on a bank card or credit card, need be specially enabled to work abroad, but it always pays to check with the issuing bank to be sure. If at the ATM you get a message saying your card isn't valid for international transactions, it's likely the bank just can't make the phone connection to check it (occasionally this can be a citywide epidemic); try another ATM or another town.

Credit Cards

Visa and **MasterCard** are now almost universally accepted at most hotels, restaurants, and shops; the majority also accepts **American Express. Diners Club** is gaining some ground, especially in Florence and in more expensive establishments throughout the region. If you arrange with your card issuer to enable the card's cash advance option (and get a PIN as well), you can also use them at ATMs.

Wire Services

If you find yourself out of money, a wire service can help you tap willing friends and family for funds. Through **TravelersExpress/MoneyGram** (☎ **800/666-3947;** www.moneygram.com), you can get money sent around the world in less than 10 minutes. Cash is the only acceptable form of payment. MoneyGram's fees vary based on the cities the money is wired from and to, but a good estimate is $20 for the first $200 and $30 for up to $400, with a sliding scale for larger sums. A similar service is offered by **Western Union** (☎ **800/CALL-CASH**), which accepts Visa, MasterCard credit or debit cards, or Discover. You can arrange for the service over the phone, at a Western Union office, or online at www.westernunion.com. A sliding scale begins at $15 for the first $100. A currency exchange rate will also apply. Additionally, your credit card company may charge a fee for the cash advance as well as a higher interest rate.

Getting **There**/Getting **Around**

By Plane

There are no direct flights from the U.S. or Canada into Tuscany, so chances are you'll land in Milan or Rome. If you'd like to continue by plane, you can either fly into Pisa (preferable if you're planning to visit northwest Tuscany) or Florence (if you want to see the city of the Renaissance or points in Central or Eastern Tuscany).

Many visitors find the 3-hour train ride to Florence from either Rome or Milan an easier and more viable option than flying.

Alitalia ☎ 055-27881 (www.alitalia.it) flies frequently from Rome or Milan to Florence or Pisa. Planes land at **Aeroporto Amerigo Vespucci** ☎ 055-30615 (www.aeroporto.firenz.it) in the suburb of Peretola, 5km (3 miles) west of central Florence. **ATAF bus #62** ☎ 800/424500 links the airport to the main train terminus in the heart of Florence; a one-way ticket costs 4€. A bus leaves every 20 minutes.

The alternative airport, **Galileo Galilei** ☎ 050-500707 is 84km (52 miles) west of Florence and 3km (2 miles) south of Pisa. Fast trains zip you from the train station into Pisa in 5 minutes, a one-way ticket costing 1€. At the Pisa airport, two to three trains per hour head for Florence, for the 1-hour trip costing 5.40€ one-way.

If you fly into Milan, try to have a ticket that lands you at **Aeroporto Malpensa** ☎ 02-2680-0613, 45km (28 miles) west of the center, rather than **Linate Airport** ☎ 02-7485-2200, 7km (4½ miles) southeast of the city. At Linate, connections are more difficult for trains to Tuscany.

Instead of flying to Tuscany from Milan, we recommend the train. From Malpensa, a 40-minute express train heads every 30 minutes to the Cadorna train station in western Milan, where most trains heading for Florence and Tuscany depart. **Malpensa Express** buses ☎ 02-9619-2301 run between Malpensa airport and the train station, a 45-minute trip costing 9€ one-way.

By Train

Every day, up to 14 Eurostar trains (reservations in London, ☎ 0875/186186; www.eurostar.com) zip from London to Paris's Gare du Nord via Chunnel (Eurotunnel) in about 4 hours. In Paris, you can transfer to Paris Gare de Lyon station or Paris Bercy for one of three daily direct trains to Milan (from which you can transfer to Florence), two to Pisa, or two to Florence. Some of the Milan runs are high-speed TGV trains, a 6½-hour ride requiring a seat reservation. At least one will be an overnight Euronight (EN) train, with reservable sleeping couchettes; the Euronight leaves Paris around 10pm and gets into Milan around 8:45am. The two Euronight trains directly from Paris to Pisa take about 10 hours; to Florence, it takes 12½ hours.

The main Tuscan rail stations, receiving trains from most parts of Italy, are Florence and Pisa, and Siena is also an important hub. Most arrivals in Florence are at **Stazione Santa Maria Novella,** Piazza della Stazione, ☎ 848-888088; ☎ 892021 for nationwide phone rail information. Some trains stop at the less convenient Stazione Campo di Marte, on the eastern side of Florence; a 24-hour bus service (#12) links the two rail terminals. Trains arrive from Milan in 3½ hours, costing 22€ for a one-way ticket; and from Rome, also in 3½ hours, costing about 16€ for a one-way ticket.

In Pisa, trains arrive at the **Stazione Pisa,** Piazza della Stazione ☎ 147-80888, at the southern end of town. Of the major terminals in Tuscany, the best links are between Florence and Pisa, with trains departing every hour. The trip between the two cities takes 1 hour, costing 5.50€ for a one-way ticket.

Twelve trains a day also run between Rome and Pisa, taking 3 hours and costing 15€ to 24€ for a one-way ticket, depending on the train.

Trains link Lucca and Pisa every hour, taking only 20 minutes and costing 1.95€ for a one-way ticket.

In Siena, trains arrive at **Stazione Siena,** Piazza Rosselli ☎ 892021. The station is only 15 minutes by frequent bus from the heart of Siena. The most popular link is between Florence and Siena, with 19 trains daily, taking 1¾ hours and costing 5.50€ for a one-way ticket.

Connections between Rome and Siena take 3 hours, routed via Chiusi. Twelve trains a day make the run between Rome and Siena, taking 3 hours and costing 16€ for a one-way.

Transfers between Pisa and Siena involve a change of trains at Florence (see above).

By Car

For motorists, the main link is the most traveled road in Italy—the Al autostrada (Italy's main express highway). This route comes in from the north and Milan, moving southeast toward Bologna before cutting abruptly south to Florence, the destination of most drivers heading to Tuscany. If you're already in the south (most likely Rome), you can travel this same road between Rome and Florence (or visa versa).

Skirting the western coast of Italy, including the Riviera, the A12 heads down the coast from Genoa. North of Pisa A12 meets up with A11, which cuts east toward

Florence. Florence and Siena are also linked by an expressway with no route number; from Florence just follow the green autostrada signs toward Siena.

For visitors heading to Arezzo and Eastern Tuscany, follow the autostrada (A1) as though you're going to Rome, until you reach the exits for Arezzo to the immediate east of the expressway.

Autostrade are superhighways, denoted by green signs and a number prefaced with an A, like the A1 from Rome to Florence. A few aren't numbered and are simply called *raccordo,* a connecting road between two cities (such as Florence–Siena and Florence–Pisa). On longer stretches, autostrade often become toll roads.

Strade Statale are state roads, usually two lanes wide, indicated by blue signs. Their route numbers are prefaced with an SS or an S, as in the SS222 from Florence to Siena. On signs, however, these official route numbers are used infrequently. Usually, you'll just see blue signs listing destinations by name with arrows pointing off in the appropriate directions. Even if it's just a few miles down the road, often the town you're looking for won't be mentioned on the sign at the appropriate turnoff. It's impossible to predict which of all the towns that lie along a road will be the ones chosen to list on a particular sign. Sometimes, the sign gives only the first miniscule village that lies past the turnoff; at other times it lists the first major town down that road, and some signs mention only the major city the road eventually leads to, even if its hundreds of miles away. It pays to study the map and fix in your mind the names of all the possibilities before coming to an intersection.

The **speed limit** on roads in built-up areas around towns and cities is 50kmph (31 mph). On rural roads and the highway it's 110kmph (68 mph), except on weekends when it's upped to 130kmph (81 mph). Italians have an astounding disregard for these limits. Nevertheless, police can ticket you and collect the fine on the spot. Although there's no official blood alcohol level at which you're "legally drunk," the police will throw you in jail if they pull you over and find you soused.

Both rental and gas prices are as high as they get in all Europe. Before leaving home, apply for an **International Driver's Permit** from the American Automobile Association (AAA; ☎ 800/222-1134 or 407/444-4300; www.aaa.com). In Canada, the permit is available from the Canadian Automobile Association (CAA; ☎ 613/247-0117; www.caa.ca). Technically, you need this permit, your actual driver's license, and an Italian translation of the latter (also available from AAA and CAA) to drive in Italy, though in practice the license itself often suffices.

Italian drivers aren't maniacs; they only appear to be. Actually, they tend to be very safe and alert drivers—if much more aggressive than Americans are used to.

If someone races up behind you and flashes their lights, that's the signal for you to slow down so they can pass you quickly and safely. Stay in the right lane on highways; the left is only for passing and for cars with large engines and the pedal to the metal. On a two-lane road, the idiot passing someone in the opposing traffic who has swerved into your lane expects you to veer obligingly over into the shoulder so three lanes of traffic can fit—he would do the same for you.

Benzina (gas or petrol) is even more expensive in Italy than in the rest of Europe. Even a small rental car guzzles between 30€ and 50€ ($39–$65) for a fill-up.

There are many pull-in gas stations along major roads and on the outskirts of town, as well as 24-hour rest stops along the autostrada highways, but in towns most stations are small sidewalk gas stands where you parallel park to fill up.

Almost all stations are closed for *riposo* and on Sundays, but most now have a pump fitted with a machine that accepts bills so you can self-service your tank at 3am.

Unleaded gas is *senza piombo*.

Car Rentals

In Tuscany, all roads lead to Florence, but you won't need a car once you get there. The historic Centro Storico is best explored on foot, but if you're venturing on to Tuscany, hang onto your car; you'll need it to get around. You're usually allowed to park in front of your hotel long enough to unload your luggage. You'll then want to proceed to a garage. (Ask the concierge at your hotel to recommend the nearest one.)

You'll save money by reserving a car before leaving home. The three major rental companies in Italy are **Avis** ☎ 800/331-1212; www.avis.com, **Budget** ☎ 800/472-3325; www.budget.com, and **Hertz** ☎ 800/654-3131; www.hertz.com. U.S.-based companies specializing in European car rentals are **Auto Europe** ☎ 800/223-5555; www.autoeurope.com, **Europe by Car** ☎ 212/581-3040 in New York; www.europebycar.com, and **Kemwel Holiday Auto** ☎ 877/820-0668; www.kemwel.com.

In some cases, members of the **American Automobile Association (AAA)** or AARP qualify for discounts.

For the U.S., we recommend www.holidayautos.co.uk. Its prepaid vouchers include insurance, which is often sky-high in Florence and Tuscany. Book online with this company for the minimum guaranteed £10 discount.

Both stick shift and automatic are commonly available today at car-rental companies. If you know how to drive stick, it's preferable for negotiating Tuscany's hilly terrain.

We'd also recommend you opt for the **Collision Damage Waiver (CDW),** even though it can cost up to $20 a day. You'll pay much less for this added insurance if you purchase it through a third-party insurer such as **Travel Guard** (www.travelguard.com).

Car-rental agencies also require you to purchase a theft protection policy. Before buying added insurance, check your own personal auto insurance policy and credit cards to see if you already have coverage.

If you're driving a rented car, the driver's license from your own country, if still valid, is acceptable. With a private car, you might want to have an International Driver's Permit.

Fast **Facts**

AREA CODES Italy no longer uses separate city codes. Dial all numbers as written in this book.

BUSINESS HOURS General hours of operation for **stores, offices,** and **churches** are from 9:30am to noon or 1pm and again from 3 or 3:30pm to 7:30pm. That early afternoon shutdown is the *riposo*, the Italian *siesta*. Most stores close on Sunday and many also on Monday (morning only or all day). Some shops, especially grocery stores, also close Thursday afternoons. Some services and business offices are open to the public only in the morning. Traditionally, **museums** are closed Mondays. Some of the biggest stay open all day, but many close for *riposo* or open only in the morning (9am–2pm is popular). Some churches open earlier, and the largest often stay open all day. **Banks hours** tend to be Monday through Friday from 8:30am to 1:30pm and 2:30 to 3:30pm or 3 to 4pm.

Use the *riposo* as the Italians do—take a long lunch, stroll through a park, travel to the next town, or return to your hotel to recoup your energies. The *riposo* is especially welcome in August.

DRUGSTORES You'll find **green neon crosses** above the entrances to most *farmacie* (pharmacies). You'll also find many *erborista* (herbalist shops), which usually offer more traditional herbal remedies along with pharmaceuticals. Most keep everything behind the counter, so be prepared to point or pantomime. Language tip: Most minor ailments start with the phrase *mal di,* so you can just say "Mahl dee" and point to your head, stomach, throat, or whatever. Pharmacies rotate which will stay open all night and on Sundays, and each store has a poster outside showing the month's rotation.

ELECTRICITY Italy operates on a 220 volts AC (50 cycles) system, as opposed to the United States' 110 volts AC (60 cycle) system. You'll need a simple adapter plug (to make our flat pegs fit their round holes) and, unless your appliance is dual-voltage (as some hair dryers and travel irons are), a currency converter.

For more information, call or send a self-addressed stamped envelope to **The Franzus Company,** Customer Service Dept., B50, Murtha Industrial Park, Box 142, Beacons Falls, CT 06403 (☎ 800/706-7064 or 203/723-6664; www.franzus.com). They'll send the pamphlet *Foreign Electricity Is No Deep Dark Secret,* with an order form for adapters and converters on the back. You can also pick up the hardware at electronics stores, travel specialty stores, luggage shops, airports, and from Magellan's catalog (www.magellans.com).

EMBASSIES/CONSULATES The **U.S. Embassy** is in Rome at Via Vittorio Veneto 119a (☎ 06-46-741; fax 06-488-2672 or 06-4674-2217; www.usembassy.it). The U.S. consulate in Florence—for passport and consular services but *not* visas—is at Lungarno Amerigo Vespucci 38 (☎ 055-266-951; fax 055-284-088), open to drop-ins Monday through Friday from 9am to 12:30pm. Afternoons 2 to 4:30pm, the consulate is open by appointment only; call ahead.

The **U.K. Embassy** is in Rome at Via XX Settembre 80a (☎ 06-4220-0001; fax 06-4220-2334; www.UKinitalia.it), open Monday through Friday from 9:15am to 1:30pm.

The **U.K. consulate in Florence** is at Lungarno Corsini 2 (☎ 055-284-133; fax 055-219-112). It's open Monday to Friday 9:30am to 12:30pm and 2:30 to 4:30pm.

Of English-speaking countries, only the U.S. and Great Britain have consulates in Florence. Citizens of other countries must go to their consulates in Rome for help: The **Canadian** consulate in Rome is at Via Zara 30, on the fifth floor (☎ 06-445-981 or 06-44598-2905; www.canada.it), open Monday through Friday from 8:30am to 12:30pm and 1:30 to 4pm. **Australia**'s Rome consulate is at Via Alessandria 215 (☎ 06-852-721; fax 06-8527-2300; www.australian-embassy.it). The consular section is open Monday through Thursday from 8:30am to noon and 1:30 to 4pm. The immigration and visa office is open Monday to Thursday 10am to noon; telephone hours are from 10 to 11:30am. **New Zealand**'s Rome consulate is at Via Zara 28 (☎ 06-441-7171; fax 06-440-2984), open Monday through Friday from 8:30am to 12:45pm and 1:45 to 5pm.

EMERGENCIES Dial ☎ 113 for any emergency. You can also call ☎ 112 for the *carabinieri* (police), ☎ 118 for an ambulance, or ☎ 115 for the fire department. If your car breaks down, dial ☎ 116 for roadside aid from the Automotive Club of Italy.

HOSPITALS The emergency ambulance number is ☎ 118. Hospitals in Italy are partially socialized, and the care is efficient, very personalized, and of a high quality. There are also well-run private hospitals. Pharmacy staff also tend to be competent health-care providers, so for less serious problems their advice will do fine. For significant but non-life-threatening ailments, you can walk into most hospitals and get speedy care—with no questions about insurance policies, no forms to fill out, and no fees to pay. Most hospitals will be able to find someone who speaks English, but there's also a Florence-based **free medical translator** available at ☎ 055-425-0126. Also see the "Doctors/Dentists" and "Hospitals" listings under "Fast Facts: Florence" in chapter 4.

INTERNET ACCESS Cybercafes are in healthy supply in most Italian cities. In smaller towns you may have a bit of trouble, but increasingly hotels are setting up Internet points. In a pinch, hostels, local libraries, and, often, pubs will have a terminal for access.

LANGUAGE Though Italian is the local language around these parts, English is a close second, especially among anyone below age 40, since they all learned it in school. Anyone in the tourism industry will know the English they need to facilitate transactions with you. Besides, most Italians are delighted to help you learn a bit of their lingo as you go. To help, I've compiled a short list of key phrases and terms later in this chapter.

LIQUOR LAWS Driving drunk is illegal and unwise on Italy's twisty, narrow roads. Legal drinking age in Italy is 16, but that's just on paper. Public drunkenness (aside from people getting noisily tipsy and flush at big dinners) is unusual except among some street people—usually among foreign vagabonds, not the Italian homeless.

LOST & FOUND Be sure to tell all of your credit card companies the minute you discover your wallet has been lost or stolen and file a report at the nearest police precinct. Your credit card company or insurer may require a police report number or record of the loss. Most credit card companies have an emergency toll-free number to call if your card is lost or stolen; they may be able to wire you a cash advance immediately or deliver an emergency credit card in a day or two.

To report a lost or stolen card, call the following Italian toll-free numbers: **Visa** at ☎ 800-819-014, **MasterCard** at ☎ 800-870-866, or **American Express** at ☎ 800-872-000, or collect ☎ 336-393-1111 from anywhere in the world. As a backup, write down the collect-call number that appears on the back of each of your cards (*not* the toll-free number—you can't dial those from abroad; if one doesn't appear, call the card company and ask).

Identity theft or fraud are potential complications of losing your wallet, especially if you've lost your driver's license along with your cash and credit cards. Notify the major credit-reporting bureaus immediately; placing a fraud alert on your records may protect you against liability for criminal activity. The three major U.S. credit-reporting agencies are **Equifax** (☎ 800/766-0008; www.equifax.com), **Experian** (☎ 888/397-3742; www.experian.com), and **TransUnion** (☎ 800/680-7289; www.transunion.com). Finally, if you've lost all forms of photo ID, call your airline and explain the situation; they might allow you to board the plane if you have a copy of your passport or birth certificate and a copy of the police report you've filed.

MAIL The Italian mail system is notoriously slow, and friends back home may not receive your postcards or aerograms for up to 8 weeks (sometimes longer). Postcards, aerograms, and letters, weighing up to 20g (.7 oz.), cost .52€ to North America, .41€ to the United Kingdom and Ireland, and .52€ to Australia and New Zealand.

NEWSPAPERS & MAGAZINES The *International Herald Tribune* (published by the *New York Times* and with news catering to Americans abroad) and *USA Today* are available at just about every newsstand, even in smaller towns. You can find the *Wall Street Journal Europe,* European editions of *Time* and *Newsweek,* and often the *London Times* at some of the larger kiosks. For events guides in English, see each individual city's "Visitor Information" listing.

POLICE For emergencies, call ☎ 113. Italy has several different police forces, but you'll most likely only ever deal with two. The first is the urban *polizia,* whose city headquarters is called the *questura* and can help with lost and stolen property. The most useful branch—for serious problems and crimes—is the *carabinieri* (☎ 112), a national order-keeping, crime-fighting civilian police force.

RESTROOMS Public toilets are going out of fashion in northern Italy, but most bars will let you use their bathrooms without a scowl or forcing you to buy anything. Ask *"Posso usare il bagno?"* (*poh*-soh oo-*zar*-eh eel *ban*-yo). *Donne/signore* are women and *uomini/signori* men. Train stations usually have a primitive bathroom, for a fee. In many of the public toilets that remain, the little old lady with a basket has been replaced by a coin-op turnstile.

SAFETY Other than the inevitable pickpockets, especially in Florence, random violent crime is practically unheard of in the country. You won't find quite as many **gypsy pickpocketing children** as in Rome, but they have started roving the Santa Maria Novella area of Florence in packs and have even shown up in cities as far off the beaten path as Cortona. If you see a small group or pair of dirty children coming at you, often waving cardboard and jabbering in Ital-English, yell *"Va via!"* (go away) or simply "No!," or invoke the *polizia.* If they get close enough to touch you, push them away forcefully—don't hold back because they're kids—otherwise within a nanosecond you and your wallet will be permanently separated.

Plenty of locals prey on tourists as well, especially around tourist centers like the Uffizi and the Duomo in Florence. In general, just be smart. Keep your passport, traveler's checks, credit and ATM cards, and photocopies of important documents under your clothes in a money belt or neck pouch. **For women:** Beware of drive-by purse snatchings, by young thieves on mopeds, in Florence. Keep your purse on the wall side of the sidewalk and sling the strap across your chest. If your purse has a flap, keep the clasp side facing your body. **For men:** Keep your wallet in your front pocket and perhaps loop a rubber band around it. (The rubber catches on the fabric of your pocket and makes it harder for a thief to slip the wallet out easily.)

TAXES There's no sales tax added onto the price tag of your purchases, but there is a **value-added tax** (in Italy: IVA) automatically included in just about everything. For major purchases, you can get this refunded. Some five-star and four-star hotels don't include the 13% luxury tax in their quoted prices. Ask when making your reservation.

TELEPHONES & FAX **Local calls** in Italy cost .10€. There are three types of public pay phones: those that take coins only, those that take both coins and phone cards, and those that take only **phone cards** (*carta* or *scheda telefonica*). You can buy these prepaid phone cards at any *tabacchi* (tobacconists), most newsstands, and some bars in several denominations from 1€ to 7.50€. Break off the corner before inserting it; a digital display tracks how much money is left on the card as you talk. Don't forget to take the card with you when you leave!

For **operator-assisted international calls** (in English), dial toll-free ☎ 170. Note, however, that you'll get better rates by calling a home operator for collect calls, as detailed here: To make **calling card calls,** insert a phone card or .10€—it'll be refunded at the end of your call—and dial the local number for your service. For **Americans:** AT&T at ☎ 172-1011, MCI at ☎ 172-1022, or Sprint at ☎ 172-1877. These numbers will raise an American operator for you, and you can use any one of them to place a **collect call** even if you don't carry that phone company's card. **Canadians** can reach Teleglobe at ☎ 172-1001. **Brits** can call BT at ☎ 172-0044 or Mercury at ☎ 172-0544. The **Irish** can get a home operator at ☎ 172-0353. **Australians** can use Optus by calling ☎ 172-1161 or Telstra at ☎ 172-1061. And **New Zealanders** can phone home at ☎ 172-1064.

To **dial direct internationally from Italy,** dial ☎ 00, then the country code, the area code, and the number. Country codes are as follows: the United States and Canada 1; the United Kingdom 44; Ireland 353; Australia 61; New Zealand 64. Make international calls from a public phone if possible because hotels charge ridiculously inflated rates for direct dial, but take along plenty of *schede* to feed the phone.

To call free national **telephone information** (in Italian) in Italy, dial ☎ 12. International information for Europe is available at ☎ 176 but costs .60€ a shot. For international information beyond Europe, dial ☎ 1790 for .50€.

Your hotel will most likely be able to send or receive **faxes** for you, sometimes at inflated prices, sometimes at cost. Otherwise, most *cartoleria* (stationery stores), *copista* or *fotocopie* (photocopy shops), and some *tabacchi* (tobacconists) offer fax services.

TIME ZONE Italy is 6 hours ahead of Eastern Standard Time in the United States. When it's noon in New York, it's 6pm in Florence.

TIPPING In **hotels,** a service charge is usually included in your bill. In family-run operations, additional tips are unnecessary and sometimes considered rude. In fancier places with a hired staff, however, you may want to leave a .50€ daily tip for the maid, pay the bellhop or porter 1€ per bag, and a helpful concierge 2€ for his or her troubles. In **restaurants,** 10% to 15% is almost always included in the bill—to be sure, ask *"è incluso il servizio?"*—but you can leave up to an additional 10%, especially for good service. At **bars and cafes,** leave a 10€ coin per drink on the counter for the barman; if you sit at a table, leave 10% to 15%. **Taxi** drivers expect 10% to 15%.

WATER Although most Italians take mineral water with their meals, tap water is safe everywhere, as are any public drinking fountains you run across. Unsafe sources will be marked *"acqua non potabile."* If tap water comes out cloudy, it's only the calcium or other minerals inherent in a water supply that often comes untreated from fresh springs.

A Brief **History**

65 MILLION YEARS AGO According to a popular theory based on evidence found at Gubbio, an asteroid strikes the earth, causing a chain reaction that drives the dinosaurs to extinction. The age of mammals begins.

1000–500 B.C. Villanovian culture thrives.

800–500 B.C. The Etruscans are a major power in central Italy.

600–510 B.C. The Etruscan Tarquin dynasty rules as kings of Rome.

506 B.C. Lars Porsena, Etruscan king of Chiusi, attacks young Roman Republic and wins.

295–265 B.C. Rome conquers Etruria and allies with Umbria. The Roman Empire spreads throughout central Italy and Latinizes local culture.

59 B.C. Julius Caesar founds Fiorentia, and Florence is born.

56 B.C. The First Triumvirate (Caesar, Pompey, and Crassus) meets in Lucca.

CA. 4 B.C. Jesus is born in Nazareth.

A.D. 313 Roman Emperor Constantine the Great, a convert himself, declares religious freedom for Christians.

476 After a long decline, the Roman Empire falls.

570–774 The Lombard duchies rule over much of Tuscany and Umbria.

774–800S Charlemagne picks up where the Lombards left off.

951 The German emperors and the pope begin to quarrel.

1125 Florence razes neighbor Fiesole to the ground. Florentine expansion begins.

1155 Frederick Barbarossa is crowned emperor of Europe and attempts to take control of part of Italy.

1173 Pisa begins its bell tower. Eleven years later, someone notices the tilt.

1215 Florentine families take sides in the conflict between the emperor (Guelf) and the pope (Ghibelline). Tuscany follows suit.

1250–1600 The Humanist era—when intellectual pursuit of knowledge and study of the classical and Arab worlds—takes precedence over blind Christian doctrine and superstition, and lifts Europe out of its medieval stupor.

1284 Genoa trounces Pisa's fleet in the naval Battle of Meloria. A long Pisan decline begins.

1290S Giotto frescoes the *Life of St. Francis* in Assisi. Painting would never be the same.

1300 The Guelfs finally win in Florence and immediately split into the White and the Black factions.

1301 Florence conquers Pistoia.

1302 Dante is exiled from Florence on trumped-up charges. He never returns.

1303–77 The pope moves from Rome to Avignon. Ambassador St. Catherine of Siena is instrumental in returning the papacy to Italy.

1308–21 Dante writes the *Divine Comedy,* which sets the Tuscan dialect as the predecessor of modern Italian.

1310 Siena runs its first Palio race on record.

1348 The Black Death rips through Italy, killing more than half the population. Siena loses more than two thirds of its citizens.

1361 Florence conquers Volterra.

1378–1417 The Great Western Schism. Avignon, Rome, *and* Pisa each appoint a pope and the competing pontiffs busy themselves excommunicating one another.

1384 Florence conquers Arezzo.

1401 Lorenzo Ghiberti wins the competition to cast the baptistery doors in Florence. May the Renaissance begin!

1406 Florence conquers Pisa.

1434–64 Cosimo il Vecchio consolidates the Medici power over Florence.

1439 The Council of Florence takes place, whereby Eastern and Western churches briefly reconcile their ancient differences.

1469–92 The rule of Lorenzo de' Medici the Magnificent in Florence, under whose patronage the arts flourish.

1475 Michelangelo Buonarotti is born in Caprese, near Arezzo.

1494 Puritanical Fra' Girolamo Savonarola helps drive the Medici from Florence and takes control of the city.

1495 The Bonfire of the Vanities. At Savonarola's urging, Florentines carry material goods seen as decadent—including paintings by Botticelli, Lorenzo di Credi, and others—to Piazza della Signoria and burn them.

1498 At the pope's urging, Florentines carry Savonarola to Piazza della Signoria and set *him* on fire.

1498–1512 The Florentine Republic is free from the Medici.

1501–04 Michelangelo carves *David.*

1505 For a few months, Leonardo da Vinci, Michelangelo, and Raphael all live and work in Florence at the same time.

1527 Charles V sacks Rome. Medici Pope Clement VII escapes to Orvieto, where by papal bull he refuses to annul Henry VIII's marriage to Catherine of Aragon and gives rise to the Anglican Church.

1530 The Medici firmly takes back power in Florence.

1550 Vasari publishes *The Lives of the Artists,* effectively the first art history book.

1555–57 Florence conquers Siena.

1569 Cosimo I de' Medici becomes the grand duke of Tuscany.

1581 The Uffizi opens as a painting gallery.

1633 The Inquisition forces Galileo to recant his theory that Earth revolves around the Sun.

1737 Gian Gastone, last of the Medici grand dukes, dies.

1796–1806 Napoléon sweeps through Italy several times, eventually declaring himself king of Italy.

1806 Napoléon gives Lucca to his sister Elisa as a duchy.

1814–15 Napoléon is exiled to Elba, which he rules as governor.

1824 Lorraine Grand Duke Leopold II starts draining Maremma. The reclamation is finished in 1950 with the defeat of malaria.

1848–60 The Risorgimento intellectual movement considers a unified Italy.

1860 Tuscany joins the new Kingdom of Italy.

1865–70 Florence serves as Italy's capital.

1922 Mussolini becomes the Fascist dictator of Italy.

1940–45 World War II. Fascist Italy participates as an Axis power.

1944 Nazi troops withdraw from Florence, blowing up the Arno bridges. At Hitler's direct order, the Ponte Vecchio is spared.

1946 Italy becomes a republic.

1946–97 Italy averages a new national government every 9 months (though until 1993, these are usually variations on the Christian Democrat Party).

1948 Italy's regions are created. Tuscany and Umbria finally get an official dividing line between them.

1966 The Arno flood in Florence. Up to 6m (20 ft.) of water and mud destroys or damages countless works of art and literature.

1985 Italy's worst winter on record; the frost hits grapevines heavily and comes close to destroying all the olive trees in Tuscany.

1988 Pedestrian zones go into effect in major cities, making historic centers traffic-free (almost).

1993 On May 27, a car bomb rips through the west wing of the Uffizi, killing five people and damaging many paintings. Italy's Christian Democratic government, in power since the end of World War II, dissolves in a flurry of scandal. In a chain reaction, far left and right also splinter; more than 16 major parties vie for power in various improbable coalitions.

1996 Italy's national government falters again, and Parliament is disbanded. The center-left Olive Tree coalition takes the lion's share of power, with Romano Prodi as prime minister.

1997 In Assisi, a series of earthquakes hit the region, and part of the basilica's ceiling collapses, destroying frescoes and damaging Giotto's *Life of St. Francis*.

1998 After an unusually long reign, Prodi's coalition dissolves and a new center-left alliance led by Prime Minister Massimo D'Alema eases into power.

1999 All Tuscany rejoices when local filmmaker Roberto Benigni, after a victory at Cannes, gathers three Oscars for his Holocaust fable *La Vita è Bella (Life Is Beautiful)*.

2001 The first cases of BSE (mad cow disease) in Italy are confirmed. Beef consumption plummets 70%, and the government considers banning such culinary institutions as the famed *bistecca alla fiorentina*. The year ends on a high note when the Leaning Tower of Pisa reopens to the public, after more than a decade of desperate measures to keep it from collapsing. (Don't worry—it still leans.)

2002 On January 2, Italy and most of western Europe adopt the euro as their currency. On January 2, prices skyrocket.

2003 Prime Minster Berlusconi—who through private media holdings and his government post controls 98% of Italian television and the country's largest publishing empire, and who last fall fired his foreign minister and declared he himself would run that office—forces through legislation to protect himself from being prosecuted for any crimes while in office. The law took effect just as one of the many bribery cases brought against him was about to come to a conclusion.

Art & Architecture

Architecture

Ambulatory Continuation of the side aisles to make a walkway around the chancel space behind the main altar of a church.

Apse The semicircular space behind the main altar of a church.

Arcade A series of arches supported by columns, piers, or pilasters.

Architrave The long vertical element lying directly across the tops of a series of columns (the lowest part of an entablature); or, the molding around a door or window.

Badia Abbey.

Baldacchino (also **ciborium**) A stone canopy over a church altar.

Basilica A form of architecture first used for public halls and law courts in ancient Roman cities. Early Christians adopted the form—a long rectangular room, divided into a central nave with side aisles but no transept—to build their first large churches.

Bay The space between two columns or piers.

Bifore Divided vertically into two sections.

Blind Arcade An arcade of pilasters (the arches are all filled in), a defining architectural feature of the Romanesque style.

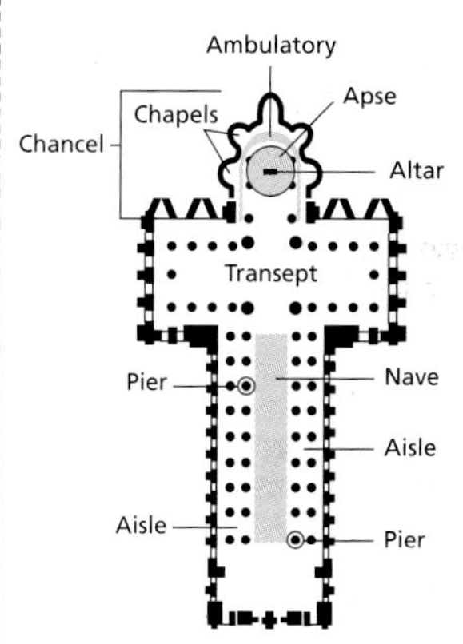

Church Floor Plan

Caldarium The hot tub or steam room of a Roman bath.

Campanile A bell tower, usually of a church but also those of public buildings; it's often detached or flush against the church rather than sprouting directly from it.

Cantoria Small church singing gallery, usually set into the wall above the congregation's heads.

Capital The top of a column. The classical "orders" (types) are **Doric** (plain), **Ionic** (with scrolls, called volutes, at the corners), and **Corinthian**

(leafy). There's also **Tuscan** (even simpler than Doric; the column is never fluted or grooved, and usually has no base) and **Composite** (Corinthian superimposed with Ionic). In many Paleo-Christian and Romanesque churches, the capital is carved with primitive animal and human heads or simple biblical scenes.

Cappella Italian for chapel.

Caryatid A column carved to resemble a woman (see also ***telamon***).

Cattedrale Cathedral (also ***Duomo***).

Cavea The semicircle of seats in a classical theater.

Cella The innermost, most sacred room of a Roman pagan temple.

Chancel Space around the high altar of a church, generally reserved for the clergy and the choir.

Chiesa Church.

Chiostro Italian for cloister.

Ciborium (1) Another word for ***baldacchino*** (above); (2) Box or tabernacle containing the Host (the symbolic body and blood of Christ taken during communion).

Cloister A roofed walkway open on one side and supported by columns; usually used in the plural because often four of them faced one another to make interior open-air courtyards, centered around small gardens, found in monasteries and convents.

Collegiata A collegiate church, having a chapter of canons and a dean or provost to rule over it but lacking the bishop's seat that would make it a cathedral.

Colonnaded Lined with columns.

Cornice Protruding section, usually along the very top of a wall, a facade, or an entablature; a pediment is usually framed by a lower cornice and two sloping ones.

Cortile Courtyard.

Crenellated Topped by a regular series of teethlike protrusions and crevices; these battlements often ring medieval buildings or fortresses to aid in defense.

Crypt An underground burial vault; in churches, usually found below the altar end and in Italy often the remnant of an older version of the church.

Cupola Dome.

Cyclopian Adjective describing an unmortared wall built of enormous stones by an unknown, central Italian, pre-Etruscan people. The sheer size led the ancients to think they were built by the Cyclopses.

Duomo Cathedral (from *domus,* "house of God"), often used to refer to the main church in town even if it doesn't have a *cathedra,* or bishop's seat—the prerequisite for a cathedral.

Entablature Section riding above a colonnade, made up of the architrave (bottom), frieze (middle), and cornice (top).

Forum The main square in a Roman town; a public space used for assemblies, courts, and speeches and on

Classical Orders

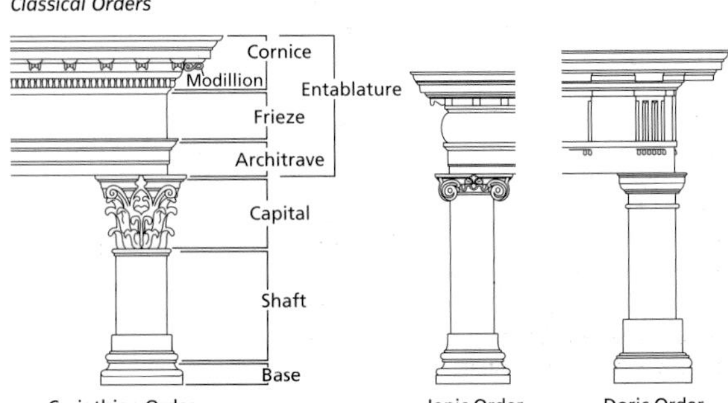

which important temples and civic buildings were located.

Frieze A decorative horizontal band or series of panels, usually carved in relief and at the center of an entablature.

Frigidarium Room for cold baths in a Roman bath.

Greek Cross Building ground plan in the shape of a cross whose arms are of equal length.

Latin Cross Building ground plan in the shape of a Crucifix-style cross, where one arm is longer than the other three (this is the nave).

Liberty Italian version of Art Nouveau or Art Deco, popular in the late 19th and early 20th centuries.

Loggia Roofed porch, balcony, or gallery.

Lozenge A decorative, regularly sided diamond (square on its corners), made of either marble inlay or a sunken depression, centered in the arcs of a blind arcade on Romanesque architecture.

Lunette Semicircular wall space created by various ceiling vaultings or above a door or window; often it's decorated with a painting, mosaic, or relief.

Matroneum In some Paleo-Christian and early Romanesque churches, the gallery (often on the second floor) reserved for women, who were kept separate from the men during mass.

Narthex Interior vestibule of a church.

Nave The longest section of a church, usually leading from the front door to the altar, where the worshipers sit; often divided into aisles.

Palazzo Traditionally a palace or other important building; in contemporary Italian it refers to any large structure, including office buildings (and has become the common way to refer to a city block, no matter how many separate structures form it).

Paleo-Christian Early Christian, used generally to describe the era from the 5th to early 11th century.

Pediment A wide gable at the top of a facade or above a doorway.

Piano Nobile The primary floor of a palace where the family would live, usually the second (American) but sometimes the third floor. It tends to have higher ceilings and larger rooms and be more lavishly decorated than the rest of the palazzo. The ground floor was usually for storage or shops and the attic for servants.

Pier A rectangular vertical support (like a column).

Pietra forte A dark gray, ocher-tinged limestone mined near Florence. Harder than its cousin ***pietra serena*** (below), it was used more sparingly in Florentine architecture.

Pietra serena A soft, light-gray limestone mined in the Florentine hills around Fiesole and one of the major building blocks of Florence's architecture—for both the ease with which it could be worked and its color, used to accent door jambs and window frames in houses and columns and chapels in churches.

Pieve A parish church; in the countryside, often primarily a baptismal site.

Pilaster Often called pilaster strip, it's a column, either rounded or squared off, set into a wall rather than separate from it.

Porta Italian for door or city gate.

Portico A porch.

Refectory The dining room of a convent or monastery—which, from the Renaissance on, was often painted with a topical *Last Supper* to aid in religious contemplation at the dinner table.

Sacristy The room in a church that houses the sacred vestments and vessels.

Sanctuary Technically the holiest part of a church, the term is used to refer to the area just around or behind the high altar.

Spandrel Triangular wall space created when two arches in an arcade curve away from each other (or from the end wall).

Spoglio Architectural recycling; the practice of using pieces of an older building to help raise a new one. (Roman temples were popular mines for both marble and columns to build early churches.)

Sporti Overhanging second story of a medieval or Renaissance building supported by wooden or stone brackets.

Stele A headstone.

Stemma Coat of arms.

Stucco Plaster composed of sand, powdered marble, water, and lime; often molded into decorative relief, formed into statuary, or applied in a thin layer to the exterior of a building.

Telamon A column sculpted to look like a man (also see ***caryatid***).

Tepidarium The room for a warm bath in a Roman bath.

Terme Roman baths, usually divided into the calidarium, tepidarium, and frigidarium.

Torre Tower.

Transept The lateral cross-arm of a cruciform church, perpendicular to the nave.

Travertine A whitish or honey-colored form of porous volcanic tufa mined near Tivoli. The stone from which ancient Rome was built.

Tribune The raised platform from which an orator speaks; used to describe the raised section of some churches around and behind the altar from which Mass is performed.

Two-light Of a window, divided vertically into two sections (see also **bifore**). A three-light window is divided vertically into three sections.

Tympanum The triangular or semicircular space between the cornices of a pediment or between the lintel above a door and the arch above it.

Painting, Sculpture & Ceramics

Ambone Italian for pulpit.

Amphora A two-handled jar with a tapered neck used by the ancients to keep wine, oil, and other liquids.

Arriccio The first, rough layer of plaster laid down when applying fresco to a wall. On this layer, the artist makes the rough *sinopia* sketches.

Bottega The workshop of an artist. (On museum signs, the word means the work was created or carried out by apprentices or assistants in the stated master's workshop.)

Bozzetto A small model for a larger sculpture (or sketch for a painting); in the later Renaissance and baroque eras, it also came to mean the tiny statuettes turned out for their own sake to satisfy the growing demand among the rich for table art.

Bucchero Etruscan black earthenware pottery.

Canopic vase Etruscan funerary vase housing the entrails of the deceased.

Cartoon In Italian *cartone,* literally "big paper," the full-size preparatory sketch made during the art of fresco.

Chiaroscuro Using patches of light and dark colors in painting to model figures and create the illusion of three dimensions. (Caravaggio was a master at also using the technique to create mood and tension.)

Cinerary urn Vase or other vessel containing the ashes of the deceased; Etruscan ones were often carved with a relief on the front and, on the lid, a half-reclining figure representing the deceased at a banquet.

Contrapposto A twisted pose in a figure, first used by the ancients and revived by Michelangelo; an earmark of the Mannerist school.

Diptych A painting in two sections.

Ex voto A small plaque, statue, painting, or other memento left by a supplicant, signifying either his or her gratitude to a saint or special Madonna, or imploring the saint's help in some matter.

Fresco The multistep art of creating a painting on fresh plaster (*fresco* means "fresh").

Graffiti Incised decorative designs, usually repetitive, on an outer wall made by painting the surface in two thin layers (one light, the other dark), then scratching away the top layer to leave the designs in contrast.

Grotesques Carved or painted faces, animals, and designs, often deliberately exaggerated or ugly; used to decorate surfaces and composite sculptures (such as fountains).

Illuminated Describing a manuscript or book, usually a choir book or bible, that has been decorated with colorful designs, miniatures, figures, scenes, and fancy letters, often produced by anonymous monks.

Intarsia Inlaid wood, marble, precious stones, or metal.

Majolica Tin-glazed earthenware pottery usually elaborately painted; a process pioneered and mastered in Italy in the 14th to 17th century.

Pala Altarpiece.

Pietra dura The art of inlaying semiprecious stones to form patterns and pictures; often called Florentine mosaic and increasingly popular from the late 15th century on.

Pinacoteca Painting gallery.

Polyptych A panel painting having more than one section that's hinged so it can be folded up. Two-paneled ones are called ***diptychs*** (see above), three-paneled ones ***triptychs*** (see below). Any more panels use the general term.

Porphyry Any igneous rock with visible shards of crystals suspended in a matrix of fine particles.

Predella Small panel or series of panels below the main part of an altarpiece, often used to tell a story of Christ's Passion or a saint's life comic-strip style.

Putti Cherubs (sing. *putto*); chubby naked toddler boys sculpted or painted, often with wings.

Sarcofagus A stone coffin or casket.

Schiacciato Literally "flattened." A sculpture form pioneered by Donatello; figures are carved in extremely low relief so that from straight on they give the illusion of three-dimensionality and great depth, but from the side are oddly squashed.

Sfumato A painting technique, popularized by Leonardo da Vinci, as important as perspective in achieving the illusion of great depth. The artist cloaks distant objects (usually landscape features like hills) in a filmy haziness; the farther away the object, the blurrier it appears, and the more realistic the distance seems.

Stoup A holy-water basin.

Tondo A round painting or sculpture.

Trecento The 14th century (in Italian, literally 1300s), often used to describe that era of art dominated by the styles of Giotto and the International Gothic (see "Art & Architecture," above).

Triptych A painting in three sections.

Useful Terms & Phrases

Tuscan, being the local lingo of Dante, is considered the purest form of Italian. (In Siena they will tell you that, actually, it's Sienese dialect that's perfect.) That means travel in Tuscany will help you learn the most letter-perfect Italian there is. Here are some key phrases and words to get you started.

Molto Italiano: A Basic Italian Vocabulary

ENGLISH	ITALIAN	PRONUNCIATION
Thank you	Grazie	*GRAHT-tzee-yey*
Please	Per favore	*PEHR fah-VOHR-eh*
Yes	Si	*see*
No	No	*noh*
Good morning or Good day	Buongiorno	*bwohn-DJOR-noh*
Good evening	Buona sera	*BWOHN-ah SAY-rah*
Good night	Buona notte	*BWOHN-ah NOHT-tay*
How are you?	Come sta?	*KOH-may STAH?*
Very well	Molto bene	*MOHL-toh BEHN-ney*
Goodbye	Arrivederci	*ahr-ree-vah-DEHR-chee*
Excuse me (to get attention)	Scusi	*SKOO-zee*
Excuse me (to get past someone on the bus)	Permesso	*pehr-MEHS-soh*
Where is . . . ?	Dovè . . . ?	*doh-VEY?*
the station	la stazione	*lah stat-tzee-OH-neh*
a hotel	un albergo	*oon ahl-BEHR-goh*
a restaurant	un ristorante	*oon reest-ohr-AHNT-eh*
the bathroom	il bagno	*eel BAHN-nyoh*
To the right	A destra	*ah DEHY-stra*
To the left	A sinistra	*ah see-NEES-tra*
Straight ahead	Avanti (or sempre diritto)	*ahv-vahn-tee (SEHM-pray dee-REET-toh)*
I would like	Vorrei	*voh-RAY*
Some (of)	Un po (di)	*oon poh dee*
This/that	Questo/quello	*QWAY-sto/QWELL-oh*
A glass of	Un bicchiere di	*oon bee-key-AIR-ay-dee*
(mineral) water	acqua (minerale)	*AH-kwah (min-air-AHL-lay)*
carbonated	gassata (or con gas)	*gahs-SAH-tah (kohn gahs)*
uncarbonated	senza gas	*SEN-zah gahs*
red wine	vino rosso	*VEE-no ROH-soh*
white wine	vino bianco	*VEE-no bee-AHN-koh*
How much is it?	Quanto costa?	*KWAN-toh COH-sta?*
It's too much.	È troppo.	*ay TRO-poh*
The check, please.	Il conto, per favore.	*eel kon-toh PEHR fah-VOHR-eh*
Can I see . . . ?	Posso vedere . . . ?	*POH-soh veh-DARE-eh?*
the church	la chiesa	*la key-AY-zah*
the fresco	l'affresco	*lahf-FRES-coh*
When?	Quando?	*KWAN-doh*
Is it open?	È aperto?	*ay ah-PAIR-toe*
Is it closed?	È chiuso?	*ay key-YOU-zoh*
Yesterday	Ieri	*ee-YEHR-ree*
Today	Oggi	*OH-jee*
Tomorrow	Domani	*doh-MAH-nee*

Breakfast	Prima colazione	*PREE-mah coh-laht-tzee-OHN-ay*
Lunch	Pranzo	*PRAHN-zoh*
Dinner	Cena	*CHAY-nah*
What time is it?	Che ore sono?	*kay OR-ay SOH-noh*
Monday	Lunedì	*loo-nay-DEE*
Tuesday	Martedì	*mart-ay-DEE*
Wednesday	Mercoledì	*mehr-cohl-ay-DEE*
Thursday	Giovedì	*joh-vay-DEE*
Friday	Venerdì	*ven-nehr-DEE*
Saturday	Sabato	*SAH-bah-toh*
Sunday	Domenica	*doh-MEHN-nee-kah*

Numbers

1	uno	*(OO-noh)*
2	due	*(DOO-ay)*
3	tre	*(tray)*
4	quattro	*(KWAH-troh)*
5	cinque	*(CHEEN-kway)*
6	sei	*(say)*
7	sette	*(SET-tay)*
8	otto	*(OH-toh)*
9	nove	*(NOH-vay)*
10	dieci	*(dee-AY-chee)*
11	undici	*(OON-dee-chee)*
20	venti	*(VEHN-tee)*
21	ventuno	*(vehn-TOON-oh)*
22	venti due	*(VEHN-tee DOO-ay)*
30	trenta	*(TRAYN-tah)*
40	quaranta	*(kwah-RAHN-tah)*
50	cinquanta	*(cheen-KWAN-tah)*
60	sessanta	*(sehs-SAHN-tah)*
70	settanta	*(seht-TAHN-tah)*
80	ottanta	*(oht-TAHN-tah)*
90	novanta	*(noh-VAHNT-tah)*
100	cento	*(CHEN-toh)*
1,000	mille	*(MEE-lay)*
5,000	cinque milla	*(CHEEN-kway MEE-lah)*
10,000	dieci milla	*(dee-AY-chee MEE-lah)*

Italian **Menu Terms**

Foods & Dishes

Acciughe or Alici Anchovies.

Acquacotta "Cooked water," a watery vegetable soup thickened with egg and poured over stale bread.

Affettati misti Mix of various salami, prosciutto, and other cured meats; served as an appetizer.

Agnello Lamb.

Agnolotti Semicircular ravioli (often stuffed with meat and cheese together).
Amaretti Almond-flavored macaroons.
Anatra Duck.
Anguilla Eel.
Antipasti Appetizers.
Aragosta Lobster.
Arista di maiale Roast pork loin, usually served in slices, flavored with rosemary, garlic, and cloves.
Baccalà (alla livornese) Dried salted codfish (cooked in olive oil, white wine, garlic, and tomatoes).
Bistecca alla fiorentina Florentine-style steak, ideally made with Chianina beef, grilled over wood coals, and then brushed with olive oil and sprinkled with pepper and salt.
Bocconcini Small veal chunks sautéed in white wine, butter, and herbs. (Also the word for ball-shaped portions of any food, especially mozzarella.)
Bollito misto Assorted boiled meats.
Braciola Loin pork chop.
Branzino Sea bass.
Bresaola Air-dried, thinly sliced beef filet, dressed with olive oil, lemon, and pepper—usually an appetizer.
Bruschetta A slab of peasant bread grilled and then rubbed with a garlic clove, drizzled with olive oil, and sprinkled with salt; often served *al pomodoro* (with tomatoes).
Bucatini Fat, hollow spaghetti. Classically served *allamatriciana* (with a spicy hot tomato sauce studded with pancetta [bacon]).
Cacciucco Seafood stew of Livrono in a spicy tomato base poured over stale bread.
Cacio or Caciotto Southern Tuscan name for pecorino cheese.
Calamari Squid.
Calzone Pizza dough folded with a number of stuffings, usually cheese and ham, before baking—like a pizza turnover.
Cannellini White beans, the Tuscan's primary vegetable.
Cannelloni Pasta tubes filled with meat and baked in a sauce (cream or tomato). The cheese version is usually called manicotti (though either name may be used for either stuffing).
Cantucci Twice-baked hard almond cookies, vaguely crescent-shaped and best made in Prato (where they're known as biscotti di Prato). The generic Italian word for them is *biscotti*.
Capocollo Aged sausage made mainly from pork necks.
Caprese A salad of sliced mozzarella and tomatoes lightly dressed with olive oil, salt, and pepper.
Capretto Kid.
Caprino Soft goat's-milk cheese.
Carciofi Artichokes.
Carpaccio Thin slices of raw cured beef, pounded flat and often served topped with arugola and parmigiano shavings.
Casalinga Home cooking.
Cavolfiore Cauliflower.
Cavolo Cabbage.
Ceci Chickpeas (garbanzo beans).
Cervelli Brains, often served *fritti* (fried).
Cervo Venison.

Cibrèo Stew of chicken livers, cockscombs, and eggs.

Cinghiale Wild boar.

Cipolla Onion.

Coniglio Rabbit.

Cozze Mussels.

Crespelle alla fiorentina Thin pancakes wrapped around ricotta and spinach, covered with tomatoes and cheese, and baked in a casserole.

Crostini Small rounds of bread toasted and covered with various pâtés, most commonly a tasty liver paste (or in Umbria *milza,* which is spleen).

Dentice Dentex; a fish similar to perch.

Fagioli Beans, almost always white cannellini beans.

Faraona Guinea hen.

Farro Emmer, a barleylike grain (often in soups).

Fave Broad fava beans.

Fegato Liver.

Focaccia Like pizza dough with nothing on it, this bready snack is laden with olive oil, baked in sheets, sprinkled with coarse salt, and eaten in slices plain or split to stuff as a sandwich. In Florence, it's also popularly called ***schiacciato.***

Fontina Medium-hard cow's-milk cheese.

Formaggio Cheese.

Frittata Thick omelet stuffed with meats, cheese, and vegetables; often eaten between slices of bread as a sandwich.

Fritto misto A deep-fried mix of meats, often paired with fried artichokes or seafood.

Frutti di mare A selection of shellfish, often boosted with a couple of shrimp and some squid.

Funghi Mushrooms.

Fusilli Spiral-shaped pasta; usually long like a telephone cord, not the short macaroni style.

Gamberi (gamberetti) Prawns (shrimp).

Gelato Dense version of ice cream (*produzione propria* means homemade).

Gnocchi Pasta dumplings usually made from potatoes or ricotta and spinach.

Gorgonzola A soft, creamy blue-veined cheese with a very strong flavor and famously overpowering aroma.

Granchio Crab.

Granita Flavored ice; *limone* (lemon) is the classic.

Involtini Thinly sliced beef or veal rolled with veggies (often celery or artichokes) and simmered in its own juices.

Lampreda Lamprey (an eel-like fish).

Lenticchie Lentil beans; Italy's best come from Umbria's eastern Castellúccio plains.

Lepre Wild hare.

Lombatina di vitello Loin of veal.

Maiale Pork.

Manzo Beef.

Mascarpone Technically a cheese but more like heavy cream, already slightly sweet and sweetened more to use in desserts like tiramisù.

Melanzana Eggplant (aubergine).

Merluzzo Cod.

Minestrone A little-bit-of-everything vegetable soup, usually flavored with chunks of cured ham.

Mortadella A very thick mild pork sausage; the original bologna (because the best comes from Bologna).

Mozzarella A nonfermented cheese, made from the fresh milk of a buffalo (but increasingly these days from a cow), boiled and then kneaded into a rounded ball; served as fresh as possible.

Oca Goose.

Orata Sea bream.

Orecchiette Small, thick pasta disks.

Osso buco Beef or veal knuckle braised in wine, butter, garlic, lemon, and rosemary; the marrow is a delicacy.

Ostriche Oysters.

Paglio e fieno Literally, "hay and straw," yellow (egg) and green (spinach) tagliatelle mixed and served with sauce.

Pancetta Salt-cured pork belly, rolled into a cylinder and sliced—the Italian bacon.

Panettone Sweet, yellow cakelike dry bread.

Panforte Any of a number of huge barlike candies vaguely akin to fruitcake; a dense, flat honey-sweetened mass of nuts, candied fruits, and spices.

Panino A sandwich.

Panna Cream (either whipped and sweetened for ice cream or pie; or heavy and unsweetened when included in pasta sauce).

Panzanella A cold summery salad made of stale bread soaked in water and vinegar mixed with cubed tomatoes, onion, fresh basil, and olive oil.

Pappa al Pomodoro A bready tomato-pap soup.

Pappardelle alle lepre Very wide noodles in hare sauce.

Parmigiano Parmesan, a hard salty cheese usually grated over pastas and soups but also eaten alone; also known as *grana*.

Pecorino A rich sheep's-milk cheese; in Tuscany it's eaten fresh and soft.

Penne strascicate Hollow pasta quills in a creamy ragù (meat-and-tomato sauce).

Peperonata Stewed peppers and onions under oil; usually served cold.

Peperoncini Hot peppers.

Peperoni Green, yellow, or red sweet peppers.

Peposo Beef stew with peppercorns.

Pesce al cartoccio Fish baked in a parchment envelope.

Pesce spada Swordfish.

Piccione Pigeon.

Pici or Pinci A delicious homemade pasta made with just flour, water, and olive oil, rolled in the hands to produce lumpy, thick, chewy spaghetti to which sauce clings. This local name is used around Siena and to its south.

Pinzimonio Olive oil with salt and pepper into which you dip raw vegetables. If the oil is flavored with garlic and anchovies, it's called *Bagna cauda*.

Piselli Peas.

Pizza Comes in two varieties: *rustica* or *a taglio* (by the slice) and *al frono* in a pizzeria (large, round pizzas for dinner with a thin, crispy crust). Specific varieties include *margherita* (plain pizza of tomatoes, mozzarella, and basil), *napoletana* (tomatoes, oregano, mozzarella, and anchovies), *capricciosa* (a naughty combination of prosciutto, artichokes, olives, and sometimes egg or anchovies), and *quatro stagione* (four seasons of fresh vegetables, sometimes also with ham).

Polenta Cornmeal mush, ranging from soupy to a dense cakelike version related to cornbread; often mixed with mushrooms and other seasonal fillings, served plain alongside game or sometimes sliced and fried.

Pollo Chicken; *alla cacciatore* is huntsman style, with tomatoes and mushrooms cooked in wine; *alla diavola* is spicy hot grilled chicken; *al mattone* is cooked under a hot brick.

Polpette Small veal meatballs.

Polpo Octopus.

Pomodoro Tomato (plural *pomodori*).

Porcini Huge tree mushrooms, best eaten grilled like a steak.

Porri Leeks.

Rape Turnips.

Ribollita A thick, almost stewlike vegetable soup made with black cabbage, olive oil, celery, carrots, and whatever else *Mamma* has left over, all poured over thick slabs of peasant bread.

Ricotta A soft, fluffy, bland cheese made from the watery whey (not curds, as most cheese) and often used to stuff pastas. *Ricotta salata* is a salted, hardened version for nibbling.

Risotto Rice, often arborio, served very watery and sticky.

Rombo Turbot fish.

Salsa verde Green sauce, made from capers, anchovies, lemon juice and/or vinegar, and parsley.

Salsicce Sausage.

Saltimbocca Veal scallop topped with a sage leaf and a slice of prosciutto and simmered in white wine.

Salvia Sage.

Sarde Sardines.

Scaloppine Thin slices of meat, usually veal.

Scamorza An air-dried (sometimes smoked) cheese similar to mozzarella; often sliced and grilled or melted over ham in a casserole, giving it a thin crust and gooey interior.

Schiacciato See "Focaccia."

Scottiglia Stew of veal, chicken, various game, and tomatoes cooked in white wine.

Semifreddo A cousin to *gelato* (ice cream), it's a way of taking nonfrozen desserts (tiramisù, zuppa inglese) and freezing and moussing them.

Seppia Cuttlefish (halfway between a squid and small octopus); its ink is used for flavoring and coloring in certain pastas and risotto dishes.

Sogliola Sole.

Spezzatino Beef or veal stew, often with tomatoes.

Spiedino A shish kebab (skewered bits of meat, onions, and slices of tomato or peppers grilled).

Spigola A fish similar to sea bass or grouper.

Spinaci Spinach (cooked to death).

Stoccafisso Air-dried cod.

Stracciatella Egg-drop soup topped with grated cheese.

Stracotto Overcooked beef, wrapped in bacon and braised with onion and tomato for hours until it's so tender it dissolves in your mouth.

Strangozzi That *a* can be any vowel; this is the name for *pici* (see above) used around Assisi, Spoleto, and southeast Umbria.

Strozzapreti Ricotta-and-spinach dumplings, usually served in tomato sauce; literally "priest chokers." Also called *strangolaprete*.

Stufato Beef pot roast in wine, broth, and veggies.

Tacchino Turkey.

Tagliatelle Flat noodles.

Tartufo (1) Truffles; (2) An ice cream ball made with a core of fudge, a layer of vanilla, a coating of chocolate, and a dusting of cocoa; order it ***affogato*** (drowning), and they'll pour brandy over it.

Tiramisù Classic Italian dessert, made by layering ladyfingers soaked in espresso (and often liqueur) with sweetened mascarpone cheese and then dusted with cocoa. Its name means "pick me up."

Tonno Tuna.

Torta A pie. *Alla nonna* is Grandma's style and usually is a creamy lemony pie; *alle mele* is an apple tart; *al limone* is lemon; *alle fragole* is strawberry; *ai frutti di bosco* is with berries.

Torta al testo A flat, unleavened bread baked on the hearthstone and often split to be filled with sausage, spinach, or other goodies.

Tortellini Rings or half-moons of pasta stuffed with ricotta and spinach or chopped meat (chicken and veal). Sometimes also called *tortelli* and *tortelloni*.

Trippa Tripe (cow's stomach lining). Served *alla fiorentina* means strips or squares of it casseroled with tomatoes and onions, topped with grated parmigiano cheese.

Trota Trout.

Umbrichelli Also *ombrichelli,* a slightly thinner version of *pici* (see above) served in Orvieto and southwest Umbria.

Vermicelli Very thin spaghetti.

Vitello Veal. A *vitellone* is an older calf about to enter cowhood.

Vongole Clams.

Zabaglione/zabaione A custard made of whipped egg yolks, sugar, and Marsala wine.

Zampone Pig's feet, usually stewed for hours.

Zuccotto A tall liqueur-soaked sponge cake, stuffed with whipped cream, ice cream, chocolate, and candied fruits.

Zuppa Soup. Popular varieties are *fagioli e farro* (beans and barley), *porri e patate* (potato-leek), *di pane* (bread and veggies; another name for ribollita), and *pavese* (eggs poached in boiling broth and poured over toasted peasant bread).

Zuppa inglese An English trifle, layered with liqueur-soaked ladyfingers and chocolate or vanilla cream.

Recommended Books & Films

Books

GENERAL & HISTORY ***Florence, Biography of a City*** (W. W. Norton, 1993) is popular historian Christopher Hibbert's overview on the City of the Renaissance, written in his extremely accessible storylike prose. Hibbert is also the author of ***The House of Medici: Its Rise and Fall*** (Morrow Quill Paperbacks, 1980), a group biography of Florence's most famous rulers.

Luigi Barzini wrote his classic ***The Italians*** (Simon & Schuster,

1996) in 1964, but the insights it gives into what makes modern Italy tick are surprisingly relevant today.

The Stones of Florence (Harcourt Brace, 1959) contains Mary McCarthy's indispensable, often scathing views on contemporary Florence (written in the early 1950s, but later editions are updated slightly).

The only favorable sequel to McCarthy's classic is ***The City of Florence*** (Henry Holt, 1995) by Yale professor R. W. B. Lewis.

Recently, a few literary histories set in Florence have enjoyed wild success. Ross King's slim tome ***Brunelleschi's Dome*** (Walker & Company, 2000) tells the fascinating story behind the building of Florence's Duomo.

Dava Sobel's ***Galileo's Daughter*** (Penguin, 2000) uses the scant documents available (letters and such) to re-create the relationship between the great Pisan scientist and one of his illegitimate daughters, whom he placed in a Florentine convent (only real place for a bastard girl in those times, other than the streets). The book deals largely with the trials and tribulations of Galileo and his fight against the Vatican's blasphemy charges, which nearly got him killed.

ART & ARCHITECTURE The first work of art history ever written was penned in 1550 (with a later, expanded edition published in 1568) by a Tuscan artist. Giorgio Vasari's ***Lives of the Artists Vols. I and II*** (Penguin Classics, 1987) is a collection of biographies of the great artists from Cimabue up to Vasari's own 16th-century contemporaries.

For a more modern art-history take, the indispensable tome/doorstop is Frederick Hartt's ***History of Italian Renaissance Art*** (H. N. Abrams, 1994). An easier, more colorful introduction, complete with illustrations, is Michael Levey's ***Early Renaissance*** (Penguin, 1967) and ***High Renaissance*** (Penguin, 1975).

Michelangelo, a Biography by George Bull (St. Martin's, 1995) is a scholarly, well-written take on the artist's life. For a livelier look, try Irving Stone's ***The Agony and the Ecstasy*** (Doubleday, 1961). Written as a work of historical fiction, it takes some liberties with the established record, but it's a good read.

LITERATURE & FICTION No survey of Tuscan literature can start anywhere but with Dante Alghieri, the 14th-century poet whose ***Divine Comedy,*** also published separately as ***Inferno, Purgatorio,*** and ***Paradiso,*** was Italy's first great epic poem since antiquity and the first major work to be written in the local vernacular (in this case, Florentine) instead of Latin. Allen Mandelbaum's edition of ***Inferno*** (Bantam, 1982) has the Italian and English side by side.

The next generation of Tuscan writers produced Giovanni Boccaccio, whose ***Decameron*** (Penguin Classics, 1995), a story of 100 tales told by young nobles fleeing the Black Death, is Italy's *Canterbury Tales*.

Tuscany also came up with the third great medieval Italian writer, Francesco Petrarca (Petrarch), whose ***Selections from the Canzoniere and Other Works*** (Oxford University Press, 1986) gives you a taste for lyrical poetry.

Even more real-world practical was Niccolò Machiavelli, whose handbook for the successful Renaissance leader, ***The Prince*** (Yale University Press, 1997), won him fame and infamy simultaneously.

If you don't have time for all of the above, pick up ***The Renaissance Reader*** (Penguin Meridian, 1987), edited by Julia Conaway Bondanella and Mark Musa, with selections from the Boccaccio's

Decameron, Petrarch's *Canzoniere,* Leonardo da Vinci's notebooks, Benvenuto Cellini's *Autobiography,* Machiavelli's *The Prince,* Michelangelo's sonnets, and others.

E. M. Forster's ***A Room with a View*** (Dover, 1995), half of which takes place in Florence, and ***Where Angels Fear to Tread*** (Dover, 1993), set in San Gimignano, are perfect tales of uptight middle-class Edwardian society in Britain and how it clashes with the brutal honesty and seductive magic of Italy.

TRAVELOGUE Wolfgang von Goethe was, by many figures, the world's first famous grand tourist, and he recorded his traipse through Italy in ***Italian Journey*** (Princeton University Press, 1994).

Mark Twain became nationally famous for his report on a package tour of Europe and Palestine called ***The Innocents Abroad*** (Oxford University Press, 1996), a good quarter of which is about Italy. Henry James's ***Italian Hours*** (Penguin Classics, 1995) pulls together essays written by the young author.

A Traveller in Italy (Dodd, Mead, 1982/Methuen, 1985) is the informed account H. V. Morton wrote of his trip through the peninsula in the 1930s, with gorgeous, insightful prose by one of the best travelogue writers of this century.

Poet and professor Frances Mayes can make us all jealous with her best-selling ***Under the Tuscan Sun*** (Chronicle Books, 1996), and its sequel ***Bella Tuscany*** (Broadway Books, 1999), which chronicle her experience of buying and renovating a Tuscan dream house outside Cortona, exploring her new neighborhood, and cooking in her new kitchen. Note that the history and art history she describes is often just a wee bit incorrect (wrong dates and such), and that the recipes which liberally sprinkle the book are as much California Cuisine as Tuscan home-cooking, but, as she's a poet by profession, it's all beautifully written. It also spawned a huge industry of "I bought a house in Tuscany/Umbria/Sicily/wherever and renovated it and here's the charming story of how I learned to fit into Italian society" books—or, rather, it breathed new life, and a more prominent placement on the bookshelves, into a tiny and largely ignored genre that had already been perfected (and done much better) by the likes of Tim Parks (in the Veneto) and the late Barbara Grizzuti Harrison (in Sicily).

Films

Tuscany's countryside and hill towns have served as backdrops for everything from Kenneth Branagh's ***Much Ado About Nothing*** (you can stay in the villa where it was filmed; see chapter 5 for more information) to 1999's ***A Midsummer Night's Dream*** and ***Tea with Mussolini.*** And, in ***The English Patient,*** Ralph Fiennes convalesces in a monastery outside Siena, and there are cameos by Montepulciano and Pienza.

The Taviani brothers' ***Fiorile (Wildflower)*** is a story within a story, reviewing the last 100 years of Italian history as a father details the lineage of a family curse.

James Ivory's ***A Room with a View*** (1986) is based on the E. M. Forster novel (see above). Though only half the film is actually set in Florence, it's the best introduction to the 19th-century British infatuation with Tuscany.

The greatest talent to come out of Tuscany in the past few years is actor, director, writer, and comedian Roberto Begnini, creator of several slapstick mistaken-identity romps *(Johnny Stecchino, Il Mostro)* available with subtitles on the foreign film shelf of your favorite video store. Then, in 1998 this Prato-area native won three Oscars, including Best Foreign Film and Best Actor (only the 2nd non-English-speaking actor to do so)—with ***La Vita è Bella (Life Is Beautiful),*** an unlikely yet successful tragicomic fable set partly in Arezzo of one Jewish father trying to protect his young son from the horrors of the Holocaust by pretending the concentration camp they've been sent off to is one big game.

Index

D

E

F

N

O

P

Q

R

S

T

U

V

W

Y

Z

Accommodations

Restaurants

Photo **Credits**

p viii: © Sam Bloomberg-Rissman/David Sanger Photography/Alamy; p 3, top: © SIME s.a.s./eStock Photo; p 3, bottom: © Ken Welch/Bridgeman Art Library; p 4, top: © Javier Delgado/AGE Fotostock; p 4, bottom: © Bluered/CuboImages srl/Alamy; p 5, top: © Atlantide S.N.C./AGE Fotostock; p 5, bottom: © Vic Bider/Getty Images; p 6, top: © Hollenbeck Productions; p 6, bottom: © Hollenbeck Productions; p 7: © Hollenbeck Productions; p 9, top: © Chuck Pefley/Alamy; p 9 bottom: © Ken Reid/Getty Images; p 11: © Ken Welch/Bridgeman Art Library; p 13, middle: © Javier Delgado/AGE Fotostock; p 14, top: © Alinari/Bridgeman Art Library; p 14, bottom: © Hollenbeck Productions; p 15, top: © SIME s.a.s./eStock Photo; p 15, bottom: © Stefano Cellai/AGE Fotostock; p 17, bottom: © Hollenbeck Productions; p 18, top: © Hollenbeck Productions; p 18, bottom: © Bridgeman Art Library; p 19, top: © Art Kowalsky/Alamy; p 19, bottom: © SIME s.a.s./eStock Photo; p 21, left: © Bridgeman Art Library; p 21, right: © Hollenbeck Productions; p 22, top: © Bridgeman Art Library; p 22, bottom: © Mooch Images/Alamy; p 23, top: © Hollenbeck Productions; p 25, top: © Giraudon/Bridgeman Art Library; p 25, bottom: © SIME s.a.s./eStock Photo; p 27, top: © Bridgeman Art Library; p 27, bottom: © Hollenbeck Productions; p 28, top: © Bruno Morandi/AGE Fotostock; p 29, bottom: © Hollenbeck Productions; p 30, bottom: © Hollenbeck Productions; p 31, top: © Hollenbeck Productions; p 33, top: © Stefano Cellai/AGE Fotostock; p 33, bottom: © Bridgeman Art Library; p 34, top: © Bridgeman Art Library; p 34, bottom: © Bridgeman Art Library; p 35, bottom: © Bridgeman Art Library; p 37, top: © Bridgeman Art Library; p 37, bottom: © Bridgeman Art Library; p 38, bottom: © Giraudon/Bridgeman Art Library; p 39, top: © SIME s.a.s./eStock Photo; p 39, bottom: © Juliet Coombe/Lonely Planet Images; p 42, bottom: © Hollenbeck Productions; p 43, top: © Hollenbeck Productions; p 44, top: © Hollenbeck Productions; p 48, bottom: © Courtesy Hotel Torre Guelfa; p 50, bottom: © Hollenbeck Productions; p 51, top: © Hollenbeck Productions; p 54, top: © Hollenbeck Productions; p 55, bottom: © Hollenbeck Productions;

p 56, bottom: © Hollenbeck Productions; p 57, top: © Hollenbeck Productions; p 60, top: © Martin Moos/Lonely Planet Images; p 61, top: © SIME s.a.s./eStock Photo; p 62, bottom: © Juliet Coombe/Lonely Planet Images; p 63: © Jon Arnold/AGE Fotostock; p 65, top: © Hollenbeck Productions; p 65, bottom: © Sam Bloomberg-Rissman/David Sanger Photography/Alamy; p 66, top: © Peter Titmuss/Alamy; p 66, bottom: © Ace Stock Limited/Alamy; p 67, top: © Hollenbeck Productions; p 67, bottom: © Navin Mistry/Alamy; p 69, top: © Kevin Galvin/AGE Fotostock; p 69, bottom: © Hollenbeck Productions; p 70, top: © Hollenbeck Productions; p 70, bottom: © Hollenbeck Productions; p 71, top: © Hollenbeck Productions; p 71, bottom: © Charlie Waite/Getty Images; p 73, top: © bildagentur-online.com/th-foto/Alamy; p 73, bottom: © Andre Jenny/Alamy; p 74, top: © Hollenbeck Productions; p 74, bottom: © Walter Bibikow/Jon Arnold Images/Alamy; p 75: © Bridgeman Art Library; p 77, top: © SIME s.a.s./eStock Photo; p 77, bottom: © SIME s.a.s./eStock Photo; p 78, top: © Alexandar Milosavljevic/Diomedia/Alamy; p 78, bottom: © Martin Rugner/AGE Fotostock; p 79, top: © Alinari/Bridgeman Art Library; p 80, top: © Bridgeman Art Library; p 80, bottom: © Hollenbeck Productions; p 81, bottom: © Hollenbeck Productions; p 83, top: © Hollenbeck Productions; p 83, bottom: © Hollenbeck Productions; p 84, bottom: © Hollenbeck Productions; p 85, top: © Hollenbeck Productions; p 86, top: © Hollenbeck Productions; p 87, top: © Hollenbeck Productions; p 87, bottom: © Targa/AGE Fotostock; p 89, top: © Hollenbeck Productions; p 89, bottom: © Steve Vidler/eStock Photo; p 90, top: © Hollenbeck Productions; p 90, bottom: © Art Kowalsky/Alamy; p 91, bottom: © Muzzi Fabio/Corbis Sygma; p 93, top: © Rail Europe; p 94, top: © LOOK Die Bildagentur der Fotografen GmbH/Alamy; p 94, bottom: © Bruno Morandi/AGE Fotostock; p 95, top: © Lee Frost/Robert Harding Picture Library Ltd./Alamy; p 97, top: © Hollenbeck Productions; p 97, bottom: © Hollenbeck Productions; p 98, top: © Mick Rock/Cephas Picture Library/Alamy; p 99, bottom: © SIME s.a.s./eStock Photo; p 100, bottom: © Martin Hughes/Lonely Planet Images; p 101: © SIME s.a.s./eStock Photo; p 103, bottom: © Corbis; p 104, bottom: © Hollenbeck Productions; p 105, top: © SIME s.a.s./eStock Photo; p 106, bottom: © Ed Gifford/Masterfile; p 107, top: © Food Features/Alamy; p 107, bottom: © Hollenbeck Productions; p 109, top: © Lauros/Giraudon/Bridgeman Art Library; p 109, bottom: © Andre Jenny/Alamy; p 110, top: © SIME s.a.s./eStock Photo; p 110, bottom: © Mark Bolton Photography/Alamy; p 111, top: © Jon Arnold/AGE Fotostock; p 112, top: © Peter Horree/Alamy; p 112, bottom: © Alessandro Chiarini/Alamy; p 113, bottom: © Nico Tondini/CuboImages srl/Alamy; p 115, top: © Brian Oxley/Alamy; p 115, bottom: © Peter Horree/Alamy; p 116, bottom: © Chris Lewington/Alamy; p 118, bottom: © Herbert Scholpp/Westend61/Alamy; p 119, top: © Alamy; p 119, bottom: © Christine Webb/Alamy; p 120, top: © Stefano Cellai/AGE Fotostock; p 121, top: © Alamy; p 122, bottom: © Hollenbeck Productions; p 123: © Hollenbeck Productions; p 125, bottom: © SIME s.a.s./eStock Photo; p 126, top: © Bridgeman Art Library; p 126, bottom: © San Rostro/AGE Fotostock; p 129, top: © Hollenbeck Productions; p 129, bottom: © Nick Higham/Alamy; p 130, top: © Hollenbeck Productions; p 130, bottom: © Targa/AGE Fotostock; p 131, top: © Bridgeman Art Library; p 131, bottom: © John & Lisa Merrill/Corbis; p 132, top: © Hollenbeck Productions; p 133, bottom: © Hollenbeck Productions; p 135, top: © PCL/Alamy; p 135, bottom: © Peter Poulides/Getty Images; p 136, bottom: © Hollenbeck Productions; p 137, top: © SIME s.a.s./eStock Photo; p 137, bottom: © Kristiane Adelt/AGE Fotostock; p 138, top: © Hollenbeck Productions; p 139, bottom: © Ron Johnson/Index Stock Imagery; p 140, top: © Hollenbeck Productions; p 141, bottom: © Chuck Pefley/Alamy; p 143, top: © Hollenbeck Productions; p 143, bottom: © Hollenbeck Productions; p 144, bottom: © Hollenbeck Productions; p 147, top: © Targa/AGE Fotostock; p 147, bottom: © John Heseltine/Worldwide Pictures Library/Alamy; p 148, top: © Hollenbeck Productions; p 148, bottom: © Hollenbeck Productions; p 151, top: © Hollenbeck Productions; p 151, bottom: © Hollenbeck Productions; p 152, top: © Bridgeman Art Library; p 152, bottom: © Javier Larrea/AGE Fotostock; p 153, top: © Bluered/CuboImages srl/Alamy; p 154, bottom: © Hollenbeck Productions; p 155, top: © Mark Thomas/Getty Images; p 157, bottom: © Bruno Morandi/AGE Fotostock; p 158, top: © Andre Jenny/Alamy; p 158, bottom: © Sam Bloomberg-Rissman/David Sanger Photography/Alamy; p 159, bottom: © Look GmbH/eStock Photo; p 160, top: © Hollenbeck Productions; p 160, bottom: © Hollenbeck Productions; p 161, bottom: © Hollenbeck Productions; p 163, bottom: © Hollenbeck Productions; p 164, top: © Simeone Huber/Getty Images; p 165, top: © Atlantide S.N.C./AGE Fotostock; p 165, bottom: © I. Vanderharst/Robert Harding Picture Library Ltd./Alamy; p 166, bottom: © Hollenbeck Productions; p 167, top: © Bruno Morandi/AGE Fotostock; p 168, top: © Lloyd Sutton/Masterfile; p 169, bottom: © Chris Lewington/Alamy; p 171, top: © Courtesy Hotel Certosa di Maggiano; p 171, bottom: © Courtesy Hotel Certosa di Maggiano; p 172, bottom: © Hollenbeck Productions; p 173, top: © Ernst Wrba/Alamy; p 175, top: © Atlantide S.N.C./AGE Fotostock; p 175, bottom: © Ernst Wrba/Alamy; p 176, top: © Enrico Caracciolo/CuboImages srl/Alamy; p 176, bottom: © Enrico Caracciolo/CuboImages srl/Alamy; p 177, bottom: © Bluered/CuboImages srl/Alamy; p 178, top: © Gianni Dagli Orti/Corbis; p 178, bottom: © SIME s.a.s./eStock Photo; p 179, top: © Matteo del Grosso/Alamy; p 179, bottom: © Hollenbeck Productions; p 180: © Guenter Rossenbach/zefa/Corbis